Knowledge of Evil

Knowledge of Evil
Child prostitution and child sexual abuse in twentieth-century England

Alyson Brown and David Barrett

WILLAN
PUBLISHING

Published by

Willan Publishing
Culmcott House
Mill Street, Uffculme
Cullompton, Devon
EX15 3AT, UK
Tel: +44(0)1884 840337
Fax: +44(0)1884 840251
e-mail: info@willanpublishing.co.uk
website: www.willanpublishing.co.uk

Published simultaneously in the USA and Canada by

Willan Publishing
c/o ISBS, 5824 N.E. Hassalo St,
Portland, Oregon 97213-3644, USA
Tel: +001(0)503 287 3093
Fax: +001(0)503 280 8832
e-mail: info@isbs.com
website: www.isbs.com

First published 2002

ISBN 1-903240-63-8 Hardback

British Library Cataloguing-in-Publication Data
A catalogue record for this book is available from the British Library

Printed by T J International Ltd., Trecerus Industrial Estate, Padstow, Cornwall.
Typeset by GCS, Leighton Buzzard, Beds.

Contents

Foreword

'Why go six thousand miles to have sex with children when you can do it in Britain?' This simple question produced a torrent of outrage and condemnation when it appeared in a charity advert in 1995. I have close personal knowledge of the response because my charity asked the question and I was the person nominated to face the ensuing torrent! Part of the anger was at the idea that some respectable towns should have been named as locations where children were involved in prostitution, part was general disbelief at the idea that such things were still happening in a seemingly civilised country.

What this book demonstrates is that the same question could have been asked at any time in Britain during the past hundred years because children have been abused through prostitution during all that time. It is chastening to consider how, at differing times, concern about the privacy of the family or unwillingness to accept the reality of the situation or fears about moral delinquency have blinded society to the abuse of young people drawn into prostitution.

In the past twenty years the public's awareness of the prevalence of child sexual abuse both in families and in children's homes has grown significantly. Yet the impression has still been that child prostitution belongs to the Victorian era as far as western Europe is concerned.

This book sweeps that complacency to one side as it sets out the continuing place of child prostitution in Britain despite major social change, increasing prosperity and the work of feminist and campaigning groups. In the past our willingness to characterise vulnerable children as evil, delinquent or disturbed closed our eyes to their exploitation and abuse. More recently, the easy labelling of 'the underclass' has led us to see it as another problem which cannot be solved.

In contrast to the Edwardian era when charities found this issue too difficult to deal with, modern children's charities, both large and small, have been at the forefront of uncovering this issue. They have also provided support and help to the young people involved in a way which is accessible, child-centred and non-judgemental.

In the Children's Society our involvement sprang from our Safe on the Streets programme which works in six areas in England and Wales. The experience of our street workers, that there were children as young as eleven and twelve who were involved in prostitution and were being cautioned or even prosecuted for this, led to our campaign called The Game's Up. This aimed, in partnership with other children's charities, the Association of Chief Police Officers and the Association of Directors of Social Services, to change policy so that young people involved in prostitution were recognised as victims of abuse rather than being prosecuted for being a prostitute. This was achieved in 1999 and the new government guidelines, though not ideal, have made some progress in the right direction.

More recently the Social Exclusion Unit's study of young runaways (some of whom are drawn into prostitution) raises hopes that we may finally have a national strategy to respond to these vulnerable young people.

However, the question that still remains is whether we are prepared to tackle the underlying causes of abuse or neglect and the poverty of opportunity and aspiration for some children which make prostitution seem like a better life than what they have experienced so far. The words of David Ramsbotham, Chief Inspector of Prisons, stand as a warning if we do not act:

> The only raw material that any nation on earth has in common is its young people and woe betide any that does not do what it can to identify, nurture and develop their talents.

Ian Sparks
Chief Executive, The Children's Society, December 2001

Acknowledgements

The creation of a book often takes on a life of its own; this one has been no exception. We started in one way, with David leading and finished with Alyson leading. We think it has made for a better book!

Alyson would like to thank staff at the several archives consulted for their invaluable expertise. Foremost among these are Ian Wakeling of the Children's Society, Nicholas Malton of the NSPCC, Lesley Hall of the Wellcome Institute, David Doughan at the Fawcett Library, Joy Eldridge at Mass Observation and Gordon Taylor of the Salvation Army. I would also like to express my appreciation to the institutions whose archives and staff I consulted. In addition to the institutions already mentioned these are the Barnardo's archives at the University of Liverpool, the Public Records Office and the British Library.

Alyson also thanks fellow author David, who was the instigator of this book, for his continued support, and those important people who gave their advice on draft chapters of this book: Susan Drinkwater, Keith Nield and Victor Bailey. Last, but not least, her thanks to Nick for his sense of humour and for his constancy.

David thanks the usual suspects – his long suffering family of Gaye, Emma and Julie, and his many friends. Neither probably appreciate their true worth to him in producing books on child prostitution. Be warned another book is at an embryonic stage. Most importantly, thank you to Alyson, the book could not have been started and certainly would not have been completed without you.

We would both like to thank our University at Luton for the support it has given this project and to our new friends at Willan Publishing, without whom none of this would have been possible.

Alyson Brown and David Barrett

Chapter 1

Introduction – concepts and contexts

Due to increasing globalisation and internationalisation of capital during the 1980s and 1990s,[1] child prostitution has become an issue of growing concern in many parts of the world.[2] Here, however, we largely confine the scope of our discussion to the situation in Britain during the twentieth century and explore the socio-economic and policy context in which child prostitution occurs, the existence of child prostitution, and legal and public service responses to child prostitution.

The twentieth century has often been referred to as the century of the child, the historical period in which the concept of childhood was clarified and elucidated in law, the labour market, education, the medical arena and a wide range of other contexts. If the idea of childhood as distinct and requiring particular accommodation and restraint was established by the end of the nineteenth century then childhood has been examined, elaborated and further provided for during the twentieth century. Certainly, the ideas and language used to express thought and action on this subject cannot be understood apart from the society and historical contexts which produced them. Indeed, this publication has paid particular attention to establishing the importance of the sometimes quite broad contexts which have determined and informed the discourses on children, and specifically on child prostitution and child sexual abuse.

While important areas of the understanding and protection of children have developed considerably, many areas have been relatively ignored. To a great extent such areas have been given little consideration because they have represented a threat to fundamental social institutions, most notably, the family. Children have been and continue to be perceived as conceptually integral to western notions of the family as the primary institution of socialisation. The avoidance of some issues regarding children has been particularly evident when violence and/or sex and sexuality, long-standing taboo subjects, have been involved, so that child sexual abuse and child prostitution remained, until the last thirty years or so, sensitive issues largely spoken about in restricted circles.

In this respect the silences, distortions and euphemisms surrounding child sexual abuse and child prostitution speak volumes and should be seen as a part of the strategies underlying discourses. This was, if anything, more especially the case for child prostitution in consequence of the long established stigmatisation of adult prostitution. The involvement of children in prostitution, and the causes and consequences of this for them, have been largely ignored between the late nineteenth century and the late twentieth century. When this issue has emerged into the public domain over the last hundred years, it has often been in a form that has been dramatised and stereotyped to such an extent that it promoted not understanding, or positive action, but an obscuring and social distancing of the problem, thus we have seen repeated moral panics caused by white slave trade accounts. This approach has also meant that the meaning of child prostitution, and the characteristics of a child involved in underage commercial sexual activity, have been abstracted largely from what it and they are not, that is to say that meaning has historically been abstracted from negatives. Child prostitutes have been perceived, therefore, as *not* asexual, dependent, moral or a 'real' child, but also *not* an adult. This tendency for negative abstraction leads to assumptions about what child prostitutes are, so that they have been seen as sexually assertive, independent, immoral, and as a distorted or perverse form of childhood or something 'other'.

One of the purposes of this publication is to examine the origins of the negative presumptions and judgements made about children involved in under-age commercial sex. To a large extent the focus of individual chapters has been led by the availability of sources. It is clear, however, that over the last century, as discourses of child sexual abuse were being constructed, those discourses relating to child prostitution have taken a distinct and separate journey more likely to lead to condemnation and criminalisation than sympathy and protection. Such distinctions between child prostitution and child sexual abuse have only been seriously challenged during the 1980s and 1990s, when the continued existence of the phenomenon of child prostitution gained academic, government and public attention. As one writer has noted 'Within the field of child welfare, the emergence of new areas of need is more often than not the rediscovery of some very old ones'.[3]

Jeffrey Weeks' comment on male prostitution, that 'much of our evidence for British prostitution is... sporadic, often the result of zealous public morality drives or of spectacular scandals'[4] can also be applied to child prostitution.

However, the evidence accumulated is sufficient to make a convincing case for the continued existence of child prostitution throughout the twentieth century and to stimulate discussion and research of a subject which has received considerable recent attention but little historical analysis. While the evidence is sometimes indirect and tangential it is significant and builds to undermine the depiction of child prostitution as purely a phenomenon of late twentieth-century society. Therefore an important aspect of this work is a laying out of some of the available sources for the consideration of the reader. A greater subjective approach which would have enabled a fuller appreciation of the individual feelings and rationales of child prostitutes, in line with the paradigm promoted by Allison James and Alan Prout,[5] would have been desirable, but is largely unobtainable for the period before the 1980s. As Harry Hendrick has pointed out, much of the history of childhood is 'really the history of what adults have thought about and done to children'[6] so that, in agreement with him, this publication seeks to offer a text which, although 'written from above' affirms an overtly sympathetic stance towards children in their relationships with adults.

The particular circumstances of children as having generally less power and self-determination than adults pervades the way in which services have been provided for them and restrictions been imposed upon them, ostensibly to defend them against exploitation. As Anna Davin has pointed out, adults at most times have the power to set the terms of childhood according to their present and future priorities.

> Whatever resistance (open or covert) young individuals might attempt, adults are always in a better position to impose their ideas and definitions, their authority in the family buttressed by emotional bonds, in other contexts by their class or function.[7]

This imbalance of power has also been used by adults to sexually abuse and/or exploit children, both inside and outside of the family.

The accumulation of new forms of knowledge through institutions and the professions has increased what Foucault has called the 'regulatory impact' of social provision for children. As the emergence and operation of the children's voluntary organisations and the development of the welfare state shows, the surveillance of children and the accumulation and usage of information regarding them has served as a means to intervene in the family, establishing new expectations and standards of child rearing and child behaviour. In this respect, Foucault maintains that the categorisations brought about by the accumulation of professional knowledge act as a control mechanism.[8] According to Foucault, the apparatus of sexuality is of central importance in modern power relations[9] and among his four strategic discourses of sexuality he cites the pedagogisation of children's sex. This is a discourse which poses a 'double assertion', that practically all children indulge in sexual activity – Foucault's focus here is upon masturbation, which is at the same time 'natural' and 'contrary to nature'. He states that such 'sexual activity posed physical and moral, individual and collective dangers' so that children were 'astride a dangerous dividing line' policed by parents, families, educators, doctors and eventually psychologists'.[10] This discourse of the dangerousness of child sexuality has been persistent in the records of social institutions and instrumental to the often un-sympathetic way in which child prostitutes have been treated. It is also a theme that has been highlighted by other prominent writers and is evident in Harry Hendrick's discussion of the dualism inherent in the portrayal of children as both victims and threats.[11]

In a debate of 1978, Foucault made clear his belief that because children were never listened to they were effectively denied the right of sexual consent. Furthermore, he maintained that due to the adult bringing their own sexuality to the child's, sexual relations between adults and children should not be condemned.[12] Foucault (1978) identified in such con-demnation what he saw as the emergence of a new penal system based on protecting populations regarded as vulnerable, in particular children at the mercy of adult sexuality. He found the rationale of professionals, especially psychologists and psychiatrists, who maintained that the sexuality of the child was 'a territory with its own geography that the adult must not enter', and that consequently 'the child must be protected from his own desires even when his desires turn him towards an adult', 'extremely questionable'. However, as Louise Jackson, following Vicki Bell, has asserted, this reasoning depends upon Foucault's exclusion of, for example, gender, class and age as fundamental categories of analysis and as determinants of power relations, some 'individuals do have more power than others'.[13] In recognition of these inequalities Roger Matthews asserts that, despite its inadequacies, legislation has served as a protective mechanism.

There can be little serious doubt that legal intervention over the past century, with all its anomalies and inconsistencies, has acted to reduce the level of prostitution and provide some protection for women and girls against exploitation.[14]

Crucially Foucault's stance, therefore, tends to negate consideration of moral frameworks or the moral legitimacy of forms of behaviour between adults and children. Nevertheless, Foucault's (1978) comment that sexuality would become 'a kind of roaming danger, a sort of omnipresent phantom, a phantom that will be played out between men and women, children and adults, and possibly between adults themselves' does have considerable modern resonance.

It is the contention of this publication that child prostitution is a form of child abuse. The language evident in historical rhetoric around child prostitution indicates that while a division between child prostitution and child abuse has been made, this division has frequently been contested, especially by feminist organisations. The legal definitions of commercial sexual transactions have continued to emphasise payment, whether in a monetary or material form. Yet not all forms of sexual transaction or payment have been perceived as prostitution, so that public opinion and police discretion have made distinctions taking into account specific circumstances, and this is especially the case with children under 16 years of age. This age is also applied here to boy prostitution, including homosexual prostitution, since the emphasis is upon the youth of some of those involved in commercial sex. Further- more, such an emphasis is not to assert that adult prostitution is considered to be a legitimate activity, but to suggest that child prostitution highlights additional and specific issues. It is important to note this since it has been suggested that concentration upon child prostitution somehow legitimates or makes tolerable the prostitution of adults. For example, Barry has asserted that separating child prostitution from that of women 'distorts the reality of the practices and conveys the impression that on some level it is tolerable to enslave women while child slavery is still reprehensible. Within that distinction lies the implication that one form of slavery is intolerable and worth attention while the other is not'.[15] This stance is denied on specific child welfare grounds.

Any definition of child prostitution must also incorporate considera- tion of the direct consequences of this activity upon the child; the rights and development of the child. Thus, the broader definition of child abuse offered by David Gil in 1970 is informative. He defines child abuse as any 'act of commission or omission by individuals, institutions, or society as a whole, and any conditions resulting from such acts or inaction, which deprive children of equal rights and liberties, and/or interfere with their optional development, constitute, by definition, abusive or neglectful acts or conditions'.[16] Definitions, therefore, must incorporate economic activity over which there has been a high degree of agreement, such as street soliciting or working in a brothel as a prostitute, but also refer to social and cultural consequences.

5

On the face of it the process of child prostitution is merely a commercial transaction, but underlying the action have been extensive and deep associations which have varied according to the social, political and economic climate: the ideologies of childhood and the family; the threat of working-class social standards; a section of the criminal underworld; the decline of morality; the threat of the foreign to Imperial Britain; the vulnerability of women moving to find work and the threat this posed to contemporary social structures. The variations in the pre-dominant depictions of child prostitution have also been reflected in the responses to child prostitution by child welfare agencies and by the police. An important factor is the malleability of such a 'dangerous' image as that of child prostitution, which has provided additional impact when related to other social problems. The difficulty has often been attempting to decipher the actuality behind the rhetoric.

Louise Jackson has been prominent in highlighting, with regard to Victorian and Edwardian England, the extent to which the language used in relation to the sexual abuse of children presents problems for the researcher. Such difficulties have led Jackson to conclude that child prostitution has been utilised as a construct, as a euphemism for child sexual abuse.[17] This may in part be the case, but it would be more accurate to suggest that child prostitution existed, and persisted, throughout the twentieth century, and to define this as a form of child sexual abuse. It is not until the late twentieth century that there has been considerable pressure and government acceptance of the construction of child prostitution as sexual abuse. Indeed, it is one of the objects of this publication to assess constructions of child prostitution through the meeting together of contemporary research with that of historical to produce an inter-disciplinary approach, one informing the other.

During the 1970s in both Britain and America, feminist priorities helped to bring previously hidden and taboo issues, including child sexual abuse and incest, into the open. However, during the late nineteenth century social workers from child protection agencies were clearly familiar with such phenomena and they were even an expected part of the caseload.[18] In England in the 1880s child prostitution received extensive official, media and public attention stoked by the now famous series of articles by W.T.Stead in the *Pall Mall Gazette*. Yet for a large part of the twentieth century, child prostitution received little or no attention outside of certain political and social circles, most prominently feminist and purity groups.[19] But as Linda Gordon perceptively observes, the decline of feminism between 1920 and 1970 (in America, but broadly a similar period applies also to the decline in British feminism) is not sufficient alone to explain this with regard to child sexual abuse and the same is true of child prostitution. Constructions not only of age but also of sexuality, gender and class had influential roles to play. Gordon cites the active reinterpretation of child sexual abuse as being responsible for the lack of social knowledge and discourse regarding these crimes against children and considers the dangers inherent in this. She states that 'I shudder when I think about what this meant: not only because of the incest victims rendered invisible and mute, but also because of its threat to us today, the threat that great achievements in consciousness-raising can be rolled back by powerful ideological tanks'.[20]

One effect of the power of ideology has been the relative invisibility of male prostitution, let alone boy prostitution, which has been a result of the framing of sexual roles and of the social construction of child prostitution, largely by social purity groups and child welfare organisations, as a female phenomenon. As Jackson notes:

> The 'discovery' of sexual abuse in England from the 1860s onwards was the product of a coalition of interests between the social purity societies and the burgeoning child welfare movement. The reason for the invisibility of boys (despite police knowledge of a market for adolescent boy prostitutes) lies in the emergence of the issue from the social purity and rescue societies' preoccupation with 'fallen' women and young female prostitutes. A woman's character, unlike a man's, was judged in relation to her sexual reputation. Girls and women could 'fall' but boys could not, according to the Victorian sexual schema.[21]

Jeffrey Weeks, a prominent writer in gender politics, also believes that no legitimating discourse has emerged for homosexual prostitution, unlike that which has been evident for heterosexual prostitution 'even as it condemns the female prostitute'.[22] No institutions for men similar to the Magdalenes directed at female prostitutes were opened and there was little suggestion that prostitutes might be male until post World War Two. Prostitution has been and to a large extent remains a gendered status.

Having suggested that child prostitution should not be considered as a distinct phenomenon unaffected by concepts and constructions such as gender and class, and that this activity should be defined as a form of exploitation coming under the umbrella term 'child sexual abuse', explanation of the persistent use of the term 'child prostitution' is required. There are several reasons for this. The first is that the age of consent for girls since 1885, and throughout the period covered by this book, has been fixed at 16. Therefore any form of consent below this age is highly problematic and sex with a girl below this age is illegal (this age is also used to define boy prostitution because the emphasis is upon youth and vulnerability). The use of this term is not to suggest that notions of the adolescent or juvenile are irrelevant, clearly they are not and indeed have played a prominent part in the way sexual activity among the young has been perceived. In addition, the term child prostitution was used by contemporaries and thus should be considered in that light and because of its long usage the term informs the nature of the activity involved in a way that no other term allows.

The term child prostitution is also used with the recognition that many recent writers have searched or made use of less value laden language which takes into account, for example, the subjective views of 'prostitutes'. In such work other terms, such as sex worker, business girl/boy, 'trade' have been preferred.[23] This is an attempt to disassociate from the 'moral arena' or judgements regarding prostitution. What is important to recognise here is that, as McCullen states, 'Engaging in acts of "prostitution" does not make one a life member to the "profession". Or, to put it even more plainly, "prostitution" is behaviour – not a person – and a "prostitute" is merely a term which describes a person's behaviour'.[24]

Contents

The starting point for any historical consideration of child prostitution during the twentieth century must be the late nineteenth century, an era of uncertainty, change and emerging forms of knowledge, when the subject of the commercial sexual exploitation of children first attracted widespread official, media and public attention. The function of Chapter Two is to offer an exposition of child prostitution during a period that was formative in constructing the images and representations of this social problem for the next century or more. Indeed, the image of the child as an innocent victim of sale or abduction to be sent overseas into prostitution on the one hand became a significant force behind early child protection measures, yet on the other hand served to obscure the reality behind the child prostitution that was occurring within the country.

Chapter Three explores the expansion of the work of children's voluntary societies, particularly the NSPCC, so that during the Edwardian period they were to consolidate their influence on childcare policies and challenge the less flexible approach of the Poor Law. By the Edwardian period the large children's charities had overcome much of the opposition to assertive social intervention and firmly established themselves as nationally recognised organisations working for the welfare of children. Problems that were previously held to be private were now increasingly perceived to be social problems in a context of concern about the strength of the nation. Through its child protection campaigns the NSPCC emphasised the prevalence of cruelty towards, and neglect of, children. The prostitution of children received limited attention, although child sexual 'assault' attracted serious concern. This, in part, revealed the persistent problems in uncovering and prosecuting such cases: the sensitivity of the subject, the often covert nature of child prostitution and the difficulties of securing evidence for prosecution. Also important were the difficulties of locating child prostitution within modern ideological concepts of what constituted the family and childhood.

The family and the relationships upon which it was founded were increasingly the subject of examination and comment during the inter-war period considered in Chapters Four and Five. In some respects women experienced an alleviation of social constraints through falling birth rates, wider employment and leisure opportunities and through the diffusion of the idea of the companionate marriage. Prostitutes, however, were subject to more criticism. The subject of child prostitution remained taboo, except in the form of the sensationalisation of white slave trade stories which, if anything, served to distance the public further from the realties of commercial sex. Child prostitutes, unless they were seen to be clear victims of parental or other adult coercion, remained likely to attract suspicion and condemnation as temptresses, at a time when it was increasingly accepted that children who experienced sexual abuse would not necessarily be able to forget and grow out of the effects of that experience. Thus early sexual abuse became a common part of explanations given for later resort to prostitution.

In the period of post-war rising social expectations and rising incomes, discussed in Chapter Six, attitudes towards prostitution shifted in that poverty was perceived to be a less justifiable and understandable reason for women selling themselves and psychological explanations were increasingly drawn upon. The spectre of child prostitution continued to be used as a symbol of moral decline and fears for the future. However, the real trade in under-age sex was highlighted by professional research. Psychiatrist T.N.C.Gibbens claimed that five per cent of the 14 to 16 year-old girls he interviewed in remand homes had been involved in commercial sex and the publication *Women of the Streets* was able to map out the areas of London in which the younger prostitutes worked. Legislation that, it was claimed, would deal punitively with habitual prostitutes, but intercept the young at an early stage, was to prove ineffective in many respects when under-age prostitutes continued to lie about their age, when they were resistant to the work of probation and social workers and when they did not work the streets.

Chapter Seven discusses the extent to which the subject of child prostitution received widespread media attention, not only because of the activity itself but also because of the social, political and economic climate of the 1970s. Furthermore, it was not until the 1970s that public and media discussion of child prostitution suggested that this social problem might even be systemic in certain environments. This was an aspect of debate on the subject of child prostitution that had not been in evidence since the late nineteenth century.

The final chapter serves to bring together and clarify, from a late twentieth-century perspective, many of the issues identified in the preceding chapters. During the 1990s more young people appear to have become involved in prostitution at younger ages, and the debate on this social problem moved forward in the sense that the existence of child prostitution was formally and widely acknowledged. Despite its contradictions the new guidance offered by the government provides some hope that things will improve for young people in prostitution and if local agencies can work co-operatively in the interests of the welfare of the child this will undoubtedly make a real difference to the lives of such young people.

References

1 B. Jordan, *A Theory of Poverty and Social Exclusion* (Cambridge: Polity, 1996); I. Robinson, 'Globilization: Nine thesis on our epoch', *Race and Class* 38 (2), 1996; A. Sivanandan, 'New circuits of Imperialism', in A. Sivanandan (ed.) *Communities of Resistance* (London: Verso, 1990).

2 See for example J. Green, *It's No Game: Responding to the needs of young women at risk or involved in prostitution* (Leicester: National Youth Agency, 1992); R. Barbaret, D. Barrett and M. O'Neill, 'Young people and prostitution: No respecter of boundaries in North Western Europe', *Social Work in Europe* 2 (2), 1995; S. Kershaw, 'Sex for sale: A profile of young male sex workers' circumstances, choices and risks', *Youth and Policy* 63, 1999; J. O'Connell-Davidson, 'Sex tourism in Cuba', *Race and Class* 38 (1), 1996; O. Calcetas-Santos, *Report of the special rapporteur on the sale of children, child prostitution and child pornography*, European Commission of Human Rights 53rd session, Item 21 (b), 1997; S. Sidorenko-Stephenson, 'Moscow street children and emerging urban marginality', paper presented to panel on Youth and Cultural Globalization in post-Soviet Russia, BASEES Conference, Fitzwilliam College, Cambridge, 27–29 March 1999; M. Melrose and D. Barrett, 'Report on a study

of juvenile prostitution', paper presented at National Vice Conference, Portishead 29–30 June 1999.

3 A. van Meeuwen, *Whose Daughter Next?* (Essex: Barnardo's, 1998), p. 3.

4 'Inverts, perverts and mary-annes: male prostitution and the regulation of homosexuality in England in the nineteenth and early twentieth centuries', in J. Weeks *Against Nature: Essays on History, Sexuality and Identity* (London: Rivers Oram Press, 1991), p. 49.

5 A. James and A. Prout, *Constructing and Reconstructing Childhood*, second edition (London: Falmer Press, 1997).

6 H. Hendrick, *Child Welfare, England 1872-1989* (London: Routledge, 1994), p. xi.

7 'What is a child?', in A. Fletcher and S. Hussey (eds) *Childhood in Question: Children, Parents and the State* (Manchester: Manchester University Press, 1999), p. 19.

8 For example see M. Foucault, *The History of Sexuality*, Vol. 1 translated by R. Hurley (Harmondsworth: Penguin, 1990) and M. Foucault, *Discipline and Punish: The Birth of the Prison* translated by A. Sheridan (Harmondsworth: Penguin, 1977).

9 J. Weeks, *Sex, Politics and Society: The Regulation of Sexuality since 1800* (Harlow: Longman, 1989), p. 6.

10 M. Foucault, *History of Sexuality*, p. 104.

11 H. Hendrick, *Child Welfare*, pp. 1–2.

12 'The dangers of child sexuality', Foucault's dialogue with Guy Hocquenghem and Jean Danet was produced by Roger Pillaudin and broadcast by France Culture on April 4, 1978. This version, taken from the internet (http://www.mindspring.com/~rainbowchild/foucault.html) is published in *Michel Foucault: politics, philosophy, culture, interviews and other writings*, L. D. Kritzman (ed.) (New York: Routledge, 1988) translated by A. Sheridan, with the title 'Sexuality, morality and the law'; also see J. R. Kincaid, *Child-Loving: The Erotic Child and Victorian Culture* (London: Routledge, 1992); L. Jackson, *Child Sexual Abuse in Victorian England* (London: Routledge, 2000), p. 11.

13 L. Jackson, *Child Sexual Abuse*, p. 11.

14 R. Matthews, 'Beyond Wolfenden? Prostitution, politics and law', in R. Matthews and J. Young (eds) *Confronting Crime* (London: Sage, 1986), p. 199.

15 K. Barry, *Female Sexual Slavery* (London: Prentice-Hall, 1979), p. 11.

16 Cited in H. Hendrick, *Child Welfare*, p. 255.

17 L. Jackson, *Child Sexual Abuse*, pp. 15–16.

18 L. Gordon, 'The politics of child sexual abuse, notes from American history', *Feminist Review* 8, 1998, p. 56.

19 C. Smart, 'Reconsidering the recent history of child sexual abuse, 1910–1960', *Journal of Social Policy* 29 (1), 2000.

20 L. Gordon, 'The politics of child sexual abuse', p. 56.

21 L. Jackson, *Child Sexual Abuse*, pp. 4–5.

22 'Inverts, perverts and mary-annes', p. 48.

23 See, for example, R. J. McMullen, 'Youth prostitution: A balance of power',

Journal of Adolescence 10 (1), 1987, p. 35; D. Barrett (ed.) *Child Prostitution in Britain: Dilemmas and Practical Responses* (London: Children's Society, 1998).

24 R.J. McMullen, 'Youth Prostitution', p. 35.

Chapter 2

Debating late nineteenth-century child prostitution

In our streets and throughout our provinces some months ago, there were circulated, emanating from the Pall Mall Gazette offices, disgusting and filthy articles – articles so filthy and so disgusting that one cannot help feeling that they may have suggested to innocent women and children the existence of vice and wickedness which had never occurred to their minds before.[1]

The starting point for any historical consideration of child prostitution during the twentieth century must be the late nineteenth century when the subject of the commercial sexual exploitation of children first attracted widespread official, media and public attention. The late Victorian period, as an era of uncertainty, change and emerging forms of knowledge, is the context for the exploration of child prostitution that follows. It should be noted that as the focus of this book is upon the twentieth century, this essentially background and contextual chapter relies largely upon secondary sources. There is a wealth of such material on this area for the nineteenth century that provides a useful and analytical starting point.

The function of this chapter is to offer an exposition of child prostitution during a period that was formative in constructing the images and representations of this social problem for the next century or more. The main purpose is not, therefore, to recount incidents of child prostitution, although some will be given. Indeed, an example of the prostitution of one Victorian child, who later achieved notoriety as the ex-brothel keeper who claimed to have purchased a 13 year-old child for W.T.Stead, will be utilised as an occurrence from which to open out this subject.

In July 1885 the attention given to juvenile prostitution was fuelled considerably by a series of articles written and published by W.T.Stead in the *Pall Mall Gazette*, (6, 7, 8, 10 and 22 July) which he edited, entitled 'The Maiden Tribute of Modern Babylon'. The sensational and salacious style of language used in these articles has rightly been subject to much historical criticism. The articles included sub-headings such as, 'Virgins Willing and Unwilling', 'Buying Girls at the East-End' and 'Strapping Girls Down'. Despite this, it is clear that Stead succeeded in highlighting a social problem to the extent that the issue continued to be the subject of comparisons in the late twentieth century. For example, Ian Sparks, chief executive of the Children's Society, stated in an article in *The Guardian* of the 24 May 2000 that 'the sexual exploitation of children during Victorian times was widespread, and little has changed since then'.[2]

The moral panic excited by Stead's revelations provided the crucial force to ensure the final passing of the Criminal Law Amendment Act in 1885 which established the age of consent at 16 years of age, from 13, and increased police powers to deal with vice. The conflicting motivations and controversies underlying the journey to the passing of the Act are suggested by the change, during Parliamentary debate, in the title of its first part from *The Suppression of Prostitution* to *The Protection of Women and Girls*. The balance between control or protection was to become an enduring feature of debates on child prostitution and on the subject of youthful delinquency generally. As well as bringing in tighter controls on brothels the Act covered the removal of women abroad. It also extended the legislation on procurement by the introduction of prosecutions against parents or other guardians who colluded with procurement. The Criminal Law Amendment Act was also effectively and notoriously to criminalise homosexuality under Labouchere's amendment.[3] In some respects this was an extension of existing legislation, for example, the Offences against the Person Act 1861 (forbidding buggery) and was more to do with policing aims rather than any innovation. Nevertheless, the 1885 Act increased willingness, in light of the reduced penalties, to convict such 'crimes' as Oscar Wilde was to discover to his cost.[4] The catchall section of the legislation stated that:

> Any male person who, in public or private, commits, or is a party to the commission of, or procures or attempts to procure the commission by any male person of, any act of gross indecency with another male person, shall be guilty of a misdemeanour, and being convicted thereof shall be liable at the discretion of the court to be imprisoned for any term not exceeding two years, with or without hard labour.[5]

Under the previous Assault of Young Persons Act 1880, the age of consent to indecent assault for both boys and girls had been set at 13 years of age, it had already been raised to 13 for cases of unlawful carnal knowledge in 1875.[6]

Thus, the period since the 1970s is not the first time that these issues have gained public recognition. It may be the case that during the 1970s the priorities of feminist organisations in both England and Wales and in the United States helped to bring what seemed at the time to be previously hidden and taboo issues, such as child abuse and incest, into the open. However, feminist organisations, and religious and voluntary societies during the late nineteenth century expressed similar concerns, including alarm over child prostitution. Late nineteenth-century social workers from child protection agencies were clearly familiar with this kind of phenomenon and they were even an expected part of their caseload.[7] George Behlmer has pointed out that the Maiden Tribute revelations had come as no surprise to the London Society for the Prevention of Cruelty to Children as it had, in the course of its work, discovered that sexual assaults upon children were 'strangely widespread' and although 'odious …   to the conscience of the country … almost unpunishable'.[8]

In response to child abuse and neglect, voluntary child protection organisations were established throughout most of the western world during the late nineteenth century. This is not to suggest that such agencies did not exist prior to the late nineteenth century; concern expressed in this form with regard to child protection and juvenile prostitution was evident from the 1830s,[9] rather children's societies experienced their most visible and significant emergence and expansion at this time. Through the work of these child protection and rescue societies the rights of the child were to be newly legitimated and so the idea that 'children possess a "right" to reasonable treatment from their parents came of age in the late nineteenth century'.[10]

During the late nineteenth century, the power of the depiction of child victims *versus* their brutal and predatory abusers became the cause which united feminists, social purity organisations and religious bodies and individuals to campaign for an increase in the age of consent and other child protection measures. The term 'white slave', in common usage by the 1870s, became the parody which denoted the abduction and violation of innocent youth by, usually foreign, evil agents, thus incorporating concerns about overseas threats to British imperialism. Loose networks of campaigning purity groups emphasised prevention and/or the, usually institutional, moral re-education of young girls, for example, the Girls Friendly Society (1874), Ellice Hopkins' Ladies Association for the Care of

Friendless Girls (1876), and the Band of Hope Mission (1879) and Josephine Butler's Ladies National Association (1869). Despite sometimes considerable disagreement between the various kinds of such organisations, they did serve to effectively highlight the sexual and physical abuse of both women and children by men and worked to eradicate moral double standards and bring about the 'purification of national life'.[11]

Purity challenged both male and female immorality and the concept of the irresistible male sexual urge. The emphasis for men, who came to dominate purity movements, was upon decency, self-discipline and control. As Frank Mort has suggested, within purity movements images of 'male sexuality twinned evangelical concepts of the struggle between flesh and sprit with an evolutionary stress on the lower and higher impulses of human nature'.[12] However, in both England and Wales and the United States, the intent to abolish prostitution was also utilised to attack the sexual behaviour and moral standards of working-class youth, poor women and homosexuals; anyone whose 'erotic activity outside of marriage placed them at odds with Victorian norms'.[13] Indeed, at this time conceptions of sexuality, childhood, social class, urbanisation and the state of the nation became closely related issues that shaped public and political debate and action.

Child prostitution became a locus upon which these broader issues converged, were debated and negotiated. The issue of child prostitution specifically became a subject of debate and campaigning in Parliament, among feminist and purity advocates, who had long been aware of such problems, particularly since the fight against the Contagious Diseases Acts,[14] within children's voluntary organisations and in the press. Juvenile prostitution was the phenomenon which elicited the first flowering of the so-called 'New Journalism' of W.T.Stead in his 'Maiden Tribute' articles.[15] The prominence of the 'Maiden Tribute' articles has presented historians with the question of the extent to which children and juveniles were involved in prostitution and they way in which this form of economic activity should be interpreted in the context of late Victorian society.

Deborah Gorham has observed that historians of the 1960s and 1970s tended to accept that juvenile prostitution was a serious social problem and that Stead's articles define and 'tell an irrefutable story of sexual exploitation that is as horrifying today as it was in the 1880s'.[16] In more recent years, however, historians have been more circumspect as to the rationale and dimensions of juvenile prostitution in late Victorian England and Wales. Gorham accepts that many young girls were engaged in prostitution in that period through economic necessity, not as the 'passive, sexually innocent victims', depicted by Stead, 'but because their choices were so limited'.[17] Louise Jackson, however, treats the claims of the prevalence of juvenile prostitution with scepticism and to some extent considers them to have been euphemistic descriptions of child sexual assault by a society that was not yet able to bare openly the emotional scars of child sexual abuse and incest.

> It is clear that the term 'juvenile prostitution' had become, by the late Victorian period, yet another euphemism – along with those of 'moral outrage', 'corruption' and 'immorality' – to refer to what we now describe as child sexual assault. The story of the child prostitute was simply the most acceptable articulation of the problem; it was clear who was 'good' and who was 'evil' and it did not open up the moral and emotional can of worms that a narrative of incest would have involved.[18]

To an extent this may have been the case. Martin Wiener has noted, for example, much of the upsurge in prosecutions for sexual abuse of minors after the Criminal Justice Amendment Act concerned girls assaulted by neighbours or family members.[19] Jackson effectively highlights the problems of interpretation concerning the vague and evasive language often used in relation to sexual issues at the time. However, since the term child prostitution represented a defined mode of behaviour, albeit often subject to dramatisation, rather than the much more obscure or nebulous terms like 'corruption', it would be more accurate to encompass an acceptance of child prostitution within the definition of child abuse.

In an approach influenced by the emphasis upon meaning derived from cultural studies, Judith Walkowitz offers a different perspective. In her 1992 publication, *City of Dreadful Delight*, she explores the cultural and political effects of the ways in which discourses around sexual danger were produced and disseminated in Victorian society. Walkowitz describes the way in which W.T.Stead took a melodramatic formula, in existence since the 1840s, and extended it to a wider public. In so doing he elevated sexual narratives to the level of social drama and produced 'a contradictory, obsessive discourse around sexuality that remain a legacy for the modern era' in the form of New Journalism.[20] In this domestic melodrama, the sexual exploitation of the daughter was, according to Walkowitz, a means to personalise class exploitation by posing a threat to the family hierarchy and male working-class prerogative, but also helped to place women on the political agenda.[21] Women mounted the political stage in defence of women and children, in respect most notably to the movement to repeal the Contagious Diseases Acts and around the issue of prostitution. In this way discourses on sexual knowledge proliferated and new definitions and categories of sexual danger emerged, most publicly in the form of the child or juvenile prostitute.

Yet these constructions were in many ways distant from the lived experience of such young people. As Walkowitz notes, 'there undoubtedly were some child prostitutes on the streets of London, Liverpool, and elsewhere [however] most of these young girls were not victims of false entrapment, as the vignettes in the "Maiden Tribute" would suggest'.[22] The 'Maiden Tribute' articles and the 'shifting of the cultural image of the prostitute to the innocent child victim' operated, Walkowitz states, to mystify wider issues of sexuality.[23] It is claimed here that these discourses and the stereotypical images they presented also operated to mystify, and in the longer term hide, the phenomenon and realities of child prostitution itself.

The mystification of child prostitution also underlies the misleading representations of adult prostitution during the period as constituting a profession followed by outcasts who lead brief and unpleasant lives. Such definitions were, in part, a mechanism to label the prostitute as outside of social norms and as polluting. The prostitute, 'literally and metaphorically, becomes her body and, albeit at times in a contradictory manner, is culpable in some way'.[24] Philippa Levine has observed of the nineteenth and early twentieth centuries that 'a vast literature sought to identify the prostitute, to examine the causes of her (and it was always her) waywardness and assess the possibility of her reform, to castigate the class from which she was assumed to have been drawn and to ram home the evils of poverty, idleness, frivolity and alcohol'.[25]

One example of the more informed of such contemporary literature on prostitution was produced by Rev G.P. Merrick, Chaplain of HMP Millbank in *Work Among the Fallen, As Seen in the Prison Cell* (1890). Merrick collated information on some 16,000, 13,915 of whom, he stated, had led an 'immoral life'. Of those who gave a previous occupation 8,001 had been domestic servants, 1,122 laundresses, 2,667 needlewomen, 1,050 barmaids, and 1,617 'trade girls'. Of 14,563 cases 1,763 were 'seduced before the age of 16 years old', eleven of these before they were 11 years old, 36 before they were 12 and 62 before they were 13.[26]

Access to the sources generated by the operation of the Contagious Diseases Acts have, in the late twentieth century, enabled a much more nuanced and analytical consideration of nineteenth-century prostitution. Walkowitz concludes that most prostitutes seem to have moved onto the streets in their late teens and remained there for no more than a few years. Most were single, living away from their families, and local to the region, often originating from casual domestic employment although this later became more diverse to include shop girls, waitresses and barmaids. Many would have been half or full orphan and before going onto the streets had already had non-commercial sexual relations with a man of their social class.[27]

Walkowitz emphasises how little contemporaries knew or attempted to know about the relationship between the prostitutes and the communities in which they operated. This would have required a questioning of the pathological approach and a 'whole new set of postulates' to see them as 'neither pollutants nor the polluted, but as persons who could and did exercise some rational control in their lives'.[28] Social integration depended upon complex factors including the character of the local community and the external pressure placed on these communities with regards to sexual respectability. Walkowitz notes, for example, the presence of parents who encouraged and/or consented to their daughters becoming prostitutes.[29]

Widespread concern about child prostitution was inextricably linked with the ideologies of childhood that were being formulated. According to Gorham, in the context of uncertainty about the concept and boundaries of childhood and adolescence, and the proper relationship of children to the family and wider society, reformers revealed a duality in their motivations, on the one hand wanting to protect young girls and on the other wanting to control them.[30] Linda Mahood's analysis of female reform institutions in Glasgow and Edinburgh takes a more social control oriented approach, emphasising the subjective experiences and resistances of the children. She states that reformers' desire to protect working-class girls was part of 'a larger programme to control their sexual and vocational behaviour, which reflects the desire to impose a middle-class social code on working-class women'.[31]

In her study of *Child Sexual Abuse in Victorian England*, Louise Jackson has also highlighted uncertainty at this time regarding the transition from childhood. She states that the Criminal Law Amendment Act of 1885 raised three questions, 'When in sexual terms, did a girl become a woman? What was the difference between girl child and woman? What marked the transformation?'[32] It is clear then, that at the heart of the revelations of child prostitution lay deep social uncertainties about age, sexual knowledge and the family.

The Maiden Tribute

Information about a traffic in English girls to Belgium, from Alfred Dyer, a Quaker and radical purity reformer, and George Gillet, his cohort, in

1879-1880, resulted not only in the establishment of the London Committee for Suppressing the Traffic in British Girls for the Purposes of Continental Prostitution but also in the setting up of a House of Lords committee to investigate. Indeed, following public revelations of girls being held captive in brothels in Brussels, already widely known in purity circles, 'white slavery' firmly and permanently took on the connotation of the 'abductor and the hypodermic syringe'.[33] This was despite the fact that most of the cases uncovered involved girls over 16 years of age who had already been prostitutes and who then travelled abroad. Upon arrival some had been brutally treated, yet public concern continued to be based, and reinforced with the help of purity propaganda, not on the actual plight of these girls but upon fear of abduction into white slavery.

The House of Lords' inquiry (1881) concluded that most English inmates of brothels overseas had been professional prostitutes before they embarked but that juvenile prostitution was a real problem in England. Reverend Horsley had, for example, stated to the inquiry that of a sample of 3,074 prostitutes imprisoned in Clerkenwell Prison, where he was chaplain, nearly a quarter were 17 years of age or younger. The Lords Committee recommended an increase in the age consent from 13 to 16, that police be empowered to search private premises for suspected prostitutes, that the age of abduction for immoral purposes be raised from 16 to 21 and that street soliciting be made illegal.[34] Under the auspices of the London Committee for Suppressing the Traffic in British Girls, a number of purity reformers, including Josephine Butler who had led the campaign to repeal the Contagious Diseases Acts, and W.T.Stead, presented a petition to the Foreign Secretary. This called for a change in the law to make it impossible to deprive any young girl of her liberty by force or fraud.[35] There were two loopholes in the law that allowed this at the time. If a girl was over 13 years old it was not illegal to induce her to become a prostitute and, even if this was done by deception, if the prostitution took place overseas no English law had been broken.

A Criminal Law Amendment Bill was drafted and several versions debated in the House of Commons between 1882 and 1885 but allowed to die. The required public and political pressure was only generated as a result of Stead's 'Maiden Tribute' articles. The series of articles, written and published by W.T.Stead in the *Pall Mall Gazette* in July 1885, were based on events set in motion by Stead and the persuasive force of Bramwell Booth and the Salvation Army. For the Booths, child prostitution was the representation of the moral depths to which English society had sunk. Bramwell Booth's notes record a visit to Stead of which he states that 'we were convinced that the only thing to be done was to rouse the public and that could only be accomplished by the testimony of witnesses of what they had actually seen with their own eyes'.[36]

The aim was to prove that girls under the age of 16 were being sold in London for the purposes of prostitution, or 'white slavery', by undertaking the purchase of a girl themselves. Thus they emulated the methods of early nineteenth-century abolitionists who had bought slaves at market to free them,[37] in order to bring pressure to bear upon the government to pass the Criminal Law Amendment Bill. Indeed, in 1890 William Booth compared the prostitution of young girls in this way to the violation of women by slave traders.[38] Stead later maintained in court that what he did was 'to commit the mere semblance of a crime in order to render the perpetration of actual crime more difficult, its detection more certain, and its punishment more severe'.[39]

To facilitate the purchase of a child Stead co-opted, through the Salvation Army, the reluctant services of Rebecca Jarrett. Jarrett had once been a child prostitute and then a brothel-keeper until rescued and helped to overcome her alcoholism by the Salvation Army. Using her old contacts, Jarrett claimed that she obtained and purchased from a woman her 13 year-old daughter, Eliza Armstrong. The girl was then taken to a midwife who examined her to verify her virginity in the same manner that it was believed genuine procurers would behave. Stead then went so far in the charade as to have the girl removed to a rented room in a brothel and chloroformed to quieten her. Following his masquerade to the last, he then entered the room. He did not touch or assault the girl, although she was frightened by his appearance, but played his role to the finale to prove that a girl could be purchased and sold into prostitution. He then published his account of a white slave trade in young girls, centring upon the experiences of Eliza Armstrong. The furore and public pressure consequent upon the Maiden Tribute articles became decisive in the passing of the Criminal Law Amendment Act.

As a result of the purchase of Eliza Armstrong, Stead, Jarrett, Bramwell Booth, Jacques Elizabeth Combe, the Salvation Army Officer who afterwards had escorted Eliza to France, and the midwife who had examined her, Madame Mourez, were charged with the abduction of a girl under 16 years of age from her parents' home. With the exception of Bramwell Booth and Combe, they were also charged with assault in relation to the medical examination. Stead believed that there was a kind of 'brothels lobby' at work behind the bringing of these charges. Certainly, the Maiden Tribute articles caused significant official embarrassment as well as public outrage. Furthermore, in both the Maiden Tribute articles and in the court, Stead accused the legislature of deliberately blocking reforms which might interfere with the pleasures of the aristocracy whom he depicted as providing the bulk of the demand for young girls.[40]

The trial began at the Central Criminal Court on 23 October 1885 and continued for nineteen days in total (including committal proceedings). On the tenth day the judge, in the face of proof that the mother had consented to the removal of the girl, ruled that it was the father's consent that was required before removing any child and it was clear that the father had not been informed prior to the removal of his daughter.[41] This judgement has since been referred to as a 'legal nicety',[42] however, although this was not the issue that the defence had wanted the case to focus upon, it indicated the social priorities of the contemporary legal system: the sanctity of the patriarchal family. Stead received three months imprisonment and Jarrett six months. Madame Mourez was given six months hard labour and died in prison. Bramwell Booth and Combe were discharged.

Walkowitz has stated that it is impossible to decipher the truth of the case in respect to the supposed sale of the child as so much is left unsaid, particularly with regard to the female protagonists.[43] Jarrett certainly felt that an agreement clearly understood by the participating parties had been made for the sale of Eliza Armstrong. 'That Mother,' Jarrett asserted, 'never asked me what I wanted her for or where I was going to take her she never even asked when she would see her again, she had got the money there I could take her where I liked [sic].'[44] Jarrett also resented the way in which Stead had proceeded to undermine the credibility of her story in defence of his own methods in the case. Significantly, he had not written down what she had told him regarding the proceedings of buying Eliza Armstrong until much later, a fact which surprised the court since Stead had claimed absolute accuracy for his narrative.[45] For Bramwell Booth the benefits of the 'Maiden Tribute' events later became clear and he recorded them in his notes. His list included, 'Act passed'; that the issue was brought 'before all classes in all countries as never before'; 'Inspired hundreds that was body [the Salvation Army] with energy and courage to go into maelstrom of iniquity'; brought in thousands of pounds; and didn't lose a single friend worth having and made a lot of new ones'.[46]

Child prostitution

The extent of social pressure and campaigning to abolish child prostitution denoted in part the symbolism that became attached to the phenomenon as a social evil, particularly in the stylised and stereotyped image of the child prostitute. Judith Walkowitz has described this as a gripping but familiar melodrama constructing the innocent child, her dissolute mother and the evil procurer as well as the aristocratic rake who formed the demand for this juvenile trade.[47] The reality for the reformers and police who did come into contact with child prostitutes was that, in many cases, they bore little relation to the fragile and coerced image portrayed by Stead. As Gorham has suggested:

> The real young girls who emerged from the interstices of that rhetoric have two characteristics. In the eyes of their would-be reformers, they are unmanageable and flighty. In the privacy of their minute books and printed annual reports, organisations which managed rescue or 'preventive' homes reveal that one of their biggest problems was controlling the unruly behaviour of the girls with whom they came into contact.[48]

The historian of the Children's Society, John Stroud, has observed that the staff running the homes in some cases had to cope with what he describes as, 'wild, foul-mouthed, undisciplined children, many of them steeped in the practices of crime and prostitution'.[49] There are clear similarities here with the problems faced by social workers in trying to help young girls involved in prostitution in the late twentieth century. Patrick Ayre and David Barrett note that child prostitutes a century later may not be adequately provided for by welfare agencies largely because of the challenge they pose to the victim concept. As they state 'aggressive, streetwise, anarchic young people who steal and do drugs as well as prostitution do not conform obviously to our idealised image of a child in need'.[50] The difficulties in coping with children from disturbed and/or abusive backgrounds was, and continues to be, reflected in the persistent problem of children absconding from children's homes.

Walkowitz asserts that there undoubtedly were some child prostitutes on the streets of London, Liverpool and elsewhere, but that the numbers were grossly exaggerated by purity propaganda, nor were most of these girls victims of false entrapment.[51] There certainly was a brisk trade in Victorian child pornography. Gorham confirms the existence of child prostitution during the late nineteenth century and illustrates this with evidence from a police witness before the Lords Committee of 1881, regarding a juvenile couple who were living together. The boy was charged with theft and the girl had gone down to the police station,

'she said she was waiting to see "her man" go down.' The police witness estimated the girl's age as thirteen and said she was 'a little child that had high boots … very short petticoats … she had her fingers covered with rings, a child of that age.' When asked if he thought that she was 'kept' by the boy, he said 'no, more likely she was assisting in keeping him'.[52]

Howard Vincent, Director of Criminal Investigations with the Metropolitan Police also suggested to the Committee that children of 14, 15 and 16 years of age were openly soliciting at night in the streets around Haymarket and Piccadilly. He asserted:

There are houses in London … where there are people who will procure children for the purposes of immorality and prostitution, without any difficulty whatsoever above the age of 13, children without number at 14, 15 and 16 years of age… Now it constantly happens, and I believe in the generality of cases it is so, that these children live at home; this prostitution actually takes place with the knowledge and connivance of the mother and to the profit of the household.[53]

The problem is that much of the available evidence is unsubstantiated and based on witness accounts. The Committee on Sexual Offences Against Young Persons which reported in 1925 was even then critical of the limitations of criminal statistics for extracting information regarding sexual offences against or by children.[54] Yet there is qualitative evidence, which originates, for example, in the rescue work of organisations like the Salvation Army, from institutional records and from parliamentary papers. Salvation Army workers confronted juvenile prostitution in the first rescue homes they opened in 1883 and 1885. In a story in the Salvation Army magazine, *The Deliverer*, one member prominent in the opening of the first rescue home, Hanbury Street Refuge, recalled how:

Some of the men who were after the girls I'd got would wait for me and get hold of my bonnet and drag it off; or they'd throw me into a passage, or kick me in the shins, and when a man is wearing blucher boots they can give a bad kick.[55]

Other incidents have also emerged from historical research in this subject area, for example, the supposed cover-up and protection of Mrs Jeffries who was accused by a former servant of permitting the rape of 13 year-old girls in her string of high-class brothels.[56] Also, the newspaper cutting found by Ellice Hopkins concerning a procurer in Hull who was claimed to have kept fifteen young prostitutes between the ages of 12 and 15 in a so-called 'infant school'.[57]

In her memoirs, Rebecca Jarrett states that she told Stead that she was 'sorry to say some of those men don't mind what her age so they know she has not been used before [sic]'. Jarrett may well have been willing to assist Stead in part because her own history resonated so much with children like Eliza Armstrong, but she came to resent the 'public show' made of the events and Stead's use of her as a 'poor tool'. She also claimed that in Millbank Prison she was approached by a woman who told her that 'me and my man has got seven years to do for doing what you have done'.[58] It is difficult to believe that her gratitude to the Salvation Army for helping her and the passage of time (she was nearing 80 when she recorded her memoirs) would have completely distorted events that figured so strongly in her life.

The issue here is that some of the evidence regarding late Victorian child prostitution has been discredited by undoubted exaggeration and even overt manipulation of child prostitution as a powerful image in purity and feminist campaigns. The most well-known, or infamous, of such misrepresentations being that constructed by Stead, although even here there remains grounds to suggest that, despite the embellishments and salaciousness of Stead's writing in the 'Maiden Tribute' articles, the initial transaction concerning Eliza Armstrong may have been implicitly understood to be for the purpose of prostitution.

The drama in the Eliza Armstrong case, according to Plowden, derived from the human predicament, 'out of the relationship between two societies living side by side and yet so totally separated, that neither ever really began to understand the other'.[59] Significantly, Plowden highlighted the social and economic structure which could produce a hidden but underlying, and unspoken, acceptance of child prostitution. This was a 'delicately balanced piece of social machinery – machinery which was geared to making life bearable in the appalling environment of Charles Street'.[60] This was not the child prostitution of melodrama, but the involvement of children under 16 years of age in commercial sex, either at or near home and not necessarily being the consequence of, or resulting in exclusion from, their family.

It's only fair to say that even if Mrs Armstrong had sold Eliza, neither she nor the street had reckoned on losing touch with her altogether … assuming that Mrs Armstrong was guilty, that she'd sold her child into prostitution, she'd also committed the more serious crime of being found out … and had exposed herself and Charles Street to public disgrace.[61]

In this respect then, the legal case following the Maiden Tribute articles may not be the counter drama observed by Walkowitz, but a submerged drama centring around Jarrett and the community of Charles Street. While Jarrett's memoir does seem to oscillate between the duality of 'mothers who saved and mothers who betrayed',[62] it is suggested here that there were social circumstances and economic pressures that made such dichotomous images of good and evil contentious and inappropriate. In the interstice between the confines of the language of contemporary middle class ideologies and the harsh realities of widespread poverty, an economically poor mother could in fact be both one who saved and one who betrayed, a factor at the core of social misunderstandings. Jarrett loved and defended her mother who lead her into prostitution and appeared not to have felt betrayed by her. It is suggestive that in Josephine Butler's biography of Jarrett, *Rebecca Jarrett* (1886) it was felt necessary to significantly change the story-line and an upper-class seducer was blamed for Jarrett's 'fall' when in, fictitious, service at the age of 15.[63] It is important that an acceptance of exaggeration in accounts of child prostitution in late Victorian England be incorporated with a recognition that the sexual exploitation of children was one consequence of economic and social circumstances. While Roberts appears to favour the latter over the former and overstates the extent to which 'gentlemen' clamoured for underage sex, nevertheless, the following is insightful:

> The sexual exploitation of Victorian working-class children is neither more nor less shocking than the facts of their day-to-day struggle for existence. To side step the issue of poverty that made them so vulnerable to abuses *of all kinds* is sadly, to persist in doing so.[64]

Society in the Cremorne Pleasure Gardens

The pleasure garden as a form of outdoor resort had a history dating back into the late seventeenth century, but by the nineteenth century was competing in a much more complex and developed urban leisure industry. The Cremorne Pleasure Gardens in Chelsea, west London, experienced their most successful commercial period in the 1860s. Lynda

Neal notes that the 'history of Cremorne in the middle of the nineteenth century is the history of the speculative and entrepreneurial management of metropolitan leisure and entertainment'.[65] The range of entertainment laid on was depicted in advertising posters, newspapers and paintings and included balloon displays, dances, an orchestra, theatre, music-hall, the circus, fireworks and the freedom for diverse public social contact; 'it gave people what they wanted'.[66] Open to the public during the day and lit by gaslight at night for carousers, Cremorne became 'a mini-metropolis', 'a schizophrenic social space, associated equally with peaceful family outings and explicit prostitution and public distur-bance'.[67] Particularly after the 1850s, the prostitute had taken her trade to the increasingly fashionable casinos, night-houses and pleasures gardens like the Argyll Rooms, Kate Hamilton's, and Cremorne.[68]

The Cremorne Pleasure Gardens became part of the conflict over cultural and social standards and values during the 1870s as opponents of the Gardens, including the Chelsea Vestry, eventually succeeded in bringing about its closure in 1877. Bristow directly associates the closure of this venue, along with the Argyll Rooms and the Highbury Barn, with campaigns to close down other well-known locations of prostitution, such as the 'night houses'. This served to increase the numbers of prostitutes on the streets and in the music-halls which then became the focus of purity campaigners.[69]

Within the diverse space of Cremorne the career of a prostitute, later to become fundamentally and notoriously associated with W.T.Stead and the Maiden Tribute articles, was initiated. Rebecca Jarrett who was later persuaded by Stead to purchase a child had herself begun as a prostitute at a very young age. In her memoir Jarrett reveals not only her own life as a prostitute and Madame but the family circumstances that were instrumental in bringing this about. As a child during the 1860s, Rebecca Jarrett was prostituted by her mother for money to buy alcohol. However, she blamed not her mother but her father for deserting them both. Indeed, she implored 'some of you will say as read this what a *bad Mother* she must have had but Please *dont* she was a good Mother it was my wretched Father doing [sic]'.[70] According to Jarrett, her father had left his wife and eight children several times to live with other women. In many ways the stark and generally unreflective manner, with little punctuation, in which she recounts her life adds to the impact of her words.

> While they [her brothers] were away [at sea] my Mother took me to
> Cremorne garden which was then opened you could spend days in
> those gardens drink as much as you like there were lonely walks
> you could be lost for hours there it were I first see the degraded life

of immorality it was there not on the street … I was 12 … My Mother was a bit proud of Me. I was inclined to be tall very fair Hair blue eyes. I remember had round my neck a string of great blue beads she kept me clean so Cremorne Gardens was My ruin before I was 13 I was used in a life of impurity [sic].[71]

It is clear from this account that in parent-child, or at least mother-daughter, relationships during a period in which severe poverty was widespread, economic considerations were crucial and were sometimes a focal issue in familial affections. As Hendrick has suggested 'maternal affection was conditional upon children playing their expected roles in the economic calculus'.[72]

Ellen Ross's examination of motherhood in 'outcast London' also emphasises the extent to which economic considerations remained a primary consideration in child rearing at this time. For working-class mothers, children continued to be a vital economic resource as well as a significant economic drain. As Ross states 'the need to help mother thus continued to dominate the lives of cockney children into the twentieth century. For the majority it was errands and other forms of "mother's work"; for the poorest it was the drudgery of home manufacturing'.[73] Girls expected to share in the household labour and, as Anna Davinn has suggested, parents expected their children to 'do all they could and sometimes more'.[74] More was expected and received from girls than boys and they also identified more closely with the worries of the mother. Ross observes that while fathers were often resented for the labour intensive lives of many children, resentment against mothers was less openly expressed.[75] In Helen Gordon's important study of social work records from Boston, *Heroes of their own lives* (1988), she identifies this kind of allegiance in American society with respect to incest. Gordon states that cases of father-daughter incest were sometimes seen as a legitimate form of self-sacrifice by the daughter within the patriarchal family. 'In working-class and particularly immigrant poor families, it was expected that children should work to spare their mothers; and mothers expected to be able to count on daughters for self-sacrifice'.[76]

Children who were subject to abuse from family members were forced to make a choice between obeying parental authority and adhering to social norms.[77] This issue also arises in Linda Mahood's examination of the records of Scottish children's voluntary societies in the late nineteenth and early twentieth centuries. In the cases of girls found wandering it was recognised that this was sometimes the result of fear of sexual and physical abuse from their fathers.[78] However, references to actual or suspected sexual abuse in case notes were usually couched in ambiguous terms about concern regarding wandering or the number of beds in the house.[79]

The inability, or at least extreme reluctance, scientifically and culturally for the nineteenth century medical establishment to contemplate that sexually transmitted diseases in children could be acquired through sexual contact exemplifies this kind of conflict or alienation experienced by children who were abused. Acquired venereal disease in children tended to be interpreted as a consequence of innocent contact, such as breast-feeding or hugging, or shared clothing or bedding.[80] Child protection societies in most western societies began to question these interpretations during the late nineteenth century and the knowledge being accumulated gradually strengthened their case. As Taylor notes, 'only gradually did the accumulation of scientific, sociological, and psychological evidence begin to force physicians to abandon their noncommittal stance'.[81] However, this was not only a slow and non-linear shift but where the existence of abuse was accepted it was identified with less-than-respectable groups and in the United States was seen as 'un-American' behaviour.[82]

Of course, considerations other than the purely economic directed child-parent relationships and also influenced the moral and disciplinary standards maintained by families even in the most difficult of circumstances; respect and respectability were powerful control mechanisms often powerfully enforced.[83] Such attitudes were reinforced by children's voluntary societies, which upheld the idealised vision of the family as protective, nurturing and as instilling social virtues in the private sphere. The NSPCC, especially, helped to reshape public opinion away from the view that the family was inviolate and towards the acceptance of interference by private and public bodies. These societies in both England and Wales, and the United States, sought to reconstruct the family towards a model of male supremacy that included state, and later professional, regulation 'limiting parental rights and prescribing new standards for proper child-raising,'[84] and by which children were regarded as citizens in their own right.[85] One of the main ways in which this was achieved was through legislation. The first major NSPCC success in this respect was the Prevention of Cruelty to Children and Protection of Children Act 1889, legislation which was later extended and consolidated in 1894 and 1904. This declared that:

Any person over 16 years of age, who having the custody of a child, being a boy under the age of 14 years or being a girl under the age of 16 years, wilfully ill-treats, neglects, abandons or exposes such a child or causes or procures such a child to be ill-treated, neglected,

29

abandoned or exposed, in a manner likely to cause such a child unnecessary suffering, or injury to is health, shall be guilty of a misdemeanour.[86]

A conviction for an offence of this nature became liable to a fine of up to £100 or two years in prison and the court could make an order committing the child to the care of a relative or other fit person.

Childhood experiences, therefore, continued to be submerged within and beneath the icon of the family. The NSPCC continued to maintain that its role was not to replace parental authority and responsibility but to reinforce it. Parents were given two warnings before legal action was taken, except, significantly, in the case of girls found living in brothels in danger of 'moral corruption'. In her examination of the construction of 'the social' as institutional and ideological space in England 1850-1940, Linda Mahood suggests that the familial ideal which reified the autonomous nuclear family, the dominant male breadwinner, his nurturing wife and dependent children, operated as a normalising mechanism used by the 'child-savers' (children's societies) to press for new legislation.[87] She states that 'this ideology established the para-meters whereby the "normal" and "abnormal" family culture could be distinguished and families (by definition poor families) that deviated from this normative ideal were judged as deviant, pathological and productive of juvenile delinquency'.[88] Thus these 'social' ideologies, spaces and practices functioned to discipline gender and sexuality in the context of familial and childhood ideologies.

One prominent theme in the rhetoric around juvenile delinquency thus constructed was that of the vicious and sexually promiscuous girl, drifting into prostitution by association with vice. The strategy of the children's societies was to separate delinquents from 'normal' children by relating to them concepts of dirt and filth, wage earning and indepen-dence and forms of knowledge, especially sexual knowledge, 'social problems were regarded as the outcome of individual weaknesses and vice, although certain situations might exacerbate tendencies and frailties'.[89] Thus sexual knowledge and its association with dirt and contamination, general social behaviour that was perceived to be undisciplined, and independent earning capacity were characteristics which became used to make the distinction between the 'normal' and the 'abnormal', 'moral' and 'immoral'. These images were also common in Europe. Alain Corbin has examined images of the prostitute which helped to inspire the need for regulation in France at this time. These images largely related to her smell, to disease (syphilis) and the indefensible way in which the prostitute was seen to enable 'the social body to excrete the excess of seminal fluid that causes her to stench and rots her'.[90]

The moral panic regarding child prostitution during this period can be seen as part of social discovery and ideological exploration of the constitution of childhood and of sexuality. It was, Jackson has noted, 'part of a move to naturalise and normalise the childhood condition amongst all social classes'.[91] Thus the middle-class idealisation and sentimentali-sation of children in both England and America during the late nineteenth and early twentieth centuries has been described as 'sacralization' by Viviana Zelizer, an American sociologist.[92] Prominent in this was the removal of children from the economic sphere and shielding of them from sexual knowledge.

It is contended here that child prostitution was one means by which a child might add to the family purse and/or lend the child some or, where family support was not available, complete economic autonomy. Of course, this was much less common than the more usual avenues of child employment, and it is impossible to estimate how frequent child sexual exploitation was, yet there is little doubt that it continued to exist throughout and beyond this period. During the late nineteenth century, child prostitution may well have been a route taken, or forced upon, the poorest families or individuals and/or those less influenced by the emerging conventions of social morality. Street children between the ages of 13 and 16 years who were without family or support were unprotected from sexual exploitation because, as was pointed out by purity campaigners, they were already out on their own. The police were often pressed by the public to clear particular areas of London, public indecency in Hyde Park was a subject of recurring public complaint. In twelve months in 1893–4, 147 prostitutes were charged with various offences in the park and nineteen 'young girls' were charged with sleeping in the open air without visible means.[93]

Certainly, a high proportion of the children taken into state care or custody had no parents. At the turn of the century, over half of those sent to industrial schools were orphaned or deserted.[94] During the 1880s, members of the Church of England Waifs and Strays Society would go 'Waif Hunting' in the early hours of the morning to find children sleeping in the streets because they were 'by this time unable to find anywhere better than the streets, some turned out by parents who have been unable to provide for themselves, others turned out of kitchens of lodging houses when they are locked up'.[95] Thus the Church of England was prompted to name its society for the rescue and protection of children the Waifs and Strays Society, after the medieval term 'wayves and streyves' meaning pieces of ownerless property.[96]

The Stead trial highlighted the fact that it was illegal only to take a child from its parents or guardian without their consent. The large numbers of destitute and homeless children and juveniles, or waifs and strays, that more or less found a living in the streets of London, like the street children of late twentieth-century South America or Thailand, had few options and capitalised on any economic opportunity available.[97] Indeed, prostitution has been termed an applied kind of 'penny capitalism', one of the available 'forms of private enterprise' for the most poor and vulnerable.[98]

Social anxiety centred upon representation of the children of the poor as savages that were subject to being depicted as either uncivilised, dangerous and precocious, morally and otherwise, or as revered innocents free from social convention but requiring protection. [99] Yet both of these images were often perceived as alien, in need of discipline and control and were used as a 'wedge to prise open families'.[100] Cunningham observes that in an age of racism and imperialism, an age which continued well into the twentieth century, the 'representation of the child as a savage was much more likely to lead to policies which emphasised the subordination, incapacity and undesirable traits in children'.[101] Indeed, it was in part racist and ideological preconceptions that delineated the images of savages utilised in relation to the children of the poor. The aims of reformers were, although to some extent motivated by humanitarian impulses, 'to anchor unclaimed, drifting and potentially dangerous children so that they could be surveyed, controlled and corrected'.[102]

Conclusions

As Hendrick has noted, many of the social stereotypes that have become familiar in the twentieth century were formulated and confirmed by the late nineteenth century. He asserts that by the 1890s a clear notion of 'the child' was beginning to be formed which focused childhood as more uniform and coherent among all children, within the context of the development of the domestic ideal among the middle classes, as 'the principal institutional influence'. In addition to this, Hendrick cites as important the evolution of a compulsory relationship between the state, family and welfare service. This elucidates much of the context of change discussed in this chapter. However, more specifically this chapter has been an exposition of another broad aspect of the work of Hendrick,[103] the way in which children have persistently been perceived through dualities, as representations of good and evil, as victims and threats; as hope for the future or representations of social degradation. In many respects child prostitution provides one of the more explicit expositions of such dualities. The image of the child as an innocent victim of sale or abduction into prostitution on the one hand became a significant force behind early child protection measures, yet on the other served to obscure the reality behind the child prostitution that was occurring within the country. Because child prostitutes did not meet the picture of innocence betrayed, they were often defined by a very different imagery, that of a vicious and sexually promiscuous threat to society. To a lesser extent, judgements were made with regard to children who were seen to live or spend a large part of their lives in the streets. Danger was seen in the realities of the lives of poor urban families where children were likely to use and know the streets and have independent earning capacity.

The commercial sexual exploitation of children was one way in which children could earn money, whether to keep themselves or to contribute to the family. In contemporary discussion of the problem, child prostitutes did not appear to 'become' their body in the same way as adults but this was prevented only by the persistence of the representation of child prostitutes as wholly victim and as wholly without agency in a world in which children commonly worked from very young ages, and thus as not posing a threat to ideologies of childhood and the family.

References

1 Judge in the trial of W. T. Stead cited in A. Plowden, *The Case of Eliza Armstrong: 'A Child of 13 Bought for £5'* (London: BBC, 1974), p. 123.
2 Also see D. Barrett and P. Ayre, *Guardian* 24 May 2000 and R. Hattersley, *Guardian* 16 October 1999.
3 F. B. Smith, 'Labouchere's amendment to the Criminal Law Amendment Bill', *Historical Studies* 67, 1976.
4 Ibid, p. 165; L. A. Jackson, *Child Sexual Abuse in Victorian England* (London: Routledge, 2000), p. 101.
5 Cited in F. B. Smith, 'Labouchere's amendment'.
6 Offences against the Person Act, 38 and 39 Vict., C.94.
7 L. A. Jackson, *Child Sexual Abuse*, p. 3; G. Behlmer, *Child Abuse and Moral Reform in England 1870-1908* (California: Stanford University Press, 1982), preface; for the United States see L. Gordon, *Heroes of Their Own Lives: the politics and history of family violence: Boston 1880-1960* (New York: Viking, 1989), p. 56.
8 G. Behlmer, *Child Abuse and Moral Reform*, p. 73.
9 E. Bristow, *Vice and Vigilance: Purity Movements in Britain since 1700* (Dublin:

Gill and Macmillan, 1977); R. Dingwall, J. M. Eekelaar and T. Murray, 'Childhood as a social problem: A survey of the history of legal regulation', *Journal of Law and Society* 11 (2), 1984; L. A. Jackson, *Child Sexual Abuse*, pp. 14-15.

10 G. Behlmer, *Child Abuse and Moral Reform*, preface.

11 F. Mort, *Dangerous Sexualities: Medico-Moral Politics in England since 1830* (London: Routledge and Kegan Paul, 1987), p. 113.

12 Ibid, p. 115.

13 A. Snitow, C. Stansell and S. Thompson (eds) *Powers of Desire: The Politics of Sexuality* (New York: Monthly Review Press, 1983), p. 22.

14 Under the Contagious Diseases Acts of 1864, 1866 and 1869, women in named garrison and port towns were subject to being arrested by police on suspicion of being 'common prostitutes' and could then be ordered to undergo an internal medical examination, often carried out in poor conditions, and if infected by venereal disease, were detained until deemed to be cured. These Acts were finally repealed in 1886. See J. Walkowitz, *Prostitution and Victorian Society: Women, Class and the State* (Cambridge: Cambridge University Press, 1980), S. Kingsley Kent, *Sex and Suffrage in Britain 1860-1914* (London: Routledge, 1987) and W. Acton, *Prostitution*, P. Fryer (ed.) (London: MacGibbon and Kee, 1968).

15 J. Walkowitz, *City of Dreadful Delight: Narratives of Sexual Danger in Late-Victorian London* (London: Virago Press, 1992).

16 'The "maiden tribute of modern Babylon" re-examined. Child prostitution and the idea of childhood in late-Victorian England', *Victorian Studies* 21, 1978, p. 362; see for example, M. Pearson, *The Age of Consent* (London: David and Charles, 1972); R. Pearsall, *The Worm in the Bud: the world of Victorian sexuality* (London: Weidenfeld and Nicholson, 1969); C. Terrot, *The Maiden Tribute: A Study of the White Slave Traffic of the Nineteenth Century* (London: Frederick Muller, 1959).

17 D. Gorham, 'The "maiden tribute of modern Babylon"', p. 355.

18 L. A. Jackson, *Child Sexual Abuse*, p. 16.

19 M. Wiener, 'New women *vs* old men?: sexual danger and 'social narratives' in later Victorian England'. Roundtable on *City of Dreadful Delight*, *Journal of Victorian Culture* 2 (2), 1997, p. 307.

20 J. Walkowitz, *City of Dreadful Delight*, p. 85.

21 Ibid, pp. 86-7.

22 J. Walkowitz, *Prostitution and Victorian Society*, p. 145.

23 J. Walkowitz, *City of Dreadful Delight*, p. 84.

24 P. Levine, 'Rough usage: prostitution, law and the social historian', in A.Wilson (ed.) *Rethinking Social History: English Society 1570-1920 and its Interpretation* (Manchester: Manchester University Press, 1993), pp. 269-70.

25 Ibid, p. 269.

26 G. P. Merrick, *Work Among the Fallen: As Seen in the Prison Cell* (London: Ward, Lock and Co, 1890), pp. 27–8 and 34.

27 J. Walkowitz, *Prostitution and Victorian Society*, pp. 14–23.

28 Ibid, p. 47.
29 Ibid, pp. 23, 29–30 and 207.
30 D. Gorham, 'The "maiden tribute of modern Babylon"', p. 355.
31 L. Mahood, *The Magdalenes: Prostitution in the Nineteenth Century* (London: Routledge, 1990), p. 163; also see P. Bartley, *Prostitution: Prevention and Reform in England, 1860–1914* (London: Routledge, 2000), pp. 12–18.
32 L. A. Jackson, *Child Sexual Abuse*, p. 17.
33 E. Bristow, *Vice and Vigilance*, pp. 86–7.
34 Ibid, p. 90; Mort, *Dangerous Sexualities*, p. 128.
35 F. Mort, *Dangerous Sexualities*, p. 126–7.
36 Salvation Army Archive, 'Maiden Tribute' material.
37 P. Bartley, *Prostitution: Prevention and Reform*, p. 88.
38 W. Booth, *In Darkest England and the Way Out* (London: Carlyle Press, 1890), p. 13.
39 G. S. Railton, *The Truth about the Armstrong Case and the Salvation Army* (London: Salvation Army, 1885), p. 5.
40 A. Plowden, *The Case of Eliza Armstrong*, p. 50.
41 Ibid, p. 116.
42 R. Hattersley, *The Guardian*, 16 October 1999.
43 J. Walkowitz, *City of Dreadful Delight*, p. 107.
44 Salvation Army Archive, 'Maiden Tribute' material.
45 A. Plowden, *The Case of Eliza Armstrong*, p. 97.
46 Salvation Army Archive, 'Maiden Tribute' material.
47 J. Walkowitz, *City of Dreadful Delight*, pp. 85–102.
48 D. Gorham, The "maiden tribute of modern Babylon"', pp. 374–5.
49 J. Stroud, *Thirteen Penny Stamps: The Story of the Church of England Children's Society (Waifs and Strays) from 1881 to the 1970s* (London: Hodder and Stoughton, 1974), p. 106.
50 P. Ayre and D. Barrett, 'Young people and prostitution: an end to the beginning?' *Children and Society* 14, 2000, p. 55.
51 J. Walkowitz, *Prostitution and Victorian Society*, p. 248.
52 D. Gorham, 'The "maiden tribute of modern Babylon"', p. 374.
53 PP 1881 (IX) 355, Evidence to the House of Lords Committee, Qu.579, 19 July 1881: 63, cited in C. Smart, 'Disruptive bodies and unruly sex: the regulation of reproduction and sexuality in the nineteenth century', in C.Smart (ed.) *Regulating Womanhood: historical essays on marriage, motherhood and sexuality* (London: Routledge, 1992), p. 27.
54 PP 1924–5 [Cmd.25611] XV, p. 905.
55 May 1921, p. 37.
56 D. Gorham, 'The "maiden tribute of modern Babylon"', pp. 360–1.
57 E. Bristow, *Vice and Vigilance*, p. 107.
58 Salvation Army Archive, 'Maiden Tribute' material.
59 A. Plowden, *The Case of Eliza Armstrong*, pp. 13–4.
60 Ibid, p. 65.
61 Ibid.
62 J. Walkowitz, *City of Dreadful Delight*, p. 116.

63 Ibid, p. 117.
64 N. Roberts, *Whores in History: Prostitution in Western Society* (London: Grafton, 1993), p. 198.
65 *Victorian Babylon: People, Streets and Images in Nineteenth-Century London* (New Haven: Yale University Press, 2000), p. 109.
66 Ibid, p. 130.
67 Ibid, pp. 113 and 109.
68 E. Trudgill, 'Prostitution and Paterfamilias', in H. J. Dyos and M. Woolff (eds) *The Victorian City: Images and Realities Vol.2* (London: Routledge and Kegan Paul, 1973).
69 E. Bristow, *Vice and Vigilance*, p. 168.
70 Jarrett memoir, n.d, p. 1, Salvation Army Archive.
71 Ibid, p. 1.
72 H. Hendrick, *Children, Childhood and English Society 1880–1990* (Cambridge: Cambridge University Press, 1997), p. 20.
73 E. Ross, *Love and Toil: Motherhood in Outcast London, 1870–1918* (Oxford: Oxford University Press, 1993), p. 152.
74 A. Davin, 'What is a child? In A. Fletcher and S. Hussey (eds) *Childhood in Question: Children, Parents and the State* (Manchester: Manchester University Press, 1999), p. 22.
75 E. Ross, *Love and Toil*, pp. 154–5.
76 L. Gordon, *Heroes of their own lives*, p. 237.
77 Ibid.
78 L. Mahood, *Policing Gender, Class and Family: England 1850–1940* (London: UCL, 1995), p. 107.
79 Ibid.
80 K. J. Taylor, 'Venereal disease in nineteenth-century children', *Journal of Psychohistory* 12 (4), 1985, p. 439; C. Smart, 'Reconsidering the recent history of child sexual abuse, 1910–1960', *Journal of Social Policy* 29 (1), 2000.
81 K. J. Taylor, 'Venereal Disease', p. 448.
82 Ibid; for twentieth century see L. Gordon, *Heroes of their own lives*.
83 J. Burnett, *Destiny Obscured: Autobiographies of Childhood, Education and Family from the 1820s to the 1920s* (London: Routledge, 1982), p. 48.
84 L. Gordon, *Heroes of their own lives*, p. 57.
85 I. Pinchbeck and M. Hewitt, *Children in English Society, Vol.II* (London: Routledge and Kegan Paul, 1973), p. 611.
86 Cited in R. Dingwall, J. M. Eekelar and T. Murray, 'Childhood as a social problem: A survey of the history of legal regulation', *Journal of Law and Society* 11 (2), p. 220.
87 L. Mahood, *Policing Gender*, p. 10.
88 Ibid.
89 Ibid, pp. 20 and 36; H. Cunningham, *The Children of the Poor: Representations of Childhood since the Seventeenth Century* (Oxford: Blackwell, 1991), p. 133; also see M. Douglas, *Purity and Danger: An analysis of the concepts of pollution and taboo* (London: Routledge, 1966).

90 Alain Corbin, 'Commercial sexuality in nineteenth-century France: A system of images and regulations', *Representations* 14, Spring 1986, p. 211.

91 L. A. Jackson, *Child Sexual Abuse*, p. 17.

92 Cited in H. Hendrick, *Children, Childhood and English Society*, p. 10.

93 PRO MEPOL 2/5815.

94 J. Springhall, *Coming of Age: Adolescence in England 1860–1960* (Dublin: Gill and Macmillan, 1986), p. 172.

95 *Our Waifs and Strays*, August 1886 (26).

96 J. Stroud, *Thirteen Penny Stamps* (London: Hodder and Stoughton, 1971), pp. 61–2.

97 H. Montgomery, 'Abandonment and child prostitution in a Thai slum community', in C. Panther-Brick and M. T. Smith (eds) *Abandoned Children* (Cambridge: Cambridge University Press, 2000); T. Hecht, 'In search of Brazil's street children', in *Abandoned Children*.

98 Biggs *et al*, *Crime and Punishment in England: An Introductory History* (London: UCL Press, 1996), p. 198.

99 T. Linehan, 'Pollution and purification: child prostitution and the age of consent in late Victorian England', MA Dissertation, London School of Economics, 1999.

100 L. Mahood, *Policing Gender*, p. 2.

101 H. Cunningham, *The Children of the Poor*, pp. 131–2.

102 T. Linehan, 'Pollution and Purification', p. 8.

103 H. Hendrick, *Child Welfare*, pp. 7–13.

Chapter 3

Edwardian England and the ideal family

Carry the purpose of the law into the mind and heart and the tissues of the bodies of children.[1]

The expansion of the work of children's voluntary societies, particularly the NSPCC, meant that during the Edwardian period they were to influence childcare policies and challenge the less flexible approach of the Poor Law. In purely numerical terms the number of children who received practical help and assistance from voluntary societies was impressive. To illustrate this point, during December 1910 the NSPCC inquired into 4,745 complaints of children being ill-treated, of these 4,301 were found to be true and to be affecting the welfare of 13,240 children. At the end of 1910 Dr Barnardo's had 9,130 children in residence[2] and the Church of England Central Society for Providing Homes for Waifs and Strays (hereafter the Waifs and Strays Society) had 4,169 children in its care.[3] These figures do not, of course, include the other forms of provision made for children by these and countless other charities, including free or cheap food and clothing. Furthermore, during this period most Reformatory and Industrial Schools were administered and managed by voluntary societies with grants from central government. At the end of 1909 the number of children and young persons under 17 detained in Reformatory Schools was 5,878, in Industrial School 20,133 and in Day Industrial Schools the number attending was 3,269.[4]

Although the child protection and rescue strategies of individual charities varied according to their specific objectives and resources, the major children's charities had in common a vision of a shared, responsible social order and an ultimate belief in the power of environment over heredity.[5] At this time perceptions of rescue work became increasingly infused with concerns about national efficiency and expanding knowledge about the lifestyles, health and education of the poorest classes and their children. Such knowledge was accrued through social surveys,[6] government commissions, the increasing range of social institutions that were established to deal with the problems of the poor, compulsory education and, of course, the voluntary societies themselves. One consequence of such knowledge was to help reinforce the image which had emerged during the later nineteenth century, of children as essentially similar whatever social class they derived from.[7] Harry Hendrick also emphasises the growth of the Child Study movement (1880s–1914), as a consequence of rising anxiety about the quality of the child population, which was combined with an interest in human development. He concludes that the 'movement served to position the social, educational, psychological and racial importance of childhood, and of children, in terms of education, social welfare and mental and physical health'.[8]

Among the most difficult problems that the children's societies came across in their work were the children perceived to be at risk of 'moral degradation', sexual abuse or exploitation. This was also increasingly considered to be one of the most serious crimes against children and among the most urgent rationales for the removal of children from their homes. In 1911 the monthly paper of the Waifs and Strays Society, called *Our Waifs and Strays*, declared that:

> The Society accepts children, absolutely according to the relative urgency of their claims, between the ages of one and sixteen. The greatest urgency being that on behalf of those whose lives are in the midst of moral temptation, and where the danger is literally a *soul-danger*, a large number of the 'family' [residents of their children's homes] are therefore drawn from such surroundings.[9]

Sexual experience in children and young people transgressed the fragile boundaries between what constituted adult and child. In an age where sex before marriage was commonly defined as sinful, for women at least, such behaviour was associated with criminality and criminal women were suspected of 'abnormal' sexual conduct. However, while the response to the sale of sex by adult women could be ambiguous, in that it was depicted as undermining and polluting but also as upholding the cult of domesticity, by providing an outlet for male sexual need, there was less ambiguity around views of the sexuality of children. The morally innocent, dependent child of middle-class cultures seemed far-removed from children who from a very young age earned their own living and who were inured in street life. The existence of child prostitutes therefore transgressed two interdependent sets of values, the ideal of childhood and the ideal of the family, leaving voluntary societies unsure and indeed unwilling to deal directly with the problems of such children once they had been 'rescued'. Any engagement with the social and economic mechanisms which perpetuated such practices was also limited.

Intervention and resistance: the work of the children's charities

Many of the problems and criticisms that had beset the major children's charities during the late nineteenth century continued into the twentieth. The strength of mainstream Victorian morality and philosophy was evident in the persistence of *laissez-faire* opposition to state interference and in debates about the degree of interference in the private sphere that was legitimate and consistent with the economic liberalism that lay behind much charitable endeavour. The more *laissez-fairist* stance was scathingly referred to by one commentator as 'that mistaken notion of liberty which recognised the parent's rights and ignored the child's wrong'.[10] The 'Englishman's home is his castle' and his castle, that symbol of middle-class property and domestic ideology, included his children. In defence of the family-centred policies and action of the NSPCC, the Society brought and won a libel suit in 1902 against the author of letters published in *The Cheltenham Examiner*. These letters claimed that the NSPCC 'wrecks the homes of the poor by false, lying, and exaggerated statements which are presented to the magistrates as evidence, and which teaches children to give false evidence against their parents'.[11] During the early twentieth century the NSPCC continued to assert that its role was one of reinforcing and elevating family life, through the strengthening of family ties and responsibilities, rather than destroying it; that they 'were not a set of plain-clothes policemen; they were not a sort of inquisition; they were rather a moral mission, seeking to instigate a better love of family, and a higher ideal of the family life'.[12] Indeed the 1900-1901 annual report of the NSPCC had asserted what was seen as the fundamental differences between the work of the police and that of the Society. The main concern of the police was 'the public peace' whereas that which most concerned the NSPCC was 'family happiness'.

This is not to present a picture in which voluntary and state provision were disassociated during this period, rather they acted in a form of partnership and co-operation. As Jane Lewis has stated, the voluntary sector was a part of the body politic 'working with the same principles as government in respect of social problems while carving out a separate sphere of action'.[13] Hence, in recognition of the prominence of its work, the NSPCC obtained from the government 'authorised person status' under the Prevention of Cruelty to Children (Amendment) Act in 1904. This meant that the Society had the right to remove a child from the home without the police but with the consent of a magistrate. The same piece of legislation (sections 20 and 131) also gave power to the local authority to remove children to a 'place of safety', a strategy fundamental to modern child protection practice. Possible places of safety included the children's societies, the workhouse, police station, any hospital or surgery, if the occupier was willing to receive the child. This caused problems between the NSPCC and local Poor Law Boards of Guardians reluctant to take on children likely to be a long-term burden, until the 1908 Children's Act determined that it was the duty of the Guardians to provide for children brought to the workhouse as a place of safety.[14] The 1908 Act was largely consolidating and amending legislation but it expanded the definitions of cruelty, and thus augmented the role of the children's societies, to include neglect, the failure to 'provide adequate food, clothing, medical aid or lodging' or to seek poor law help to obtain these. The core of the legislation was, therefore, to increase and extend surveillance of parental responsibility.[15]

Hendrick has referred to the interventionist methods of the children's charities, and asserts that the giving of limited 'rights' to children was 'an important part of the general strategy to discipline the family through the application of selected liberal democratic principles, while simultaneously avoiding economic reform'.[16] Thus, the late nineteenth-century tendency to highlight individual cases of parental inadequacy, alcoholism, and promiscuity as deserving moral condemnation and punishment persisted into the early twentieth century. This is not to say that the causes of such social problems were not recognised, they increasingly were, only that, for many, to intervene in the economic *status quo* was perceived to be more harmful. The Charity Organisation Society, for example, epitomised an approach which inextricably linked an early social casework method with its individualistic ideology to rationalise provision, a philosophy referred to as 'scientific philanthropy'.[17]

The publications of the children's charities, therefore, sometimes offered an undifferentiated mix of factors to explain the poor treatment of children. Thus, in a series of articles in the monthly paper of the Church of England Waifs and Strays Society, *Our Waifs and Strays*, the 'Enemies of Childhood' were identified as drink, common lodging houses, overcrowded accommodation, child vagrancy, child labour, and street trading by children.[18] The policy of the Waifs and Strays Society emphasised, that 'indiscriminate alms-giving is an evil … every indis-criminate alms-giver is doing harm'[19] and also that it 'is no part of our work to aid directly in the solution of the problem [in this case overcrowding], but it is our work to migrate, so far as lies in our power, some of the worst effects of the evil'.[20] The NSPCC, the greatest political campaigner of the children's charities, was also oriented towards the immediately practical. The NSPCC continued to press for legislation to outlaw practices perceived to promote the neglect of children, such as baby-farming and the tramping of children, or to expand the range of offences against children that could be punished under the law, and to improve the process of the law in such cases.

A major achievement of the children's charities was the important role they played in promoting the public recognition of the rights of the child as distinct from their parents, and in particular the father because for them, children were 'born into the State as well as into the home'.[21] The rights of children not to be subject to cruelty, abuse and exploitation were in part a reflection of the prevailing international economic competition facing Britain, and the level of public alarm that this produced. Publicity given to the poverty surveys and the physical condition of recruits for the Boer War had heightened concerns over national efficiency and the state of the nation. Arnold White in his publication of 1901, *Efficiency and Empire,* claimed that of the 11,000 men in the Manchester district who had offered themselves for war service between October 1899 and July 1900, 8,000 were found to be 'physically unfit to carry a rifle and stand the fatigues of discipline'.[22] Another contemporary who was directly involved in sanctioning the discharge of unfit men from the army reported that, of those who were accepted into the army at this time, two out of every five did not last longer than two years.[23] Fears about physical efficiency were compounded by the report of the Inter-Departmental Committee on Physical Deterioration (1904), the year following the publication of the report saw a rush of philanthropic planning 'to found or revivify race-strengthening programmes'.[24] The NSPCC's own study of the physical condition of children in London, however, concluded that there was no perceptible decline in the physical stature of these children and these findings were passed on to the Tory government via the Royal College of Surgeons.[25]

It is clear, nevertheless, that the hidden hand in economic and industrial growth had failed to distribute the benefits effectively to the bottom quarter of the population. Increasingly, contemporary debate concentrated not only upon the responsibility and role of the family and of voluntary organisations but also of the state. In answer to political and philosophical challenges to the Liberal Government, after 1906, and to liberalism itself, a number of milestone social welfare measures were introduced which provided old age pensions (subject to a means test), unemployment insurance, and meals and medical examinations for school children for the first time. This signalled an important expansion of state responsibilities and, in some areas, a parallel reduction in the responsibilities of voluntary organisations. Indeed, the late nineteenth and early twentieth centuries witnessed what has been referred to as a reformulation of the state. Within this gradual shift of responsibilities, the children of the poor, the street children and the children born to those who were perceived to be criminal or immoral were represented in several ways; as the key to the future prosperity of the Empire, as victims of their environment and heredity and, more negatively, as a threat to the nation. Indeed, the annual report for Dr Barnardo's for 1900 warned against 'the absolute madness, of leaving the potential citizens of tomorrow so entrenched in the environment of evil in which vast multitudes enter upon life … that they grow up to constitute a danger to the body politic'.[26]

Given the generally individualist and self-help philosophies of the large children's charities it was not surprising that, initially at least, there was some opposition to the plans to extend social provision for children embodied in the Liberal welfare reforms of 1906-1911. Between 1906 and 1908 in particular, reforms providing not only for the feeding and medical inspection of school children but for the early notification of birth, the probation of young offenders and the establishment of juvenile courts were implemented. Although the NSPCC accepted that some of its supporters might find this opposition difficult to understand, state provision was seen by some societies, most vociferously by the Charity Organisation Society, as indiscriminate and reckless charity that would nurture dependence and encourage degradation. Indeed, Behlmer has suggested that greater prosperity was shifting the NSPCC towards a more conservative stance and greater emphasis upon the enforcement of parental duty.[27] Thus, in coercive vein, one NSPCC article claimed that to 'prepare the school tables for hungry children's breakfasts and for hungry children's dinners, and hungry children for them will increase. But prepare the prison fare for neglectful men, and neglectful men will diminish. Children before they go to school will be fed'.[28] The more extreme views of this kind criticised, as encouraging reckless marriages and the neglect of children, not only the state social legislation of the early twentieth century but provision given under the auspices of the Poor Law and also by societies, like Dr Barnardo's and the Waifs and Strays, that provided homes for children. Such Malthusian philosophies were certainly expressed by a minority within the NSPCC.[29] This was despite the fact that the Waifs and Strays Society often took children into their homes who were referred to them by the NSPCC as well as Poor Law Guardians, the Charity Organisation Society and various local rescue societies.

Childhood, 'moral danger' and prostitution

The diffusion of the cult of domesticity and respectability during the late nineteenth and early twentieth centuries to the working classes was to increase the social divide between the 'reputable' and 'disreputable' sections of society. This divide had long been policed by a deterrent Poor Law and was increasingly perceived as being demonstrated by sexual knowledge and behaviour, especially on the part of women. Legislation implemented during the late nineteenth century (1885) ostensibly to protect female children and young people from procurers for the traffic in child prostitutes was, according to Walkowitz, used for the systematic repression of brothels in most major cities.[30] By 1914, legal repression had significantly affected the nature and structure of prostitution. The power structures within prostitution may even have altered and, with increased general standards of living, prostitutes became more socially distanced from their local communities. Robert Roberts recalls in his *Classic Slum*, in Salford, the enduring taint of prostitution and their resignation to the base of the 'social pyramid' along with 'idlers, part-time beggars and petty thieves'.[31] Walkowitz suggests that:

> Cut off from any other sustaining relationship, they [prostitutes] were forced to rely increasingly on pimps for emotional security as well as protection against legal authorities. Indeed, with the wide prevalence of pimps in the early twentieth century, prostitution shifted from a female- to a male-dominated trade. Further, there now existed a greater number of third parties with a strong interest in prolonging women's stay on the streets.[32]

Although the role and input of pimps with prostitutes has historically been over-simplified, prostitution during the twentieth century has certainly capitalised upon the growth of particular forms of commercialisation. Night clubs, cafés and massage parlours have become new or increasingly important sites for prostitution and have attracted a wider range of third party interests.

Given the difficulty inherent in determining the actual extent of prostitution, whether during the 1910s or the 1990s, the degree to which this transition had occurred by 1914 cannot be accurately assessed, and can be even less accurately assessed with regard to child prostitution. The limited evidence obtainable from the archives of the large children's charities does, nevertheless, indicate that child prostitution was in evidence and was in some cases practised from within the family. Conclusions, however, must be tentative as in many cases the sensitivity of the issue meant that it was referred to by implication only. For example, the following appeared in the NSPCC annual report of 1915:

> In a town in Central Asia, where the people are of a low type, and where the position of women is little better than that of slaves, it is recorded that parents who were proved to have sold their daughter for immoral purposes were put to death. Hideous wrongs done to defenceless children in this country are frequently hidden until it is too late to render help to the victim or to bring the offenders to justice.

However, it is also clear from such accounts that not only was this considered fundamentally and morally wrong by those involved in voluntary social work but that there was a distinct rejection of child prostitution from the 'respectable' working classes.

The children of the poor were more and more thought to be entitled to the same kind of childhood and the same kind of rights that were being constructed in middle-class society for their own children. Child prostitution not only offended the sexual morality of the day but also assaulted ideologies regarding the dependence and innocence of childhood and also of the primary social institution, the family. The moral corruption of 'unprotected' children was, according to the NSPCC annual report of 1911 'of all the corrupt things in life … the most dastardly and contemptible'. The practice of prostitution among the very young was condemned in Europe. The investigation into *Prostitution in Europe* carried out by Abraham Flexner, and then published in 1917, highlighted evidence from France and Germany. Between 1880 and 1903, 975 minors (in this context those under 21 years old) were arrested by the Paris police for prostitution – however 91 of them were under 16 years of age.[33] Flexner maintained that despite variations in the law, official and public attitudes towards prostitution were similarly liberal across Europe. However, when prostitution became linked to disorder, the contamination of the very young (prostitutes as young as 15 and 16 were to be found in small numbers on the lists of regulated prostitutes in Prussia and Germany in the late nineteenth century) and/or exploiting third parties, it was perceived and treated in a more serious light.[34]

There were several pieces of legislation passed prior to the First World War in England that were important expressions of contemporary concern linking morality with the state of the nation. The Children's Act of 1908 was a major piece of consolidating legislation that clarified and re-emphasised pre-existing law and confirmed the importance of child protection legislation. The Act had several clauses which related directly to the subject of moral danger to children (under the Act those under 14 years old) and young persons (14 and 15 year-olds). These included measures to prevent the seduction or prostitution of girls and to prevent children and young people living in or frequenting brothels, or children from frequenting 'the company of any common or reputed prostitute'. Inherent in this legislation was an assumption that prostitution was a lifetime profession or at least irrevocably contaminating and that prostitute mothers would therefore inevitably introduce their own children into it. The concept of the 'professional' prostitute was envisaged as a career when it was often a temporary or last resort for the poorest classes of women and largely a consequence of social deprivation, family breakdown and a lack of alternative means of earning a livelihood. The annual reports of Dr Barnardo's consistently show that around half of all the children admitted into their care before the First World War came from families in which the father was recorded as dead.[35]

The 1908 Act reinforced concentration upon the criminalisation and closure of brothels forcing prostitutes onto the streets and making them more vulnerable to harassment by the police. Prostitutes were widely perceived to be responsible for the spread of venereal disease, in particular social purity and feminist organisations were important in the growth of a movement concerned with public health, called social hygiene. As Evans has suggested, 'VD was one of the *racial poisons* (along with alcoholism and feeblemindedness) that social hygienists saw as linked with *racial*, economic and imperial decline'.[36] Concerns about morality and national efficiency served to heighten fears about the extent and effects of venereal disease and put pressure on government to increase its interest in the sexual health of the nation because 'Sex conduct was not merely about morality or personal well-being but about national virility'.[37] Although the arsphenamine drug, Salvarsan, which 'stopped the clock' of syphilis was discovered in 1909, the resources and facilities to enable the widespread use of the drug to treat the disease were not organised until after the First World War. Nevertheless, for the first time the matter of venereal disease was openly discussed in the press and after enquiries and a Royal Commission into the problem, the Public Health (Venereal Disease) Act of 1917 was passed. This legislation restricted the administration of Salvarsan to authorised, trained doctors and criminalised the purveying of purported remedies by any but qualified doctors.[38]

Paradoxically, the existence of venereal disease itself had nurtured a belief, which, according to middle-class observers in both England and the United States, survived well into the twentieth century, and which may have helped to maintain the demand for sex with young girls. This belief held that if a man who had contracted venereal disease had sex with a virgin he would pass the disease on to her and be cured of it himself.[39] Unusually, in the debate on the Criminal Law Amendment Bill (1922) in the House of Commons, one speaker suggested that women were also infecting young boys for this reason. It was claimed that:

> any medical man will tell you that he has had experience in hospitals of boys of very tender years who have been infected for no other reason than the prevalence of that belief and others may have lingered on, perhaps longer than equivalent beliefs relating to other diseases, because of the secrecy and shame in which venereal diseases and sexual matters generally were shrouded.[40]

The social prejudices of the medical professional may well have contributed to the survival of such beliefs. Taylor suggests that the willingness in America to attribute the existence of venereal disease in the children of immigrants and the poor to sexual contact constituted an unwillingness to come to terms with the reality of children becoming infected.[41] Of course, much of the evidence of the belief that sex with a virgin cured venereal disease comes from social commentators, particularly in Parliament, referring to what the lower orders believed. There is little evidence that this was ever used as a plea of mitigation in court, although unless it was thought likely to elicit sympathy it would not have been used. But the credibility of such superstitions might have increased for an individual facing a debilitating disease like syphilis. The survival of the belief that sex with a virgin could cure venereal disease may also indicate the extent to which the concept of young children as sexual objects or indeed subjects of desire was perceived as problematic. As Smart has pointed out, the framing of this abuse in non-sexual terms did not absolve the abuser from condemnation but the children involved would still be defined as victims. According to Carol Smart, such a problematic concept was also evident in the fact that obliging a child to touch a man's genitals was not constituted by law as a form of sexual assault until 1959.[42]

In contrast it is the strength of the moral rejection of sexually experienced or knowledgeable children, and certainly of the phenomenon of child prostitution, that is among the most emotive aspects of the records of the children's charities. One case file held in archives of the Children's Society (previously the Church of England Waifs and Strays Society) is unusually forthcoming on the details of the behaviour which resulted in a young girl being sent to the St Saviour's Home for Girls at Shrewsbury. St Saviour's was specifically intended for 'children whose characters may have been affected, in some way or other, by exceptional knowledge of evil'.[43] The Waifs and Strays Society also had Industrial Schools at Mumbles, near Swansea (1882-1902) and the Beckett Home at Meanwood, near Leeds (1887) (see cover photograph) which served a similar purpose, 'to enable and aid these polluted little streams of life to run clear'.[44] In fact there was a shortage of industrial school accommodation for girls under 14 'with knowledge of evil'. As Pam Cox has noted, girls aged between 14 and 16 were too old to be admitted to industrial schools and, unless they had committed an offence could not be placed in a reformatory. These girls would sometimes be charged with other offences, such as theft. The shortage of places for girls under 14 sometimes resulted in months in places of detention on remand.[45] The separation of the 'fallen', with the allusion to the original fall, from other girls exemplified fears about moral contamination as did the separation from adult prostitutes in rescue homes who might contaminate these abused children further. Caught between ideologies of what were considered to be appropriate adult and child experiences, the girls in these separate homes for those with 'exceptional knowledge of evil' must have also experienced stigmatisation in the locality of their care homes. No such homes were established for boys.

In some cases, the behaviour of young girls described in the Children's Society case files do strongly suggest that abuse has taken place. One girl of ten had been living with her mother who was a domestic servant. Into their one-roomed home, described as a 'hovel', a prostitute was taken in, probably as a lodger, who appears to have looked after the girl while the mother was at work. After a year or so the mother's employer required that the mother sleep in and an arrangement was made whereby the children, three in all, would be looked after by another woman. This woman stated that the girl acted:

> in a very immoral manner she pulled up her clothes for boys to see her private parts and asked the other girls to do the same she also took boys into the bedroom to have sexual communication with her them to pay her a penny a time she as [sic] stood at the Bedroom Window quite naked and called to boys in the street come for she was ready for them.[46]

The implication was that the girl in question was sexually active, although the application form does not actually state that she had sexual intercourse with the boys that were invited to pay 'a penny a time'. The least that can be discerned is that the girl probably witnessed at close quarters the behaviour of women prostitutes at work.

There are some instances where girls have been deemed to be unmanageable, keeping bad company, staying out at night or generally described as 'wild', 'depraved' or having 'knowledge of evil'. Yet, the information provided by those who completed the application form to request that the Waifs and Strays Society take children in is often derived from community-based hearsay, in many cases little or no effort was made to verify this information. In this respect the application forms to the Waifs and Strays Society are useful for assessing social values and attitudes to perceived sexual precocity, particularly of individuals who were influential in their localities, including local clergymen, Poor Law Guardians, police court missionaries (precursors of probation officers) and rescue workers. In many cases, the rather limited factual information given and the vague and evasive language used, is insufficient to establish the actual character of the behaviour of the child and indicates the contemporary sensitivity of such issues. One case file describes a mother as 'most immoral, and it is feared the child inherits this sin',[47] another refers to a girl of 13 who had 'fallen', 'poor child taught to sin in ignorance at first'.[48] A more informative file pronounced a girl of 12 to be out of control and an 'immoral child. Born in immorality'. According to the case notes this child was born in prison to a mother who was 'ninety times in cells and prisons, for being drunk and disorderly'.[49] Judgements made regarding the mother often, therefore, clouded views about the child.

Clearer cases of child prostitution are occasionally recorded, even if the term itself is not applied. A court case reported in the supporter's magazine of the NSPCC, the *Child's Guardian* in June 1902, concerned a charge against a mother for ill-treating and neglecting her six children, aged one year and nine months to 15½. The report is a prime example of the frequent associations that were made at the time between physical and moral cleanliness, or lack of it. The home was described as 'filthy' and the upstairs as being in 'a state of horrible, indescribable filth'. A doctor also determined that the eldest daughter (aged over 16 and therefore out of the purview of the court case) looked very ill and was 'suffering from a loathsome disease'. The daughter aged 15 was also described as 'very filthy, and made certain admissions, alleging she had handed money to her mother'. When the mother was spoken to on the subject she smiled, and apparently 'looked on it as a matter of course'.[50] A few years later, a case in Bradford passed on to the NSPCC, and taken from the quarterly report of the Women Sanitary Inspectors under the Bradford Corporation, was reported in which two under-nourished girls were found living alone in a house which 'resembled a pigsty'. The elder girl of 15 years of age was, according to the report, 'being encouraged to earn her living by immorality'. Their mother was described as 'a habitual drunkard' and was sentenced to six months imprisonment, the children were handed over to the poor law guardians.[51] An important conviction under Section 17 of the 1908 Children's Act resulted in a twelve-month prison sentence in 1912 for a mother who had 'deliberately set herself to bring about the defilement of her daughter' of 11 years. This was only discovered to be the case during prosecution by the NSPCC of a man 'for an outrage' on the girl concerned.[52] In 1913, a further case of this kind was reported in which a father had forced his 15 year-old daughter, under threats of violence, into prostitution and had been living on her earnings for at least the previous year. Indeed, he had even 'accompanied the girl on her journeys, waiting for her in the nearest public-house'.[53]

Children perceived as having 'knowledge of evil', including victims of incest or sexual assault, were subject to removal from their family and school, as a source of contamination, and ostracised from their communities. In children's homes little had changed regarding the treatment of children with any kind of sexual experience since the second half of the nineteenth century. They were expected never to talk about or refer to such experiences, no matter how distressing. One girl in the care of the Waifs and Strays Society was not considered 'in any sense a depraved child' but because 'her past experiences [were] too vivid to be forgotten' she was felt to be 'a dangerous influence… in any Home' and was then sent to St Saviour's.[54] In common with the reformatory system one purpose of a home like St Saviour's was 'to restrain and suppress unsuitable behaviour and beliefs pertaining to sexual conduct, and substitute an alternative set of values'.[55]

As Jackson has pointed out, 'Victorians and Edwardians used a wide range of euphemisms – "ruin", "corruption", "outrage", "molestation", "indecency" – to describe sexual acts and assaults committed on children'.[56] In articles in the *Child's Guardian* the term 'assault' was used by definition rather than with reference to the forced or consensual, although this concept is particularly problematic with regard to children, or commercial context of the offence, albeit that the complexity of the circumstances of some 'assaults' was recognised. It was maintained, for example, that the 'law rightly recognises that these girls have sometimes to be protected against their own weaknesses',[57] but assertive sexuality on the part of the child was often judged harshly. In a court case at the

Derby Assizes a girl, under 16 years of age, was said by the presiding magistrate to be of 'a most depraved character'. He suggested 'some form of restraint or punishment for such children, who should not be allowed to associate, at least for a time, with other children at school, and they should be taught the errors of their ways in that interval'.[58]

In some cases the strongest conclusion must be the recognition of the deprived and abusive family background experienced by some children and the mix of condemnation and repulsion evident in the language to describe their circumstances, indicating the conflicting set of judgements upon which child protection and rescue strategies were based. The comment below, regarding a child of nine years old, is worth quoting in full as it typifies the moral tenor of some of the comment made in the Children's Society's case files.

> The child … is another gutter child and has been brought up to know every charitable person in her neighbourhood and to think all religion cant, she can hardly read and hates school and will do anything to get off being sent to school … worst of all she has been continually sexually assaulted by her own father, while her mother has allowed her to see and hear things which any decent mother would have been careful to keep from the poor little child. The poor little thing has never had a childhood … The discovery of his [the father's] conduct was made about 18 or 20 months ago by [her] giving a disease to two little boy schoolmates.[59]

Terms such as 'moral danger' or 'moral wrong' were commonly used by voluntary workers, philanthropists and politicians alike. To a large extent, they were used specifically to refer to the children, almost always girls, who were believed to have or be in danger of gaining knowledge or direct experience of sex. Thus, a man who was found guilty of offences against five girls, one of whom became pregnant, was described, rather lightly by late twentieth century standards, as a 'moral pest'.[60] However, as the annual reports of Dr Barnardo's show, their use of the term moral danger could encompass a broad range of activities and environments and could justify rescue 'from an actual street life, from sleeping-out, from common lodging-houses, or from the custody of thieves or persons of abandoned life, or who have been used for begging purposes'.[61] Like the word prostitute, 'moral danger' could be a label or censure encompassing a range of behaviour that moral reformers found objectionable.[62]

Despite some different interpretations of the meaning of 'moral danger' it was, by the early twentieth century, well established as a legitimate reason, or rather body of reasons, for removing children from their homes and families. The flexibility of the term made it valuable in the work of the organisations undertaking rescue work and enabled them to summon up images of the worst of scenarios without having to legitimate the quality of the information with which these societies sometimes operated. This is not to say that there were not large numbers of children saved from lives of cruelty, abuse or exploitation. However, the values and assumptions upon which decisions to extract children from their environments were often unsympathetic to the cultures of the poorest classes. The environment in which it was feared sexual knowledge would be acquired, whether it was the street, the common lodging house, the brothel or the public house, was important in the construction of a picture which was, in effect, ascribing immorality to much of the way of life of the poorest classes.

Publicity, prosecution and public awareness

In some respects the flexible or vague usage of language was an obstacle to an increased awareness of the problems some children faced, particularly with regard to sexual abuse and exploitation, and contemporary child welfare workers were aware of this. Concern was expressed in the *Child's Guardian* suggesting that the use of 'guarded' language was allowing a false impression to arise that the cruelty and neglect of children had decreased since the late nineteenth century. Generally, however, consideration of the sensitivity of these issues took precedence along with acceptance of the 'perils in publicity'.[63] The use of vague and euphemistic language might well have tapped into popular understanding of its meaning[64] but the precise nature and therefore the differences in the causes, consequences and indeed perpetrators of such crimes were blurred. This was exacerbated by the fact that the descriptive silence around sexual crimes against children fed into a kind of sensationalism that was sometimes used by children's voluntary societies to enhance their legitimacy and support base, so that 'silence becomes a highly meaningful space to which the imagination is conspicuously drawn and left to roam'.[65]

The nature of the language used in public discussion of such sensitive subjects was not, however, the only hindrance to increasing awareness in this area. Obstacles stood in the way of bringing cases of sexual abuse, incest or prostitution to light through the courts. In order to protect the reputation of young girls thought to be involved in prostitution, those under 16 were brought before the courts under the 1908 Act as 'being beyond control', 'living in circumstances likely to cause corruption', 'being without visible means of support', 'association', or theft.[66] Also people involved in rescue work were reluctant to allow the child victim to give evidence in court. In common with the prevailing ethos it was felt better not to allude to the experience again in any way in order to encourage the child to forget as soon as possible and so in some way retrieve their childlike innocent. The linkages made between sexuality and evil are clearly evident along with the assumption that if the knowledge of sexuality were removed so too would the evil. Another obstacle was that in some cases the abuser would pay off the child's, often poor, family so that they would not agree to a prosecution.[67] Other, longer-term, problems revolved around the difficulty in proving that such offences had occurred and controversy surrounding the reliability of children's testimony in court, as well as around the appropriate arrangements for hearing the evidence of children.

During this period, concessions over the way in which children gave evidence in court were very much at the discretion of the magistrates or judge, and some were less sympathetic than others. During a court case in 1913, involving a charge of criminal assault against a girl of 11, the girl was made to stand on a chair before a bench of magistrates, the press and the men in court, the women had been asked to retire, and recount the full details of what had happened to her. A doctor, called to give evidence in the case, wrote a disgusted letter to the Director of the NSPCC:

> It seems to me that if this publicity is to be given to such cases as these, any parent knowing the ordeal to which their child would be subjected would shrink from the exposure, and in this way the end of justice would be defeated. I must apologise for troubling you, but feel most strongly that this is a matter which your Society should take up. It strikes me as absurd to have Children's Courts where petty offences are tried, and then to subject a child to an ordeal like the one I witnessed yesterday.[68]

Evidence of the difficulties that these kinds of cases met with in a courtroom can be found in the successes and failures in prosecuting them. For example, out of a total of 144 prosecutions for 'moral offences' brought by the NSPCC during 1909-10, 29 were dismissed. Out of a total of 2,135 prosecutions for neglect, starvation, manslaughter, abandonment and exposure during the same year there were only 32 dismissals.[69] Nevertheless, the NSPCC were attentive to the prosecution of sexual cases against children and its greater attention to legal matters in general was reflected in its long-term relationship with William Moreton Phillips, a London lawyer. In 1912, nearly a third of all sexual assault cases brought to the attention of the Society were prosecuted and conviction rates were relatively high.[70]

The NSPCC in London had also built up effective working relations with the police since the nineteenth century and perceived this as an important part not only of their monitoring and/or prosecution of cases but also as a means to increase their reputation and access to child cases. The Society was notified of every case of actual or suspected unlawful conduct towards a child coming to the knowledge of the Metropolitan Police. Indeed, by 1907, Nottingham was one of the few large towns left in England whose police took unilateral action in matters of child protection.[71] Yet, from the beginning the Society stressed the distinctions between the two organisations. It was assumed that the police were constrained by the priorities of the Watch Committees and the ratepayers, thus proving the need for a strong and independent child protection society. The police, according to the NSPCC, were feared by children and lacked 'adaptation to the tiny and timid and helpless'.[72] NSPCC Inspectors were promoted as able to negotiate the intricacies of the urban familial and community environments as well as the networks of local agencies effectively.[73] There is the assertion here of professional specialisation in the work of child protection and the need for particular skills in reaching the abused and/or exploited child. Harry Fergusson sees in such assertions and their corresponding practices, the 'mapping out and standardisation of procedures and policies for child protection' which, although not uncontested, occurred during the period from 1880 to 1914.[74] The importance placed on NSPCC Inspectors developing such skills was emphasised in the Inspector's Directories, the practices and rules by which they operated. The 1901 Directory stated, for example, that 'children accustomed to injustice are very acute in perceiving the mood of the judgement-seat'.

Public awareness of children being involved in prostitution was once more raised to the heights of moral panic during the Edwardian era with the resurgence of white slave trade stories. Merchants and brothel owners, it was feared, were dealing in innocent young girls on an international scale, duping them into prostitution overseas. In the United States the Bureau of Social Hygiene was established in 1911 as a result of an investigation by the Special Grand Jury into the white slave traffic in New York. In England, due to fears and melodrama regarding prostitution and the abduction of young girls, purity movements, most prominently the National Vigilance Association (NVA), pressed the government for further legislative action which was implemented in the punitive Criminal Law Amendment (White Slave Traffic) Bill 1912. This further tightened up the law regarding prostitution, allowed for the whipping of men convicted of procuring young women and required landlords to evict any tenants convicted of using the premises for the purpose of prostitution. Similar to the events of the 1880s, it was the sensationalist accounts that reached the press and were used as warnings to girls and young women. A branch of the Metropolitan Police was even set up in 1912 to work on white slavery despite the widespread belief that forces designated to such work were easily corrupted and the lack of evidence of an organised system of trafficking. The work of this branch, which had actually concentrated upon those making a living out of prostitution, was suspended on the outbreak of the War.[75]

Purity movements tended to combine the traditional focus of reformers on preventive and rescue work with an emphasis on what could be achieved through legislation. In this latter respect they overlapped with suffrage organisations in both objectives and personnel. Indeed, issues of male immorality and white slavery were an important part of the campaigns of the Pankhursts' Women's Social and Political Union in 1913.[76] However, feminist organisations emphasised not only sexual morality but the right of women to control their own bodies and the extent to which prostitutes, and potentially all women, were victims of male lust.[77] During this period there was increasing recognition of the consequences of sexual intercourse, primarily with regard to the physical dangers of repeated pregnancy and of the passing of venereal disease from husbands to their wives. Denials that prostitution protected the institution of marriage by acting as a safety valve for men's greater and less controllable sexual urges increased. The double standard which still applied in sexual morality was highlighted by a critical article in the *Westminster Review* which condemned the values by which a man might 'gratify his sexual feeling very much as it pleases him' and even be proud of his 'conquests' whereas a 'girl's one lapse from virtue' rendered her a social pariah.[78] An alternative picture was given by feminist organisations in which prostitution and the sexual abuse of children and women were consequences of men perceiving women primarily as a sexual function. One of the arguments behind why women needed the vote was to endow them with the power to effect a change in men's sexual behaviour. In her much quoted pamphlet *The Great Scourge and How to End It* Christabel Pankhurst declared 'Votes for women and chastity for men'.

The fact that the aims of both purity and feminist organisations were state-centred is an indication of their middle-class values. Their membership came largely from a background and a class in which 'the state was viewed as an instrument for enacting their own class specific demands'.[79] However, in the broadest sense both types of organisations campaigned for what they saw as the welfare of women. In July 1910 *The Shield*, published by the Association for Moral and Social Hygiene, referred to this common ground. It stated that 'the belief which hinders the recognition of women's citizenship is the same which underlies the acceptance of prostitution as a necessary social institution. It is the belief that women are not individual human beings in the fullest sense, or at least the appendages – of men'.

The feeble-minded and other perceived causal factors

Another prominent debate of the period regarding sexual behaviour concerned the extent to which mental illness or disability led women into immoral behaviour and prostitution. Indeed, the use of the term 'moral defective' made a clear link between mental capacity and immoral behaviour and the largest group of feeble-minded women were often assumed to be prostitutes. One writer asserted in 1910 that 'many of these women, sometimes even mere girls, are possessed of such erotic tendencies that nothing short of lock and key will keep them off the streets'.[80] In 1910 a report in the *Child's Guardian* suggested there should be powers of compulsory detention for life in some cases.[81] Hence, the Mental Deficiency Act 1913 was an important and revealing piece of legislation in respect of the eugenicist and neo-Darwinian links made between mental and moral deficiency.

During the late nineteenth century the falling birth rates among wealthier sections of society relative to the urban poor encouraged the view that a degenerate race apart was being nurtured, passing on their defective inheritance, and causing their poverty, through the generations. From the end of the nineteenth century the word 'feeble' was, as Simmons suggested, often used 'to characterise the weak, the sickly, and the unfit who would not have survived if the State had not come to their aid at every crisis'.[82] The concept of the feeble-minded was included, therefore, in the search for explanations of immoral behaviour, which to many commentators appeared irrational. For example, Mary Dendy, an early worker in mental deficiency in Manchester and founder of the Lancashire and Cheshire Society for the Permanent Care of the Feeble-Minded, made a revealing statement to the Royal Commission on the Care and Control of the Feeble-Minded in 1906. She stated that 'The first test [for mental deficiency] I think is that if a woman comes into the workhouse with an illegitimate child it should be considered evidence of weakness of mind; there is certainly evidence of lack of moral fibre'.[83] It was generally assumed that feeble-minded women were more fecund and less morally restrained than normal women. These women were also perceived to be vulnerable to sexual or criminal exploitation. The picture that was presented was that of large families of feeble-minded women being supported by poor relief and posing 'a deep threat to existing middle-class and respectable working-class notions of sexuality and familial morality'.[84]

The Charity Organisation Society had worked with other organisations to establish homes for feeble-minded adolescent girls from the 1880s. Certainly, the belief that institutionalisation was a solution was followed through in the Mental Deficiency Act of 1913, although this aspect of policy was severely restrained by cost considerations. Those children who were deemed incapable of benefiting from education provided by the Local Education Authorities became the responsibility of the local mental deficiency committees and were liable to be institutionalised. This seemed to offer a straightforward solution to social problems of poverty, illegitimacy, prostitution and crime in the form of incarceration of the 'feeble-minded'. However, uncertainty over definitions of 'feeble-minded' and an increasing recognition that the linkages between feeble-mindedness and social problems were not as clear as had been portrayed, as well as a shift in priorities in the years immediately prior to the First World War, hindered the uptake of this institutionalisation.

Public and political alarm over the perceived social problems of the white slave traffic and the immoral propensities of the 'feeble-minded' joined with a list of other fundamentally individualistic interpretations of the causes of poverty, deprivation, prostitution (of women and children), and child assault and cruelty. Children's charities were prominent in identifying these causes, many of which had a distinctively moral or sexual aspect to their perceived dangerousness. One of these issues concerned the dangerousness of public space within the cities, especially the urban streets. In an article entitled 'Dangers of the streets', published in the *Child's Guardian* September 1908, it was stated that 'familiarity with certain sights and sounds tends to develop habits of precocity in quite young children, whilst association with men and youths of evil manners and debauched minds can have only the worst results'.[85]

Knowledge of the streets itself was perceived to surely lead on to 'vice in some form or other'.[86] It is likely that the streets could form a context for the informal passing of information about sex and also the potential for making contacts with the immoral or criminal. In his interviews with people who had pre-marital sex during the period 1900-1950, Stephen Humphries confirms that the street culture of the working classes 'provided them [the young] with a vocabulary, a knowledge and experience of sexuality that was denied elsewhere'.[87] The degree of dangerousness that this was seen to pose, however, was determined and expressed through class related standards of behaviour. For example, for the poor the streets were a place to socialise outside of their crowded houses and also were a place in which a living could be earned. The NSPCC, however, was critical of children's involvement in street trading and campaigned against it. For boys the dangers were believed to be contact with criminals and dead-end employment and for the girls, moral degradation and ruin.[88] In 1911, the London County Council introduced new bye-laws regarding street trading explicitly to protect children and by which no girl under 16 or boy under 14 could be employed in street trading.

Further issues highlighted by the voluntary societies were the housing conditions and extreme overcrowding suffered by the poor in both urban and rural areas, although the cities provoked most concern. One reason for this concern, in addition to the implications for health and sanitation, was the immorality that was felt followed from several members of a family sharing the same room and possibly the same bed; ideas which influenced housing reform of the time. Specific legislation to criminalise incest was not implemented until 1908, and prior to 1908 incest came under the jurisdiction of the ecclesiastical courts which were virtually inactive in this respect (previous attempts to pass incest legislation had failed in 1899-1900, 1903 and 1907). The NVA and the NSPCC had actively prosecuted fathers for incest before this, under the Criminal Law Amendment Act 1885, but this was made difficult because a prosecution had to be brought within three months of the offence and also because parental consent was needed to allow a medical examination of the child.[89] Incest had been a taboo subject and offensive to the idealised standing of the Victorian family. Furthermore, without more statistical evidence of incest, state interference in the home and family was felt to be premature and counter to 'the grain of *laissez-faire* practice in the sphere of social policy'.[90] The NSPCC came across or reported on several cases of incest. In 1908 a 15 year-old boy was charged with 'a terrible offence upon his little sister, who was just over seven years of age', with whom he shared a bed. The boy was imprisoned but his father was also convicted of 'gross and criminal neglect'. The Society commented that:

> It is much to be feared that little is known and less believed of the flagrant indifference that exists in the land, not only as to the ordinary rules of decency, but also of the ghastly frequency with which the Society is called on to intervene to rescue quite young children from the gravest dangers.[91]

In most cases, however, such offences were hidden within families leaving a legacy that stayed with the child victims for the rest of their lives.[92]

Conclusions

In many respects the large national children's charities came of age during the Edwardian period. They had overcome much of the opposition to assertive social intervention and firmly established themselves as nationally recognised organisations working for the welfare of children. The NSPCC, it has been suggested, was by the First World War recognised as 'the primary organisation in the formulation of child-protection policy and practice'.[93] In this respect the NSPCC had been successful in building on a measure of existing social consensus with regard to the treatment of children. Yet the extensive social poverty that remained also began to expose the inadequacies of voluntary and philanthropic welfare and was to face increasing substantial challenges from state provision.

In another sense it was the First World War itself which marked a significant change in social attitudes and a gradual distancing, which continued during the inter-war period, from the non-interventionist ideas that had left a significant minority of the population in extreme poverty. The challenges made to dominant ideologies by an array of groups as diverse as voluntary charitable societies, feminist and purity movements, New Liberals, Socialists and Irish Nationalists irrevocably changed the social and political landscape of England. Problems that were previously held to be private were now increasingly perceived to be social problems in a context of concern about the strength of the nation. The quantity and quality of the nation's population had become of primary importance. The level of investment in the nation's children had risen dramatically through compulsory state education and the provision, albeit limited, of school meals and medical inspection and treatment. Furthermore, changes in legislation and the extension of the forms of behaviour, especially of the young, which could be policed by the police, the courts and the voluntary societies, increasingly defined what constituted proper behaviour. The cruelty and abuse of children was held to be damaging the future prosperity of the country and also the well-being of the family as the basis of national stability. This linked campaigns to protect children with motivations to repress criminal vice and public immorality generally. Within these wider concerns the existence of child prostitution tapped into and undermined middle-class idealism regarding the family and the proper roles of those within it. Children should be innocent, dependent and passive and anything that was perceived to subvert this was vigorously criticised by the national children's charities.

The publications of the major children's charities in Edwardian England reflected the social attitudes of the time and often cited moral and individual factors as being the primary root causes of the cruelty, abuse and sexual exploitation of children. The factors cited as indicators of 'morally reprehensible and condemnatory lifestyles' included drunkenness, vice, immorality, idleness, gambling and ungovernable temper.[94] As part of its child-protection campaigns, the NSPCC emphasised the prevalence of the cruelty and neglect of the young and pressed, for example, for more legislative restrictions on baby farming, on adoption, on the tramping of children and, more controversially, on children's life insurance. Relative to these areas the sexual prostitution of children received limited attention. This may well have been a part of a conscious directing of the resources and efforts of children's charities into areas in which they could achieve the most for the greatest number of children, although child 'assault' attracted serious concern. But it was, no doubt, also a function of the sensitivity of the subject, the covert nature of such practice and a sense of inevitability with regard to the practice of prostitution as well the difficulties of securing evidence for a prosecution. Perhaps most important, however, were the increasing difficulties of locating child prostitution within modern ideological concepts of what constituted the family and childhood. For all of these reasons there has been a lack of recognition during the twentieth century of the prostitution of those under the age of consent.

References

1 *Child's Guardian* 1902 XVI (10), p. 114.
2 Barnardo's annual report 1910, D239/A3/1/45.
3 Waifs and Strays 30th annual report, p. 10.
4 Report on reformatory and industrial schools, cited in *Child's Guardian* 1910, XXIV (12), p. 141.
5 H. Hendrick, *Child Welfare: England 1872-1989* (London: Routledge, 1994), p. 78.
6 C. Booth, *The Life and Labour of the People in London.* First series (London: Macmillan, 1969); S. B. Rowntree, *Poverty: A Study of Town Life* (London: Macmillan, 1901); A. Mearns, *The Bitter Cry of Outcast London: An Enquiry into the Conditions of the Abject Poor*, introduction by A. S. Wohl (Leicester: Leicester University Press, 1970).

7 H. Cunningham, *The Children of the Poor: Representations of Childhood since the Seventeenth Century* (Oxford: Blackwell, 1991), pp. 2-5; C. Steedman, 'Bodies, figures and physiology: Margaret McMillan and the late nineteenth-century remaking of working-class childhood', in R. Cooter (ed.) *In the Name of the Child: Health and Welfare 1880–1940* (London: Routledge, 1992).

8 H. Hendrick, *Children, Childhood and English Society 1880–1990* (Cambridge: Cambridge University Press, 1997), p. 49.

9 November 1911 (319), pp. 195–6.

10 Anon, 'The cry of the children', *Quarterly Review* 205, 1906, p. 43.

11 *Child's Guardian* 1902 XVI (6), pp. 61–2.

12 *Child's Guardian* 1904 XVIII (1), pp. 1–2.

13 'The voluntary sector in the mixed economy of welfare', in D. Gladstone (ed.) *Before Beveridge: Welfare Before the Welfare State* (London: IEA Health and Welfare Unit, 1999), p. 15.

14 Children Act 1908 8 Edw 7, Ch.67 section 126.

15 J. Stewart, 'Children, parents and the state: The Children's Act 1908', *Children and Society* 9 (1) 1995, pp. 92–3 and 95.

16 H. Hendrick, *Child Welfare*, p. 59.

17 J. D. Smith, 'The voluntary tradition', in J. D. Smith, C. Rochester and R. Hedley (eds) *An Introduction to the Voluntary Sector* (London: Routledge, 1995), p. 20; A. W. Vincent, 'The Poor Law reports of 1909 and the social theory of the Charity Organisation Society', in D. Gladstone (ed.) *Before Beveridge: Welfare Before the Welfare State* (London: IEA, 1999).

18 February 1902 (214), pp. 229–230; March 1902 (215), pp. 257–9; December 1902 (224), pp. 412–3; March 1903 (227), pp. 45–7; June 1903 (230), pp. 101–3.

19 *Our Waifs and Strays* December 1902 (224), p. 413.

20 *Our Waifs and Strays* April 1902 (216), p. 275.

21 *Child's Guardian* 1904 XVIII (1), p. 2.

22 Cited in E. J. Evans, *Social Policy 1830–1914: Individualism, Collectivism and the Origins of the Welfare State* (London: Routledge and Kegan Paul, 1978), p. 225.

23 F. Maurice, 'Where to get men', *Contemporary Review*, 1903, p. 42; also see F. Maurice, 'National Health: A soldier's study', *Contemporary Review*, 1902.

24 G. Behlmer, *Child Abuse and Moral Reform in England 1870–1908* (California: Stanford University Press, 1982), p. 206.

25 Ibid, p. 207; NSPCC Annual Report 1905.

26 D239/A3/1/35, p. 20.

27 G. Behlmer, *Child Abuse and Moral Reform*, p. 207.

28 *Child's Guardian* 1905 XIX, no.5, p. 54.

29 *Child's Guardian* 1911 XXV (11), p. 129.

30 J. Walkowitz, *Prostitution and Victorian Society: Women, Class and the State* (Cambridge: Cambridge University Press, 1982), p. 85.

31 R. Roberts, *The Classic Slum: Salford Life in the First Quarter of the Century* (Manchester: Manchester University Press, 1971), pp. 8–9.

32 J. Walkowitz, *Prostitution and Victorian Society*, p. 85.

33 A. Flexner, *Prostitution in Europe* (New York: The Century Co, 1917), p. 77.

34 Ibid, pp. 112–118 and 153–4.

35 For example, 1900, 1905 and 1910 D239/A3/1/35.
36 D. Evans, 'Tackling the 'hideous scourge': The creation of the venereal disease treatment centres in early twentieth-century Britain', *Social History of Medicine* 5, 1992, pp. 414–5; also see L. Bland, 'Cleansing the portals of life: The venereal disease campaign in the early twentieth century', in M. Langan and B. Scwartz (eds) *Crises in the British State, 1880–1939* (London: Hutchinson with the Centre for Contemporary Cultural Studies, The University of Birmingham, 1985).
37 R. Porter and L. Hall, *The Facts of Life: The Creation of Sexual Knowledge in Britain, 1650–1950* (New Haven: Yale University Press, 1995), p. 228.
38 Ibid, p. 232.
39 *Royal Commission on Venereal Disease*, Cd.7475, 1914, para.2822, cited in Porter and Hall, *The Facts of Life*, p. 226; C. Smart, 'The historical struggle against child abuse', occasional paper, The University of Leeds, 1998, pp. 7–8; K. J. Taylor, 'Venereal disease in nineteenth-century children', *Journal of Psychohistory* 12 (4), 1985, p. 450; see L. DeMause, 'The history of child abuse', *Journal of Psychohistory* 25 (3), 1998 for a more universalist view.
40 Cited in C. Smart, 'Disruptive bodies and unruly sex: the regulation of reproduction and sexuality in the nineteenth century', in C. Smart (ed.) *Regulating Womanhood: Historical Essays on Marriage, Motherhood and Sexuality* (London: Routledge, 1992), p. 44.
41 'Venereal Disease', p. 450.
42 'A history of ambivalence and conflict in the discursive construction of the 'child victim' of 'sexual abuse'. *Social and Legal Studies* 8, 1999, p. 393.
43 Children's Society [CS] Case File 115. Case files from the Children's Society Archive have been renumbered and any names changed or omitted in consideration of the sensitive nature of these documents.
44 *Our Waifs and Strays* April 1888 (48), p. 10 and November 1890 (103), pp. 9–10; also see L. Jackson, *Child Sexual Abuse in Victorian England* (London: Routledge, 2000), p. 139.
45 P. Cox, 'Rescue and reform: Girls, delinquency and industrial schools, 1908–1933', Ph.D Cambridge University 1996, p. 31.
46 CS Case File 101.
47 CS Case File 114.
48 CS Case File167.
49 CS Case File 108.
50 *Child's Guardian* 1902 XVI (6), pp. 62–3; also see *Child's Guardian* 1910 XXIV (4), p. 39, for reference to similar case.
51 *Child's Guardian* 1906 XX (7), p. 84.
52 *Child's Guardian* 1912 XXVI (11), p. 126.
53 *Child's Guardian* 1913 XXVII (1), p. 4.
54 CS Case File 104.
55 M. Cale, 'Girls and the perception of danger in the Victorian reformatory system', *Historical Association* 78 (253), p. 204.
56 'Singing birds as well as soap suds': The Salvation Army's work with sexually abused girls in Edwardian England', *Gender and History* 12 (1), p. 107.

57 *Child's Guardian* XXIV (12), p. 139.
58 *Child's Guardian* December 1910 XXIV (12), p. 141.
59 CS Case File 156.
60 *Child's Guardian* January 1900 XIV (1), p. 7.
61 Barnardo's Archive, D239/A3/40: 18.
62 L. Mahood, *The Magdalenes: Prostitution in the Nineteenth Century* (London: Routledge, 1990), p. 68.
63 *Child's Guardian* 1911 XXV (1), p. 5.
64 Jackson, *Child Sexual Abuse*, p. 55.
65 Ibid, p. 56.
66 P. Cox, 'Rescue and Reform: Girls, delinquency and industrial schools, 1908–1933', Ph.D Cambridge University 1996, p. 32.
67 *Child's Guardian* 1911 XXV (1), p. 5.
68 *Child's Guardian* September 1913 XXVII (9), pp. 103–4.
69 *Child's Guardian* 1911 XXV (1), p. 6.
70 NSPCC Annual Report 1912–13; also cited in Jackson, *Child Sexual Abuse*, p. 59 also see p. 61.
71 G. Behlmer, *Friends of the Family: The English Home and its Guardians, 1850–1940* (California: Stanford University Press, 1998), p. 110.
72 *Child's Guardian* April 1889 III (8).
73 H. Fergusson, 'Cleveland in History: the abused child and child protection, 1880–1914', in R. Cooter (ed.) *In the Name of the Child: Health and Welfare, 1880–1914* (London: Routledge, 1992), pp. 154–5.
74 Ibid, p. 148.
75 S. Petrow, *Policing Morals: The Metropolitan Police and the Home Office 1870–1914* (Oxford: Clarendon, 1994), p. 173.
76 F. Mort, *Dangerous Sexualities: Medico-Moral Politics in England since 1830* (London: Routledge and Kegan Paul, 1987), pp. 140 and 145.
77 S. Kingsley Kent, *Sex and Suffrage in Britain 1860–1914* (London: Routledge, 1987), ch.II.
78 H. R. Boyle, 'Sexual morality', *Westminster Review* 166, 1906, p. 337.
79 F. Mort, *Dangerous Sexualities*, p. 141.
80 Tredgold cited in L. Zedner, *Women: Crime and Custody in Victorian Britain* (Oxford: Oxford University Press, 1991), p. 275.
81 March 1910 XXIV (3), p. 27.
82 H. G. Simmons, 'Explaining social policy: The English mental deficiency Act of 1913', *Journal of Social History* 3, 1978, p. 390.
83 Cited in Ibid, p. 392.
84 Ibid, p. 394.
85 XXII (9), p. 105.
86 Anon, 'The cry of the children', Quarterly Review 205, 1906, p.38; also see J. H. Whitehouse, 'Street trading by children' in J. H. Whitehouse (ed.) *Problems of Boy Life* (London: King, 1912), p. 167.
87 *A Secret World of Sex: Forbidden Fruit, the British Experience 1900–1950* (London: Sedgwick and Jackson, 1988), p. 40.

88 *Child's Guardian* 1910 XXIV (9), pp. 94–5.
89 V. Bailey and S. Blackbourn, 'The punishment of Incest Act 1908: A case study of law creation', *Criminal Law Review* 1979, pp. 711–2.
90 Ibid, p. 709.
91 *Child's Guardian* 1907 XXII (7), pp. 78–9.
92 S. Humphries and P. Gordon, *Forbidden Britain: Our Secret Past 1900–1950* (London: BBC Books, 1994).
93 H. Fergusson, 'Cleveland in History', p. 148.
94 *Child's Guardian* 1903 XVII (7), p. 73.

Chapter 4

War and the 1920s

The mature girls under 16 or the professional prostitute under 16 who is herself responsible mainly for the man committing this offence. You do not want to protect her.[1]

During the inter-war period, the domestic sphere was becoming more attractive in part due to increasing standards of living in many areas and the continued decline in the birth rate. Between 1900–9 and 1930 the percentage of couples with one or two children had increased from 33.5 per cent to 51 per cent.[2] The domestic sphere was increasingly perceived to be the normal place where the family spent much of its time outside of work or school hours. Of course, this must be balanced by the severe poverty experienced in particular by those families and communities suffering the worst effects of unemployment in the staple industries during the inter-war years (*ie* coal, steel, shipbuilding, textiles). Pre-First World War eugenic fears persisted that, as the birth rate of the poorer classes was greater than that of the wealthier, the 'more progressive' classes would be out-bred by 'the thriftless, the unthinking, or, more particularly, the mentally deficient'.[3] As early as 1911, the report of the Registrar General showed that the birth rate was declining faster among the middle and upper classes than among the working classes, largely because working-class women were marrying earlier and were less likely to use birth control. These significantly differential birth rates had more or less gone by the late 1930s, although it took some time for contemporaries to recognise this.

During the war years and the 1920s there also began a gradual redefining of sexual morality in England. The war years, in particular, accelerated change in cultural attitudes and in the diffusion of sexual knowledge that was, in part, reflected in the changing fortunes of campaigning groups. Purity organisations, with their emphasis upon a high moral standard for both sexes and a positive approach to state responsibility in moral and sexual issues, were weakened, although their influence was felt into the 1930s. There was a shift towards greater individual responsibility and a more positive image of the sexuality of young people. Within the sanctity of marriage, sex was put forward as a normal and progressive force by the increasingly popular social hygiene movement.[4] Marie Stopes' quite explicit publication, *Married Love* (1918), with its assertion of mutual sexual fulfilment in marriage and of 'women's sexuality, the eroticisation of marriage, and … [women's] rights in marriage and as mothers' became a best-seller and went through 22 editions in five years.[5] Several works of this type followed on; G.Courtney Beale's *Wise Wedlock* (second edition 1922) and Isabel Hutton's *The Hygiene of Marriage* (1923), for example. This more 'eroticised' ideal of marriage may have made it more attractive for men compared to resorting to a prostitute.[6] Indeed, Hall has suggested that the:

> new eroticism being adumbrated in the thinkers during the 1910s and 1920s was not something capable of being embodied in the commercial relationship of a man with a prostitute. In thinkers as disparate as the old-fashioned liberal Havelock Ellis and the anarchic revolutionary Wilhelm Reich, the idea of the fulfilling sexual relationship involved the free engagement of two autonomous individuals.[7]

There is evidence to suggest that, following the war, resort to prostitution and prostitution may have declined although the nature of this activity means that such a conclusion must be tentative. The causes of this decline are complex, prominent among these changes were improved standards of living for many people and a representation of marriage involving mutual sexual satisfaction and companionship, although the oral history work of Stephen Humphries testifies, for example, to the persistence of wide-scale ignorance on sexual matters.[8] The Victorian claims that prostitution helped to uphold the marriage were now rarely heard. A degree of relaxation in the sexual behaviour of young people was also evident and was the subject of criticism partly through the rhetoric around the 'amateur' prostitute. Higher cultural standards of behaviour may have increased intolerance of sexual exploitation but this persisted nevertheless. It is clear that there was considerable community condemnation of child prostitution, perhaps especially when carried out within the family making it in some respects more visible. Yet, there were many factors which inhibited the bringing of such cases to the attention of the child protection agencies or the law and their prosecution in court, many of which continue to provide obstacles to convictions. What could be termed a legal traffic in children was carried on, for example, through unregulated adoptions into and even beyond the 1920s. There is no way of knowing how many of the thousands of children who were transferred from adult to adult in this way later suffered sexual or physical abuse or whether this was intended at the time of the 'adoption'. The proportion is likely to be small, and the extent to which unregulated adoptions provided good homes should not be underestimated, however, a small number of these children came to the attention of voluntary or state child welfare institutions in consequence of their abuse and exploitation.

The First World War

The effects of the First World War upon voluntary organisations was contradictory. On the one hand the immediate demands of the war effort provided a stimulus to voluntary societies as one of the resources of the nation that were accounted, mustered and utilised. On the other hand, the stimulus that the war provided to state provision and action also challenged the traditional spheres of action of the voluntary sector. As has been suggested elsewhere 'the experience of total war saw the state assuming a greater role *vis-à-vis* the lives of citizens than ever before and there was a feeling that relations between the state and its people would never be the same again'.[9] Nevertheless, the negative effects upon the children's charities should not be overstated. Not only did they fulfil a much needed role during the war but they proved to be flexible and increasingly professional in the face of social and economic change in the post-war decades.

During the First World War the patriotism of the children's charities was reflected in their taking on additional workloads. In common with other organisations and institutions, the war service of male employees forced internal restructuring and the role of paid women workers expanded. The first woman NSPCC inspector (in Lincoln) was, in January 1915, reported to be doing her husband's job well.[10] Although the shortages of resources affected charitable giving and also the publication of some of the literature of the children's voluntary organisations, they continued to promote themselves and to influence government policy and practice. The children's charities reported the numbers of previous employees who were serving in the military, their promotions, injuries and deaths. They were also proud of the numbers of 'old boys' and 'old girls' who were perceived to have rewarded the work and faith of the Societies by serving their country at a time of crisis. We are now 'breeding the next generation of patriots!' the Waifs and Strays Society pronounced.[11]

During wartime, children were more valued and revered as representing the future of the country. One of the most emotive rationales for the children's charities at this time was to protect the offspring of those who were fighting to preserve the freedom of the nation. A speech in 1915, published in *Our Waifs and Strays,* asserted that 'it is unthinkable that the child of anyone of our gallant defenders should suffer, be it in the direction of poverty or of unwholesome surroundings, if such can possibly be avoided'.[12] The children's charities helped to cope with family dislocation caused by voluntary enlistment, and later by conscription, and the fact that there was little requisitioning of the homes or offices of the large children's charities signalled government recognition of the importance of their activities.

As part of its additional workload, the NSPCC undertook work for the Soldier's and Sailor's Families Association and the War Office. This involved investigating the claims for separation allowances, which took some time to be established as a right, and other relief and helping to secure, for those seeking the separation allowance, including unmarried mothers, marriage and/or birth certificates where necessary. In some cases, where the capabilities and even morality of a woman in receipt of separation allowances were in doubt, individual local NSPCC inspectors administered them along with a measure of controlling influence, help being dependent in part upon personal moral judgement. This type of work was largely undertaken by voluntary charitable societies until administration was passed over to the War Pensions Statutory Committee, and then the Ministry of Pensions in 1917. Separation allowances and pensions to the wives and widows of solders and sailors continued to be subject to their moral behaviour and the kinds of ideological remit instituted under the administration of the system by charitable bodies. However, priority was upon maintaining and protecting the rights of the absent husband.[13]

In the context of the war and the expansion of the military services, morality campaigners came into conflict with the government over the appropriate methods to use in the prevention of venereal disease. These concerns were intensified by fears about 'amateur' prostitutes who conferred their 'sexual favours' for non-monetary and non-contractual gain, usually seen in terms of a gift, dinner or a night out. According to

Frank Mort, the concern over these young 'amateurs' amounted to a moral panic during the war years.[14] In 1916 the Royal Commission established in 1913 to investigate venereal disease reported, and although its evidence was taken before the rise of widespread concerns about VD its findings informed later government action. The Commission estimated that in large cities more than ten per cent of the population was infected with syphilis and that gonorrhoea, often not considered to be a serious affliction, had serious physical consequences and both had considerable costs for the state. Such considerations helped to overcome opposition within the medical arena and, amongst other initiatives, treatment centres began to be opened from 1917, although insufficient provision for women remained a significant problem.[15]

After the war, in parallel with the decline in the levels of venereal disease, the panic subsided, although VD remained one of the most frequently referred to factors in criticism of the perceived post-war relaxation of morality. The existence of 'amateurs' may have, according to Lesley Hall, resulted in 'a growing public sense of the lack of acceptability of male resort to prostitutes after the war' and they were often cited as the reason behind a perceived decline in 'professional' or 'habitual' prostitution.[16]

During the war sexual behaviour in public and 'undesirable women' were among the targets for surveillance by the new women's patrols.[17] These private organisations policed open spaces and areas near military camps on the look-out for 'loose' behaviour. Women's patrols were established from quite early in the war by a number of women's organisations and were said to have 'exercised a salutary influence, especially in regard to young women and girls'.[18] By 1917 there were 2,284 voluntary patrols; some paid for out of police funds. Voluntary Women's Patrols established by the National Council of Women at the beginning of the war became, by 1918, a small section of the Metropolitan Police which, by 1923, had full powers of arrest and prioritised duties, such as advising young girls and investigating sex offences.[19] However, the responsibilities of women police remained very much related to women and children. As a *Report of the Commissioner of Police of the Metropolitan Police* noted for 1923, 'the duties they [police women] perform are not strictly Police duties, but more in the nature of rescue work among young women and girls'.[20]

Much of the contemporary concern still centred on the 'professional' prostitute, although less attention was given to making distinctions between stereotyped career prostitutes and women who prostituted themselves only on an occasional basis or in times of need. It has been suggested that the concentration upon prostitution, the character of those involved and the associating of it with an increase in venereal disease during the war made it far less easy to glamorise.[21] According to Hall, the 'grim' realities of the regulated brothels for the troops in France, *maisons tolerées*, in one of which fifteen women daily served 360 men, and which attracted such criticism in Britain, brought home to many men the actual sordid nature of prostitution and influenced the willingness to resort to them after the war.[22] Through their publication, *The Shield*, the Association for Moral and Social Hygiene (AMSH) expressed concern in 1916 about public reaction to the increase of prostitution and venereal disease. This concern was specifically with regard to Shorncliffe military training camp, Folkestone, which had 'rallied many supporters to methods abhorrent to Abolitionists'. It was asserted that the accepted increases in prostitution and venereal disease did not mean that they had to give way to 'a vicious demand to subordinate one sex to the other or to make promiscuous sexual indulgence safe and easy for our soldiers'.[23]

The Association (AMSH) was critical of the impulse to regulate prostitution and expel 'undesirables' as the solution to the problem, pointing out that these women did not compose a definite class and that the only way to exclude them would be to exclude all women. Under the Defence of the Realm Act (DORA) the government had introduced strict and far-reaching measures, most notably Regulations 13A and 40D, in February 1916 and July 1918. By these regulations, prostitutes and those who managed brothels could be expelled from military areas under pain of imprisonment (13A) and it became a criminal offence for any women infected with venereal disease to engage in or invite sexual relations with a member of the armed forces (40D). A woman could be remanded into custody for up to a week for medical examination. Furthermore, under Regulation 40D, no prohibition was placed upon publishing the names and addresses of accused women, even though DORA enabled other forms of press censorship. The identity of an accused soldier was, however, withheld as a matter of course. The latter of these regulations (40D) especially proved to be very unpopular, if short-lived since it was withdrawn at the end of the war. Nevertheless, the 1918 Regulation had not only placed all of the responsibility for instigating sexual intercourse and for spreading venereal disease upon women but it also meant that the wives of members of the services could also be policed for their sexual behaviour.[24]

There were, however, earlier examples of local restrictions being placed on the movements of prostitutes. In 1914 the military commander in Cardiff had issued an order banning women from public houses between 7pm and 8am and had placed what was in effect a curfew on women of 'bad reputation' preventing them from going out of doors between those times. A similar curfew was instituted at Grantham. Significantly, men living off the immoral earning of prostitutes were not included in these regulations and curfews, nor was there any consideration made for prostitutes under the age of consent. These restrictions were seen as reintroducing the kind of regulation experienced under the Contagious Diseases Acts, and were opposed by feminist and purity groups including the NVA, the AMSH as a 'demand to subordinate one sex to the other'[25] and caused a split in the Women's Voluntary Patrols.

The considerable publicity about the increase of prostitution during the war, particularly in London, capitalised on the youth of some of those believed to be involved. Indeed, the alarmism of newspaper articles about prostitution was comparable to that regarding previous 'white slave traffic' scares during the 1880s and in 1912.[26] In June 1917 *The Daily Mail* claimed that, over a three-month period, 50 Australian soldiers had been drugged and robbed in the area in and around Leicester Square, Charing Cross Road and the Strand, by women, with the implication they were prostitutes, in order to buy cocaine. In a series of articles for *The Weekly Dispatch* entitled 'The Grave Sex Plague', Max Pemberton had written that on the route from a hotel to Piccadilly Tube a young officer was:

> accosted sixteen times – sometimes by those who appeared to be mere children. To a relative who met him later he said: 'No healthy lad could long withstand this kind of temptation'. It is a true saying. They cannot, and we should not expect it of them. It is our part to remove that temptation from their path.[27]

An article in *The Nineteenth Century* referred to a South African soldier whom, it claimed, said 'I had to wait twenty minutes at Waterloo Station, and for not one of those minutes was I free from women who spoke to me. Some of them were girls apparently of only 12 or 13, painted, got up, and with all the manners and phrases of professionals'.[28] The AMSH raised the subject of the temptation that these men held out to 'young girls of 16, 17 and 18'. They urged that the same moral standard, 'the same sturdy resistance to temptation', should be expected of men as of women.[29] Issues of prophylactic means of dealing with venereal disease were raised but as a politically sensitive issue were not followed up. During the first years of the war Britain gave no general provisions or instructions to its troops with regard to preventing or combating venereal disease. By 1917, 55,000 soldiers were hospitalised through venereal disease.[30] It was not until 1917 that treatment centres were established.

Local and central authorities also remarked on the increase of young prostitutes during the war. In 1916 a Westminster Police Court magistrate, C.K.Francis, wrote to the Home Office to voice his concerns. He commented that the:

> most noticeable feature of this evil [prostitution] is the fact that a great number of young girls from 15 to 21 years of age hitherto unknown to the police, are now leading the lives of prostitutes, or rapidly drifting in that direction … voluntary methods are often impossible, because of the reluctance of the girls to give up a life in which a great deal of money is easily earned.[31]

Francis wanted the power to compel all women certified as suffering from venereal disease to go to the infirmary or lock hospital until certified fit, and to send young girls of 15 to 21 to institutions for six to twelve months for 'reform and training'.[32] In his response, the chairman of the Prison Commission, Evelyn Ruggles-Brise, stated that the only evidence regarding an increase in youth prostitution was figures for commitments to Holloway Prison. His example statistics did suggest a younger age profile for imprisoned women at least, however not all of these women were necessarily prostitutes and, furthermore, this did not reveal anything about possible changes in police or judicial strategies. It does suggest the extent to which the association between criminality and morality remained gender-centric. One hundred and twenty nine women were committed to Holloway Prison in June 1916, this was less than half the number committed in June 1914, 278, but of these there had been a noticeable increase, from 15 to 70, in those aged between 16 and 20 years old.

Anxiety about prostitution persisted. Letters were received from the Visiting Committee of Exeter Prison (November 1917) and Kent County Council (February 1918) asserting that some action should be taken to prevent prostitutes infected with venereal disease from being discharged from prison until they were cured.[33] Certainly the autobiography of Mary Gordon, the first woman prison inspector, suggests that magistrates made full use of their discretionary powers to control prostitutes.[34] In an account openly critical of the effects of repeated short prison sentences, Gordon noted that during the nine months to March 1920, 150 women in one prison were all remanded at least twice, of these 69 were for 'loitering' but only six for 'soliciting'. Only 24 of the 150 were sent to prison on conviction. 'We thus have a herd of girls driven into prison on remand, or left there with the main object of diagnosing and treating disease, which was not their offence'.[35] She also noted the frequent use of heavy sureties for good behaviour, which in effect meant them having to stay in prison, ensuring a period of treatment for those infected with venereal disease. Because they did not realise they had the right to refuse, most girls in prison consented to examination, even though if infected other inmates jeered at them. Gordon asserted that such girls should be protected rather than punished and believed that the existing laws condemned them and kept them in their 'hideous bondage, hall-marked as a degraded and outcast class'.[36] Gordon's stance on the punishment of prostitution was applauded by the Association for Moral and Social Hygiene and she later became a member of its Executive Committee (1922–34), she was then elected Vice-President and remained in that position until her death in 1941.[37]

The 1920s and the strategies of children's voluntary societies

Following the short post-war boom, economic recession and a persistent high rate of unemployment set in, predominantly in the pre-war staple industries. Although debate continues on the balance of the factors involved and the extent of the consequences of the Depression, it is clear that the financial and trade dislocations caused by the war, the growth of the huge North American export surplus and the widespread international imposition of trade tariffs were critical. During the 1920s the total number of unemployed workers remained at over one million and this rose to over three million in the early 1930s. Despite the recession, social conditions in the country as a whole gradually improved, partly through the expansion of new industries (e.g. electrical household goods, motor vehicle manufacture) but also due to the continued decline in the birth rate and the extension, albeit limited, of state provision. As Arthur Marwick commented 'the working class in 1914 was large and it was poor. In the early twenties it was not quite so large, and it was not quite so poor'.[38] Nevertheless, significant regional variations persisted and in many cases were exacerbated into the 1930s.

The inequalities between men and women working also reappeared following the limited expansion of women's employment during the war. In the 1920s working women continued to face a discriminatory labour market and the same problems they had faced in the 1910s. Employment opportunities were limited and the work that was available to women tended to be low paid and monotonous, even in the expanding new industries in the south east. Nevertheless, in both Britain and the United States young people were increasingly demanding to enjoy independent leisure pursuits: cinemas and clubs. In many cases this made young women reliant upon men for their access to such venues along with the possibility of, often unspoken, associated obligations but also highlighted adolescence as an increasingly distinct phase of life.[39]

Rising social expectations were reflected and reinforced in the higher standards of childcare and health aimed at by the children's charities. The NSPCC increasingly emphasised not only the need for better medical provision for children but promoted dental care and the provision of spectacles for children, neither of which were catered for under state welfare provision. The extension of the definition of 'neglect' in the 1908 Children's Act, and the inclusion in Section 12 of the failure to provide medical care as an offence, allowed proceedings to be taken against parents who refused to carry out the instructions of a doctor if this was likely to cause unnecessary suffering or injury to health.[40] The fact that during the 1920s the children charities were taking a broader view of child welfare also suggests that there had been some alleviation in the incidence of abuse and neglect of children than had been evident prior to the First World War. Certainly contemporaries within the NSPCC believed this to have been the case and a decline in drunkenness was claimed to be a decisive factor in this.[41]

The numbers of children dealt with by the NSPCC rose over this period, although the numbers were less than before the war (annual report 1920–1). In 1919–20 the Society dealt with a total of 98,624 children, ten years later (1929–30) the number had risen to 107,172. Internally, the increase was put down to the Society becoming better known and to the increase in the number of local committees and Inspectors (an additional fourteen over the 1920s). By May 1932 the Society had 260 Inspectors and a rising income.[42]

The Waifs and Strays Society was similarly optimistic about the future in their literature, although this was no doubt in part a rallying in the face of extending state provision. In the run-up to their jubilee in 1930 (50 years), a Special Jubilee Thanksgiving Fund was established which aimed to 'Strengthen and extend the existing work'. The areas to be developed were the technical education of boys and the endowing of scholarships to give children the opportunity of attending secondary schools and also the provision of hostels for boys and girls in employment. The number of children cared for by the Waifs and Strays also increased, although again this represented a decline on pre-war figures. The 40th annual report of the Society (1920) recorded 3,384 children as being resident in the Society's homes, 745 as boarded out and 140 in 'other' Church homes, that is homes not owned by the Society. In the annual report of 1930, 3,528 children were in the Society's homes, 911 boarded out and 106 in other Church homes.

The numbers of prosecutions brought by the NSPCC declined, for the year 1929–30 there were only 500 prosecutions, whereas ten years before there had been 1,051, in the context of what was claimed to be 'no change in the Society's policy'.[43] Prosecution remained a coercive tool that could be held in reserve but emphasis remained upon the power wielded by inspectors to 'persuade parents to mend their ways'.[44] Both inside and outside of the children's voluntary organisations, prosecution and criminalisation were also increasingly perceived to be inappropriate means to deal with juvenile delinquency. Concern about the effects of wartime social disruption upon children and adolescents whose fathers were in the services and whose mothers were working persisted after the war. Within a liberal philosophy emphasising parental neglect and the expansion of state services, delinquency was beginning to be seen as a child protection issue rather than one calling for the full and punitive rigours of the criminal law; control, however, remained a primary concern.

The focus was increasingly on the child rather than the offence.[45] This was perhaps most evident in the Children and Young Persons Act of 1933, however, the Departmental Committee on the Treatment of Young Offenders (1927) acted as a focus for debate on the meaning of delinquency and its appropriate treatment and was influential in the framing of the 1933 Act. The Report of the Committee categorised children into those being cared for in Poor Law institutions, those in voluntary homes and those who were dealt with under the 1908 Children Act, including those who had previously come under Industrial Schools legislation, and the victims of adult offences. The Committee recommended that in court the investigation of the history of the juvenile offender should be provided by the new child guidance clinics, or by medical examination. Specialist child guidance clinics did expand from the mid-1920s, although the extent to which they affected the attitudes of the families whose daughters were most likely to come under the surveillance of the criminal justice system is debatable.[46]

In 1927 the Children's Clinic for the Treatment and Study of Nervous and Delicate Children was established (in 1931 renamed the Institute of Child Psychology) followed by the British Paediatric Association in 1928. Yet the extent to which such institutions affected the everyday work of the juvenile courts has been questioned. Behlmer claims that such courts often had no clear conception of how to cope with delinquents, fell considerably short of the ideal and were generally inefficient in respect to both regulating the family and reducing delinquency rates. Indeed, Behlmer suggests that some magistrates and senior police officials blamed the increase in juvenile crime rates during the 1930s on the 'sentimental' provisions of the 1933 Act.[47]

Prostitution: investigation and debate

When fears about the re-emergence of an international white slave trade were voiced after the First World War, the League of Nations took on and expanded the concerns and the international work of the NVA. Significantly, the League of Nations used the term 'traffic in women and children' as opposed to 'white slave trade'. This was due to the widespread confusion and misuse of the term 'white slave trade' which operated to make a wide distinction between the abduction/procuration of the innocent to brothels overseas and the prostitution of 'fallen women'. Inherent in this oppositional image was the representation of the so-called 'professional' prostitute as separate from 'ordinary' communities and as earning their living in this way by choice for a large period of their lives as a career. This also presented the 'professional' as undeserving of practical help and sympathy and as an inevitable aspect of the urban scene.

The surveys of the League of Nations as well as of the International Bureau and the Jewish Association revealed a considerable international trade in children and young people following the widespread economic, political and social dislocation and stresses consequent upon war and poverty. The International Bureau had been established in 1899 in London to investigate the international traffic in young people and promote international co-operation to eradicate it. In effect the Bureau was an arm of the NVA.[48] A League of Nations report of 1929, building on this work, stated that little or no procurement for an international trade operating in Britain had been discovered, although their reports on the trade elsewhere did encourage speculation and exaggeration in some of the British media.[49]

With regard to Britain, the League's report stated that there was general agreement among social workers, and others working with urban social problems, that there had been a considerable diminution in prostitution over the previous fifteen or twenty years and also that, quoting from the Street Offences Committee 1928, 'their methods have become more discreet with the general improvement in public manners'. There is evidence, however, to suggest that the fall in prosecutions against prostitutes may have been due in part to changing attitudes by magistrates regarding the law appertaining to prostitution. This was particularly evident in London. An article in *The Justice of the Peace* was critical of the practice which enabled prosecutions against prostitutes on the evidence of the police only and it was asserted that the attendance at court of a witness should be ensured.[50] By law (Metropolitan Police Act 1839 or outside of London the Vagrancy Act 1824 or local enactments) it was illegal only to be in a public place for the purpose of prostitution or to solicit *to the annoyance of* inhabitants or passers by. This was to be a persistent area of conflict between the police and the courts. The Commissioner of the Metropolitan Police of the time blamed what he claimed was a deterioration of conditions on the streets on magistrates because police were now reluctant to make arrests without the support of the courts that prostitutes would then be convicted. The arrests for soliciting in London had fallen from 2,504 in 1921 to 538 in 1923.[51] In her study of female sexual delinquency in New York, Ruth Alexander has noted similar conflicts around this period. However, her evidence suggests that the police and the courts largely co-operated in the capture of prostitutes under the amended Vagancy law of 1915, which expanded the definition of vagrant to include, for example, any person who offers to commit prostitution, leaving women and girls open to entrapment and extortion by the police.[52]

The League of Nations report showed little consideration of the complexities behind the criminal statistics and rather a comprehensive list of factors was put forward to explain the unquestioned decline in prostitution, including the altered status of women in public life and in industrial and commercial employment, and the increased organisational and recreational facilities for young people, such as the Boy Scouts and the Girl Guides.[53] Reiterating long-standing associations between prostitution and the feeble-minded, the report also commented on improved provision for the 'mentally deficient'. Other preventive measures cited were the expansion of after care services related to orphanages, industrial and reformatory schools and similar institutions, the development of a probationary system and the increase of sex education in schools. A 'change in attitude' towards juvenile offenders based on the principle of 'training and reformation' was seen as particularly important as 'studies' revealed that a large proportion of girls who had become prostitutes were 'drawn from broken homes, or [were] otherwise deprived of normal family life'.[54]

Sexual offences against children and young people were the subject of considerable debate during the 1920s. In his *Causes of Sex Delinquency*, Cecil Burt stated that 'some of the youngest on my lists have become habitual little courtesans for the sake of sweets or for the money with which to buy them'.[55] In a later well-known study, Gladys Hall stated that she had found similar evidence 'in England for pennies or small sums of money by children of seven'.[56] The Criminal Law Amendment Act (1922) was the culmination of vigorous campaigning for further legislation by feminist and purity groups and of failed Private Members Bills in the years immediately following the end of the First World War. Penalties for brothel keepers were increased, the defence of reasonable cause to believe that a girl was 16 or over thereafter referred only to men of 22 years of age or younger on a first offence, and the period in which a conviction might be brought after an offence has been committed was extended from six to nine months. One of the clauses which prompted the most debate throughout the passage of the Bill was that referring to the defence that a man had reasonable cause to believe that a girl was 16 or over. In the House of Commons Major C. Lowther described this clause as a 'charter to blackmailers' and accused the government of putting forward 'stunt legislation' under pressure of agitation by 'various enthusiastic and well-meaning, but, if I may venture the criticism, unreasoning societies, composed largely, I believe, of women'.[57]

Prominent in the debates in the House of Commons during the passing of the 1922 Act was the depiction of young, particularly working-class, girls as the more sexually mature seducer of innocent, and by inference middle and upper class, young men who would then be held legally responsible and open to blackmail. It was, therefore, deemed in one case to be 'legislation against one sex more than another'.[58] In these debates many of the themes running through arguments about sexual morality since the late nineteenth century re-emerged. Perhaps one of the most interesting of the series of failed amendments that were tabled to the 1922 Act was to exclude girls who were prostitutes under 16 years old from legal protection. It was claimed that 'the danger … is the case of the mature girls under 16 or the professional prostitute under 16 who is herself responsible mainly for the man committing this offence. You do not want to protect them'.[59] Such arguments reveal not only a resistance to the idea that sexual exploitation of the young was inherently harmful but also 'the tenacity of the belief that children chose to be sexually immoral and having thus chosen should not be protected'.[60] Sir Archibald Bodkin, Director of Police Prosecutions and former NVA member, was himself 'wholly opposed' to the recommendation to remove the defence of reasonable cause to believe a girl was 16, as he was to many of the alleviations to the treatment of children in court suggested by feminist groups.[61] Although the subject of the sexual activity of boys under 16 was touched upon, in that it was stated that a 'great deal of vice which exists is engaged in by boys of comparatively tender years', the prostitution of young boys and their possible need for protection was not seriously raised.[62]

The sexual abuse of children and the legal process surrounding its detection and prosecution were investigated by the Departmental Committee on Sexual Offences Against Young Persons.[63] Such issues had been the subject of concern by several groups and individuals, including magistrates and feminist organisations. In their annual report of 1922–3, the Magistrates Association had issued a list of recommendations regarding court procedure in cases of 'child assault'.[64] Three of the seven recommendations asserted the necessity for women as figures of support for children to be present in the criminal process whether they be family, police or probation officers or magistrates. Indeed, the Home Office maintained that no court examination of children should take place without the presence of a woman relative, woman probation officer or matron. However, it was clear that, due to the judge's discretionary powers in this respect, many instances were occurring in which courts were cleared of all women in sex cases involving children. The Women's Freedom League condemned this and requested that the Home Secretary receive their deputation. The Home Office memo relating to this request pointed out that under common law women had the same right to be in court as men. But by Section 114 of the Children Act 1908 all persons, except those directly concerned with the case and the press, could be excluded from the court when a child under 16 was giving evidence. In effect, this tended to be limited to cases involving sexual crime. [65] The Home Office refused to receive the deputation surmising that trouble might arise if the Women's Freedom League were told that no woman could be 'legally excluded from a Court of Justice on account of her sex except during the time a witness under 16 is giving evce [sic] in a case that comes within S.114 of the Children Act'.[66] There remained a long way to go in addressing the unsympathetic environment of the court in cases involving children, although ironically cases in which children were the offenders would have been much more likely to have women present since, for example, women magistrates were overtly encouraged in the juvenile courts.

Despite the fact that much that was in the *Report of the Departmental Committee on Sexual Offences Against Young Persons* was considered to be 'too radical and child-centred' for implementation,[67] the publicity it received further aired these important issues. Significantly, it reported that sexual crime committed against children under 16 years was increasing and recommended long prison sentences for male offenders. The report included recommendations that the age of consent be raised to 17, that the defence of reasonable cause to believe that a girl was 16 should be finally abolished, and that the procedures in court for offences against children should be alleviated. The Committee disclosed that, based on the evidence of child welfare societies, rescue and social workers, very many cases were never brought to the police. Social workers had stated to the Committee that they did not report cases to the police either because they wanted to protect the child from a trial, or because the difficulty of providing proof was so great that it was a waste of time. Few of the recommendations of the Committee were incorporated into the Children's Bill of 1932.

According to Smart, the main focus of feminist and purity campaigners at this time 'was to extend protection to girls from forms of sexual assault that fell short of rape'.[68] They also campaigned for an increase in the age of consent to 18. Feminist and purity groups also 'sought to explain sexual precociousness in young women as an outcome of sexual abuse, rather than following the more patriarchal convention that saw precocious and immoral girls inviting sex and seducing older men'.[69] Such groups, with support from the NSPCC, had some success and, against constant resistance, managed to extend legal protection towards young girls and to increase public awareness of the subject. Indeed, the Director of the NSPCC was a member of the Sexual Offences Committee and its work was reported in the *Child's Guardian*, which also asserted the importance of addressing the 'present ignorance, carelessness, and indifference in sexual matters' with regard to children as well as the light sentences often imposed for sexual offences against children.[70]

The image of the under-aged prostitute as bearing the responsibility as the seducer and as a threat to the sexual control of men persisted however. The magistrates' periodical *The Justice of the Peace* depicted the under-aged subject of sexual assault as composing 'the helpless innocent child at one end of the scale and the precocious temptress at the other' (2 January). This is an indication of the resistance in legal circles to change in sexual legislation that has been identified by Smart. According to Smart, the legal establishment perceived the child 'as an unreliable witness who could not withstand cross-questioning and who, in any case, was likely to be partly responsible for the minor lapse in adult behaviour of which she complained' and, furthermore, was not seen as requiring special treatment.[71]

Evidence of the response to child sexual abuse and/or exploitation on a community level is relatively scarce, yet community condemnation was certainly apparent. In areas like Campbell Bunk, Islington in London, the community's women's networks concerned themselves with women's survival but also with the welfare of local children and would not disdain from reporting one of their neighbours to the NSPCC Inspector.[72] Despite considerable mistrust, such communities also resorted to the police. Relations between the poor and the police may well have been ambivalent but, as White notes, 'people needed the police – to protect the weak against the strong … ; to protect wives against husbands and children against parents'.[73] Both kinds of institutions were seen as resources for the resolution of difficulties, when other avenues had been exhausted. Linda Gordon has suggested a similar resource-based view to the way in which poor families approached welfare organisations in Boston, USA.[74]

However, in one of the best pieces of evidence on the subject of child prostitution located in this study, it appears that, despite at least one letter of complaint and considerable community disapproval, the only action taken by the local police was a single warning, until the NSPCC stepped in.[75] In the late 1920s, a woman in the south of England received six months imprisonment for allowing the carnal knowledge of her daughter. The brief for the prosecution of the trial made it clear that complaints had been received by the local police regarding the family both as to accusations that the mother beat the daughter and that soldiers were visiting their house so that the girl was 'exposed to the dangers of prostitution'. Following a letter received by the NSPCC alerting the Society to the birth of a baby to the 14 year-old daughter, and in which the mother was called 'an abusive and filthy talking woman' of whom the neighbours were afraid, investigation began. The letter to the NSPCC stated that it was not the girl's fault, as 'she has never been allowed to go out without her mother she as [sic] been taken to barracks by her mother and the soldiers brought to the house'. Once the NSPCC became involved the girl and her baby were given over into the care of the local Rescue Society as a 'place of safety' until the case could be brought before a Court of Summary Jurisdiction in pursuance of section 20, sub section 2 of the Children Act 1908. Furthermore, police visited neighbours, took statements and also gave evidence in court. The difficulties of interfering in the family and of prosecuting such cases may have made the police reluctant to intervene until the intervention of the NSPCC. In fact, during the 1930s the NSPCC itself began to withdraw from prosecutions of this nature, because it made the Society vulnerable to counter-prosecution and libel suits, forcing this prosecuting role upon the police.

The background to the case is evident from the depositions given by neighbours of the family. One neighbour stated that:

> I saw a soldier come out of Mrs [their house] ...   it was in the evening, shortly after another soldier came out and brought him back. [The mother] then came out and went up the street, leaving the two soldiers in the house with [her daughter], then one soldier came out and walked up and down. About twenty minutes later [the mother] came back and went into the house, and the soldier who had been walking up and down, went in shortly after. Since that time I have seen soldiers visit the house frequently always in the evening, and leave ...   hours up to 11pm. I have seen [mother and

daughter] go out about 9pm, the girl almost always crying, I have seen them return with other soldiers.

Similar deposition were made by several other neighbours testifying to years of 'immoral' behaviour by the mother and the fact that the pregnancy of the daughter was 'the talk of the neighbours'. Upon investigation, the NSPCC Inspector concluded that the mother was 'of immoral habits' and that 'a great number of the soldiers know this woman'. The prosecution lawyer in this case complained about the attitude of the daughter because 'it appeared that either through affection or fear she would support her mother' but he asserted the moral responsibility to prosecute such a case, in which it was said that the mother 'reeked of immorality'. He continued,

> It is obviously difficult in a case like this to produce conclusive evidence, but one must recognise that the Prosecution is saddled with the necessity of bringing home guilt to the Defendant with a reasonable certainty, and with the fact that the mind of any decent person revolts at the idea of a mother doing, or failing to do anything to deprive her daughter of her honour.

On this occasion, the NSPCC seems to have spearheaded the move to investigate complaints from the local community, with the aid of the police once investigations had begun. It was the Society and the court that elicited and confirmed the moral standards of the individuals in the community who gave evidence. The local neighbourhood proved to be the arbiters in the constructions of the mother's reputation and be-haviour. It was here that the formulation of such cases was most likely to begin. As Shani D'Cruze has noted with regard to violence against and by women during the nineteenth century, 'people occupied and moved across the grid of neighbourhood space under the regular observation of others … . Although neighbourhoods could prove a supportive and positive context for sociability, it could also be the crucible for innumerable tensions'.[76] The consequences of this prosecution were imprisonment for the mother; the daughter and her baby were sent to a Rescue home and the youngest child, an adopted son, was sent to the workhouse.

The difficulties of obtaining convictions in this area were acknowledged in the *Report of the Committee on Sexual Offences against Young Persons* 1924–5. Problems obtaining evidence regarding child abuse, and which would also have appertained to child prostitution, were compounded by contemporary views on the transmission of venereal disease. As early as 1916 outbreaks of venereal disease were being recorded in children's homes but were largely attributed to contamination through the shared use of such things as towels and lavatory seats, from a few sexually precocious and infected children entering the home undetected. This therefore raised the fear of sexual activity among children but, according to Smart, did not give rise to suspicions about sexual abuse in the home, which was for most unthinkable. With the spread of VD clinics in the 1920s, doctors increasingly dealt with venereal disease within poorer families, but the reasons given tended to be poor hygiene and the sharing of the same bed with infected adults.[78] Yet the possibility of infection in children through sexual abuse by adults was raised. For example, in evidence to the Royal Commission on Venereal Disease 1914, a matron of a hospital for women and children clearly asserts that, in her opinion, the 'little children' in her care who had acquired syphilis had 'been sinned against in every instance we have got', 'I think they are cases of assault in every instance'.[79] There did, therefore, exist a discourse, which asserted that venereal disease in children was a direct result of abuse, although by the 1940s and the resurgence in domestic ideologies, this had reverted back to denial that such a phenomenon existed.[80]

Another obstacle to obtaining evidence of child prostitution and abuse was the sanctity of parental rights. In some cases doctors faced treating young patients and staying quiet about abuse or raising suspicions and having children removed from their treatment. Even the NSPCC could not examine a child without the father's consent to obtain proof of abuse, neglect or cruelty. Even in the event of obtaining a conviction abusers could make their children live with them on release from prison.[81]

Unregulated adoptions and abuse

During this period the *Child's Guardian* also revealed cases of what might be more accurately called a traffic in children, which in some cases resulted in the sexual abuse of the child, as well as exposing them to possible cruelty and neglect. This was a traffic that was never identified as such despite the fact that there is more concrete evidence, albeit limited, relating to the procurement of children in this way than to stories of girls being drugged in cinemas and carried away that during the 1930s again attracted so much sensationalist publicity. This traffic was continued by means of unregulated adoptions. Since 1889 Poor Law, Boards of Guardians had been able to 'adopt' children and assume parental rights over them until they were 18, often fostering them out until that age. Outside of this, most adoptions were informal and without the aid of any agency, although the National Children's Home and Orphanage (established 1869) and societies such as Barnardo's and the Church of England Waifs and Strays Society had long arranged adoptions.[82] Until 1926 children could be passed from the parent/s to any other adult, whether they were members of the same family or complete strangers, without relinquishing their parental rights. A parent could not, until 1926, voluntarily deprive themselves of their rights and responsibilities regarding their children.[83] Hendrick has discussed this and pointed out the 'chattel-like' regard that such un-regulated transfers of children, which sometimes occurred repeatedly to the same child, indicated on the part of individual parents and society as a whole, particularly towards illegitimate children who made up most of this traffic.[84] Indeed, in a social context of legal and moral prejudice against unmarried mothers, illegitimate children had long been particularly vulnerable to neglect or abuse through being transferred to other adults. During the second half of the nineteenth century there were several public scandals regarding children being neglected within a system of 'baby-farming', whereby individuals might take in several children for payment. Care must be taken, however, not to exaggerate the dangers, most children transferred to the care of other adults were successfully adopted often within the same family or neighbourhood.

As a consequence of the First World War there were not only large numbers of war orphans and war babies but more middle-class couples seeking to adopt, so magnifying concerns about the lack of security evident in informal adoptions, a factor that was felt to inhibit willingness to adopt. The NSPCC was prominent among the organisations pressing for legislative change and as part of their campaign they highlighted incidences which illustrated the potential for abuse. In a case from 1922, a mother had passed her 13 year-old daughter to a young married man who then left the town. After some time, in which the girl had travelled around with the man, she was traced by an NSPCC Inspector to a common lodging house, 'where she had been for a fortnight with a young man, 24 years of age [not the one to which the girl was originally given], whose wife was in service only visiting her husband occasionally'.[85] A further case recounted the 'adoption' of a girl of ten years old by a couple. Events revealed that the couple were not married and that they slept with the girl in the same bed. In the context of the time and the continued problem of overcrowded housing this would not of itself indicate abuse. However, before reaching the age of 16, the girl had given birth to a child by the man which later died through neglect and was buried in the garden.[86]

The sad fortunes of children who were treated so casually and the potential extent of the abuse unregulated adoption exposed them to are clear in the small numbers of these cases that came to court or to the attention of voluntary or state welfare organisations. To give a further example, a little girl of about three years old was abandoned at a workhouse by her parents, her father was later traced and retrieved her. He then sold her to gypsies with whom she lived and tramped until she was about ten years old. She was then transferred to some peddlers, 'whether by gift or payment is not known' and with whom she remained for three years until abandoned. She then fell into the hands of a 'rough woman' who kept a 'house of ill-repute' where she was 'ill-treated', the girl was taken from there by a NSPCC Inspector to a children's home. The article questions, 'What this girl has been saved from no one can tell', however when the girl was handed over to the NSPCC the woman called, 'You can take the little ... for since she came into the house my husband has never taken his eyes off her'.[87]

The NSPCC campaigned to have legal adoption proceedings introduced and regulated by the state. In June 1921 the Society published an article on the Report of the Committee (Hopkinson's Committee) appointed by the Home Secretary to enquire into the adoption of children. The Committee recommended an extension of the 1908 Children Act 'so as to obtain the notification and supervision of all adoption of children under the age of 14, whether payment is made or not'. The Committee also reported that the lack of proper control over adoptions of children:

> over the age of seven years of age, and under that age unless payment is made, results in an undesirable traffic in child life with which no one can interfere, unless proceedings are taken against the adopting parent for cruelty or neglect. Children may be handed from one person to another with or without payment, advertised for disposal, and even sent out of the country without any record being kept.[88]

The Committee recommended that Section 11 of the Children's Act should be amended so as to render all homes and institutions undertaking the control and custody of children liable to inspection, a proposal which the NSPCC stated they had been pressing for. A related measure that the NSPCC also supported, and which was introduced in 1926, was that children born out of wedlock should be legitimised by later marriage. Nevertheless, in the absence of statistics regarding long-term fostering, the Committee concluded that there was no real necessity to legalise adoptions.[89] It was not until a further Committee (Tomlin

85

Committee) had been appointed and had reported in favour of legalised adoption that this was enabled, under the Adoption of Children Act in 1926.

The NSPCC later registered its dissatisfaction with the Adoption of Children Act 1926 which seemed to offer protection to 'good' people who adopt children by securing their legal rights and preventing the children being taken back when they become potential wage-earners, but did little to prevent the abuse and exploitation of adopted children. An article on the subject stated that the Committee had failed to see:

> the desirability of securing the registration of all cases of adoption, with full enquiry beforehand as to the fitness of the persons adopting, or the suitability of the premises in which it was proposed the child should be kept. Existing evils are likely, therefore, to be perpetuated, and the same old dangers surround the children whose unhappy lot it may be to fall into the hands of unsuitable adopters.[90]

As an illustration of the dangers which this change in the law would not prevent a specific case was detailed. In this case a man had applied to the Board of Guardians to adopt a boy. While the Guardians were still making enquiries the man placed an advertisement in a local paper and obtained a seven-year-old boy from a woman who left the workhouse to transfer the child to the man, signing an adoption agreement. By this time the Guardians had completed their investigation which showed that the man lived alone in what was judged to be unsuitable accommodation. Later realising her mistake the mother went to the Guardians who called in the local NSPCC Inspector. The Inspector discovered that the man 'had the boy sleeping with him' and also that:

> apart from the unsuitability of the man and the place in which he lived, the boy would be there at great risk to himself. This man has an income of about £94 per annum, is, or has been, connected with some movements amongst boys, in which he has come under police supervision because of a complaint that he had 'medically examined' a boy.[91]

The man had previously and unsuccessfully tried to obtain a boy from another Board of Guardians and from an Adoption Society. In this case the boy was retrieved by the NSPCC and returned to his mother. Following the 1926 Act, adoptions became more popular and there was a rise in adoption societies and in private adoptions. But even by the time of the *Report of the Departmental Committee on Adoption Societies and Agencies* the number of unregulated adoptions remained large, in part, the Committee felt, because of inertia or ignorance. In the case of one of the largest adoption societies only 30 per cent of the adoptions arranged in 1935 were legalised and most adoptions during the 1930s continued to be of illegitimate children; the transfer of children for money was also still being operated.[92] Despite several attempts to regulate adoption between 1926 and the 1940s many individuals and even some adoption societies continued to ignore the law, it was not until the 1948 Children Act that a more coherent and centralised structure for all homeless children was sought.[93] However, this Act did not altogether prevent unregulated adoption which persisted, neither did it prevent the adoption of male children by single men; only the adoption of female children by single men was circumscribed by the Act.

Conclusions

There is no doubt that during the years of the First World War and the 1920s issues of sexuality remained on the political and public agenda. Culturally and sexually the diffusion of literature and ideas on equal sexuality and the companionate marriage, in the context of a continued decline in the birth rate, increased the attractions of the domestic sphere and the popularity of marriage. Moral change was significant, albeit restricted to the confines of the marital and familial norm. Unmarried mothers, for example, were still subject to social censure, control and marginalisation. Prostitutes, if anything, may have been subject to more criticism and exclusion from within their neighbourhoods and communities. The effects of the war and the continued decline in birth rates served to increase the status of the child which was perhaps most evident in the passing of the Criminal Justice Amendment Act (1922). It was also clear, for example, in the NSPCC's criticisms of government reconstruction plans at the end of the war, which not only called for more child-centred policies but for a closer partnership between the state and voluntary organisations, although with the NSPCC retaining a 'controlling influence'. It was maintained that a 'broad view' was required to enable entrenched and long-standing problems to be finally tackled.

> It is not enough to know what one public body is doing or of what one voluntary association is accomplishing. More especially it is desirable that workers should come together, try to understand

each other, and beyond all other things appreciate the fact that of all the subjects now under discussion that of the child is of urgent national importance. That is why it is essential to secure a definite controlling influence in directing all action.[94]

Ambiguity remained, however, with regard to the image of precocious children and the experiences that might have resulted in their sexual activity. Unless they were seen to be clear victims of parental or other adult coercion, as in the child prostitution case discussed in detail in this chapter, child prostitutes, particularly those nearing the age of consent, remained likely to attract condemnation and suspicion as temptresses. At the same time, lack of protection for children, in particular in consequence of unregulated adoptions, left illegitimate children especially open to abuse and exploitation.

References

1 *Hansard* 5 July 1922 Vol.157, col.439, Mr Dennis Herbert.
2 J. Weeks, *Sex, Politics and Society: The Regulation of Sexuality since 1800* (Harlow: Longman, 1989), p. 202.
3 *Child's Guardian* 1928 XXXVIII (4), p. 28.
4 F. Mort, *Dangerous Sexualities: Medico-Moral Politics in England since 1830* (London: Routledge and Kegan Paul, 1987), p. 189.
5 C. Haste, *Rules of Desire, Sex in Britain: World War I to the Present* (London: Chatto and Windus, 1992), p. 59; M. Stopes, *Married Love* (London: Fifield, 1918).
6 S. Jeffreys, *The Spinster and her Enemies: Feminism and Sexuality 1880–1930* (London: Pandora, 1985).
7 L. Hall, *Impotent ghosts from no man's land, flappers' boyfriends, or crypto-patriarchs? Men, Sex and Social Change in 1920s Britain.* Social History 21(1), 1996, p. 61.
8 S. Humphries, *A Secret World of Sex: Forbidden Fruit, the British Experience 1900–1950* (London: Sedgwick and Jackson, 1988).
9 J. D. Smith, 'The voluntary tradition', in J. D. Smith, C. Rochester and R. Hedley (eds) *An Introduction to the Voluntary Sector* (London: Routledge, 1995), p. 25.
10 *Child's Guardian*, XXIX (1), p. 2.
11 *Our Waifs and Strays*, March 1917 (377), p. 36.
12 January 1915 (351), p. 20.
13 S. Pedersen, 'Gender, welfare and citizenship in Britain during the Great War', *American Historical Review* 95 (4), 1990.
14 F. Mort, *Dangerous Sexualities*, p. 191.
15 D. Evans, 'Tackling the "Hideous Scourge": The creation of the venereal

disease treatment centre in early twentieth-century Britain', *Social History of Medicine* 5, 1992, pp. 418 and 427.

16 L. Hall, *Impotent ghosts*, p. 59.
17 *Shield* 3rd ser I, January 1916, p. 90.
18 NVA 4/BVA/Box 199, 28th Report of Bristol and South Western Counties 1915, p. 7.
19 J. Weeks, *Sex, Politics and Society*, p. 215; J. Radford, 'Women and policing: contradictions old and new', in J. Hanmer, J. Radford and E. A. Stanko, *Women, Policing and Male Violence: International Perspectives* (London: Routledge, 1989).
20 PRO MePol 2/2290.
21 A. Marwick, *The Deluge* (London: Macmillan, 1973), p. 110.
22 L. Hall, *Impotent ghosts*, p. 58.
23 January 1916, 3rd ser I, p. 90.
24 R. Porter and L. Hall, *The Facts of Life: The Creation of Sexual Knowledge in Britain, 1650–1950* (New Haven: Yale University Press, 1995), p. 234; *Shield* 3rd ser II, July 1918–January 1920).
25 Ibid.
26 For comment see *Shield* 3rd ser I, Sept 1917, pp. 332–3.
27 2 June 1917.
28 M. H. Mason, 'Public morality: some constructive suggestions', *Nineteenth Century* LXXXII, p. 187.
29 *Shield*, 3rd ser I, September 1917, pp. 332–3.
30 C. Haste, *Rules of Desire*, p. 49.
31 PRO HO 45/10523/140266).
32 Ibid.
33 Ibid.
34 M. Gordon, *Penal Discipline* (London: Routledge and Sons, 1922).
35 Ibid, p. 118.
36 Ibid, p. 99.
37 *Shield* VIII (3) September 1941, p. 100.
38 A. Marwick, *The Deluge*, p. 304.
39 R. M. Alexander, *The 'Girl Problem': Female Sexual Delinquency in New York, 1900–1939* (New York: Cornell University Press, 1995), p. 2.
40 *Child's Guardian* 1920 XXX (10), p. 1.
41 For example, *Child's Guardian* 1927 XXXVII (7), p. 50.
42 *Child's Guardian* 1931 XLI (1), p. 1 and 1932 XLII (6), p. 41.
43 *Child's Guardian* 1931 XLI (1): 1–2.
44 Ibid, p. 1.
45 H. Hendrick, *Child Welfare: England 1872–1989* (London: Routledge, 1994), p. 180; V. Bailey, *Delinquency and Citizenship: Reclaiming the Young Offender, 1914–1948* (Oxford: Clarendon Press, 1987).
46 R. M. Alexander, *The 'Girl Problem'*, also makes this point with regard to New York.
47 G. Behlmer, *Friends of the Family: The English Home and its Guardians, 1850–1940* (California: Stanford University Press, 1998), pp. 266–270.

48 E. Bristow, *Vice and Vigilance: Purity Movements in Britain since 1700* (Dublin: Gill and Macmillan, 1977), pp. 176–7 and 194–5.
49 League of Nations Advisory Commission for the Protection of Children and Young People, Traffic in Women and Children Committee IV Social, 1929 Official No: C.T.F.E 336 (2), 28/2/199.
50 PRO MePol 2/2291.
51 PRO MePol 2/2290; also see MePol 2/7356.
52 R. M. Alexander, *The 'Girl Problem'*, Ch. 2.
53 IV Social 1929 Official No: C.T.F.E 336 (2), 28/2/1919, p. 85.
54 Ibid, p. 85.
55 C. Birt, *The Young Delinquent, Vol.1* (London: University of London Press, 1925), p. 14.
56 G. M. Hall, *Prostitution, a Survey and a Challenge* (London: Williams and Northgate, 1933), p. 26.
57 *Hansard* 5 July 1922 Vol.157, cols.405–7.
58 Ibid, cols.408–10, Lieut-Colonel Moore-Brabazon.
59 Ibid, col.439.
60 C. Smart, 'The historical struggle against child abuse, 1910–1960', occasional paper, The University of Leeds 1998, pp. 10–14.
61 PRO HO 45/24867.
62 *Hansard* 5 July 1922 Vol.157, cols.457–8.
63 PP 1924–5 (Cmd.2561) XV, p. 905.
64 PRO HO 45/22907.
65 Ibid.
66 PRO HO45/22907; PRO HO45/24628.
67 C. Smart, 'The historical struggle against child abuse', pp. 10–14.
68 Ibid, pp. 10–11.
69 Ibid, pp. 12–13.
70 XXXVI (1), p. 2.
71 C. Smart, 'A history of ambivalence and conflict in the discursive construction of the 'child victim' of sexual abuse', *Social and Legal Studies* 8, 1999, p. 399.
72 J. White, *The Worst Street in North London: Campbell Bunk, Islington Between the Wars*, History Workshop (London: Routledge and Kegan Paul, 1986), p. 75.
73 Ibid, p. 114; also see H. Daley, *This Small Cloud: A Personal Memoir* (London: Weidenfeld and Nicolson, 1986), p. 81.
74 *Heroes of their Own Lives: the Politics and History of Family Violence: Boston 1880–1960* (New York: Viking, 1989).
75 Special permission to view this file was obtained from the NSPCC. Due to the sensitive nature of the subject all identifying references have been excluded.
76 S. D'Cruze, *Crimes of Outrage: Sex, Violence and Victorian Working Women* (London: UCL Press, 1998), pp. 50–51.
77 *Hansard* 5 July 1922 Vol.157, col. 439.
78 C. Smart, 'The historical struggle against child abuse', pp. 4–6.
79 Quoted in C. Smart, 'A history of ambivalence', p. 396.
80 C. Smart, 'The historical struggle against child abuse', pp. 7–9.
81 Ibid, pp. 9–10.

82 *Report of the Committee on Adoption Societies*, PP 1936–7 (Cmd. 5499) IX, p. 5.
83 E. E. Bowerman, *The Law of Child Protection* (London: Pitman, 1933), p. 19.
84 H. Hendrick, *Child Welfare*, p. 237.
85 *Child's Guardian* XXXII (12), p. 91.
86 *Child's Guardian* 1925 XXXV (3), p. 19.
87 *Child's Guardian* 1922 XXXII (3), p. 20.
88 *Child's Guardian* 1921 XXXI (6), p. 48; G. Behlmer, *Friends of the Family*.
89 G. Behlmer, *Friends of the Family*, pp. 305–6.
90 *Child's Guardian* 1926 XXXVI (9), p. 61.
91 Ibid.
92 PP (Cmd.5499) 1936–7 IX, pp. 1–6 and 36–8.
93 H. Hendrick, *Child Welfare*, p. 238; G. Behlmer, *Friends of the Family*, p. 311.
94 *Child's Guardian* 1919 XXIX (3), p. 1.

Chapter 5

Prostitution, child abuse and feminism during the 1920s and 1930s

This matter of protection of children is a partnership between the dead, the living and those who have not yet been born.[1]

The 1930s were, in many respects, a period in which women, especially, experienced alleviations of long-standing expectations and restrictions. Employment and leisure opportunities for unmarried women were expanding, smaller families reduced the burden of maternity, and marriage was increasingly seen as a partnership. In other respects, society became more exclusive. The shift towards social hygiene and 'welfare feminism' prioritised the domestic role of women and, in the context of population concerns, their part in rearing the next generation. The interests of adult women who chose, or had to lead an independent life, such as those without independent wealth who remained unmarried or were separated or widowed, often received less consideration and were sometimes stigmatised.

Despite strong pressures against sexual promiscuity, more young women were having sex before marriage, although this was often to their future spouse. Fears about the consequences of greater social and sexual freedom for young women were expressed in diverse ways, including through sensationalised accounts of the white slave trade. On the other hand, the subject of the sexual abuse of women and children was raised less in public circles than it had been during the 1920s. This has been linked to the decline of militant feminism and the medicalisation of sex offenders as psychologically ill. Paradoxically, the experience of sexual abuse during childhood became a common part of explanations for the resort of young girls and women to prostitution.

Feminism and society

By the 1930s the sexuality of women was increasingly being interpreted through ideas informed by social hygiene. In both Britain and the United States, this reinforced and reflected the enhanced influence of medical power and classification, which placed sex (within marriage) in a more positive light. The idea of marriage as a partnership in which women had the right to equal sexual enjoyment was confirmed and, in the context of population concerns, the status of motherhood and domestication was heightened with the differences rather than the similarities between genders being emphasised. With regard to the young, concentration was on education and the prevention of sexual delinquency rather than the sexual suppression that had been put forward by earlier feminist groups.[2] As Ruth Alexander has noted with reference to the influence of social hygiene ideas on social workers in America, psychiatrists and psychologists, by promoting a scientific understanding of female adolescence, they hoped to 'avert self-destructive and delinquent conduct' and to spare girls the heavy personal expense of searching for a new sexual ethic by trial and error.[3] The 'new feminism' of the inter-war years, which had been heavily influenced by sex reformers, such as Havelock Ellis, was characterised less by challenges to male dominance than by more constitutional methods and pragmatic, if less ambitious, objectives.

Feminism during the inter-war period fragmented into lobbying and campaigning for specific issues. One of the most well-known feminist groups was the National Union of Societies for Equal Citizenship (NUSEC), which was established in 1918 from the non-militant feminist organisation, the National Union of Women's Suffrage Societies, and was led by Eleanor Rathbone. Indicatively, the NUSEC split in 1928 into two, one arm became the National Council for Equal Citizenship which supported equal rights for women, while the other arm became the Union of Townswomen's Guilds and supported a more educational and welfarist stance; the former quickly withered while the latter thrived.

Olive Banks describes this shift in the priorities of many feminist groups as the emergence of 'welfare feminism', which was also evident in the United States during the same period.[4] Welfare feminism was concerned primarily with the endowment of motherhood, children's health and generally with the alleviation of poverty, it was also linked to the growing socialist movement. Sheila Jeffreys is critical of this major strand of feminism. She asserts that 'Eleanor Rathbone's brand of "welfare feminism" betrayed the cause of spinsterhood and the independent woman'. Jeffreys accuses Eleanor Rathbone of deserting a genuine feminist strategy because it was too difficult and claims that she 'embraced the simpler alternative of emphasising woman's mission of motherhood'.[5] Jeffreys suggests that 'new feminism' constructed a more narrowly defined view of respectable womanhood, excluding spinsters, lesbians and any women who willingly, or were forced to, led an independent life. For example, at a time when female virtue upon marriage remained at a premium but male sexual experience approved of, and even advised in literature, such as Hendrick van do Held's *Ideal Marriage* (1930), Rathbone excluded unmarried mothers from her fight to obtain the endowment of motherhood, later emerging in the form of the family allowance. Jeffreys also makes similar criticisms of Marie Stopes amid her emphasis upon married sexual fulfillment. The widespread discussion of such issues during the inter-war period diffused the idea of women as sexually autonomous even if social morality asserted that the enjoyment of sex should still be confined within marriage. As Chow has remarked with regard to the 1920s, 'Stope's vision of women's sexuality as autonomous and deserving of respect from their lovers was in itself liberating for women'.[6] Some feminist organisations, such as the Association for Moral and Social Hygiene (AMSH), the Six Point Group and the Women's Freedom League, did continue to challenge the social and economic domination of men. The National Vigilance Association (NVA) also continued to promote purity ideals and the single moral standard. However, during the l930s these groups were struggling against a tide that was moving in a different direction.

Other factors provided contextual influences for strengthening the definitions of womanhood as being particularly suited for domesticity. The economic depression of the 1930s placed pressure on married working women to make way for the mass of men who had been made unemployed by international competition and falling demand facing the old staple industries. Sally Alexander has suggested that 'Women and migrant labour were the shock troops of industrial change, their visibility and ubiquity made them objects of ridicule and insult'.[7] As well as the economic consequences of adult male unemployment upon the family, the pride and masculinity of its men were at stake. Among all employees, insured and uninsured, the average rate of unemployment for 1921-1938 was 10.9 per cent, although the rate for 1931–2 rose to over 16 per cent.[8] Of course, unemployment patterns varied regionally with the worst affected areas being Wales and the north. For example, Hatton calculates that in 1932 the actual unemployment rate in London was 12.5 per cent while in the north-east of England it was 26.8 per cent and in Wales 37.3 per cent.[9] Concern continued to be expressed about the low birth rate in the inter-war years. By the 1930s the standard of the small family had been largely established; between 1900–9 and 1930 the percentage of couples with one or two children had increased from 33.5 to 51.1.[10] Associated with this, imperialist and eugenic ideals remained prominent so that aspects of public and political debate remained focused on national efficiency and competition as well as hereditary and environmental influences on the nurturing of the next generation.

The ideal of domestic womanhood was also reinforced by the expanding child-care literature, which emphasised the effects upon children of full-time working mothers and referred to general failures of motherhood, issues that had become prominent during the First World War. The growth in women's magazines reflected and fuelled the image of a much more attractive domestic sphere facilitated partly by smaller families which 'helped shape the meaning given to the home and led to a new family ideal'.[11] Despite these changes, informative sex manuals continued to be associated with pornography and even marriage advice manuals were still not considered suitable for mass reading. Certainly, the experiences of families, and women in particular, varied considerably across the class spectrum. Evidence to the Women's Health Enquiry, which reported in 1939, highlighted the appalling living conditions and standards of health under which some women and their families laboured.[12] Nevertheless, social pressures to conform to, largely middle-class led, standards of sexual morality and domestic respectability remained strong.[13]

In conjunction with the pressures on women to take up the mantle of marriage, motherhood and domesticity, the Depression of the 1930s also brought increased economic pressures for single women to contribute to family income and to travel to find work if necessary. For many at this time, this was still a journey into domestic service and travelling to take up live-in domestic service was a common phenomenon. For a century and more, young girls had been taking up domestic service in large numbers, sometimes at considerable distances from their homes. By the 1930s however, increasing numbers were also going into the new industries or the service sector, although the wages in these sectors at this time often remained too low to enable an independent lifestyle let alone pay for leisure activities. Nevertheless, economic constraints and 'new feminism' were competing for the moral ground with shifting social and moral standards, particularly among the young. For example, an increase in choice of employment paralleled the decline in the numbers of young girls going into domestic service, which was characterised by long hours and a restricted and often isolated lifestyle. This shortage was reflected in the fact that after 1922 women were denied social assistance if they refused a job in domestic service available through the labour exchange.

Discussion about the 'new morality' or so-called 'new woman' and changes in social life by commentators usually centred upon the loosening of sexual mores and was open to a variety of interpretations. New morality was described by one contemporary researcher as 'the pursuance of sexual gratification in long-term relationships without marriage or children'.[14] These discussions fed public debate about the potential for mishap among young girls and women subject to less social surveillance and controls than in the past, and armed with what they believed to be a more sophisticated knowledge of the world provided by the cinema and popular magazines and literature. Women were increasingly seen to be going to pubs, clubs and cafes and long-standing courtship conventions had, for many, long been interred. Some feminist organisations perceived this as a retrograde version of the decline of the double moral standard. Alison Neilans, Secretary of the AMSH, asserted in *The Shield* of June 1935 that the sexual double standard had been passed over 'by a knowledge which, for the first time in history, puts the woman, if she chooses, into the same position of moral irresponsibility as her partner'.

The white slave trade: rhetoric or reality?

The more melodramatic elements of public debate were stoked by sensational and scare-mongering stories in the popular press about the dangers facing lone women, particularly from the white slave trader. Porter and Hall have suggested that the role of the press with regard to sexual subjects was ambiguous, sensationalist and prurient with recurrent panics but that it served to disseminate knowledge.[15] With regard to the subject of white slavery, the press was less ambiguous and served to spread minor panics which put young women in fear. Such sensationalist and conspiratorial articles also sidelined the real problems being faced in England by young girls and women involved in prostitution at this time. Even without the benefit of reliable statistical evidence, the numbers working on the streets or in brothels in England because they had, or felt they had little or no alternative, must have far outnumbered the few who may have been duped or coerced into leaving the country and ended up selling themselves. In response to an enquiry from the Home Office about the prevalence of white slavery, especially among immigrants, regional police forces responded negatively. In one case the Chief Constable of Cardiff Police did state that:

During the past five years two cases have arisen in this City where white women, coloured men, and a Maltese have been concerned in the procuration of young women [including those under-age] for the purpose of carnal intercourse. The facts disclosed that between the persons charged a conspiracy existed, but I do not consider that these isolated cases justify the assumption that organised trafficking exists.[16]

Certainly, police forces were dealing with prostitution and vice between the wars. In the Home Office records held at the Public Record Office, for example, there is detailed documentation regarding police observation and raid upon the Caravan Club which police comment describes as being frequented by both female and male prostitutes.[17] None of this constituted a white slave traffic.

Nevertheless during the mid-1930s the popular press abounded with accounts of girls being abducted and smuggled overseas to be sold into sexual slavery. Many of these articles have been preserved in the archives of the National Vigilance Association (NVA), held in the Fawcett Library, which continued to show unerring concern with the sexual morality and protection of young girls and women.[18] Some of these stories publicised the numbers of girls in the country reported to the police as missing, implying that a proportion of these could have been forced into prostitution in this way but also offering an exaggerated indication of potential numbers. The 'bright lights and glittering promises' of London and other major cities were depicted as being particularly productive of immorality and vice and employment agencies in London were accused of operating as a front for white slave traffickers. An article in *John Bull* (6 June 1936) insisted that 'the offered domestic employment in London may prove nothing but the carefully arranged bait of the traffickers', the girl may refuse but once adrift without employment 'how easily these girls become the victims of traffickers is not difficult to imagine'.

Another major target was the cinema, or sometimes the theatre, in which girls were allegedly drugged, abducted and secreted abroad to work in brothels against their will. In defensive mood, the Gaumount-British Picture Corporation went so far, in 1935, as to send a confidential memoranda to its cinema managers warning against the drugging of young girls and advising them to send for a doctor or a policeman in cases of illness.[19] The purported white slave traffic became the subject of a number of special investigations by tabloid newspaper reporters in which none of the stories could be substantiated. But the stories were never completely discharged, the allure of the mystery could never quite be dismissed in the interests of future newspaper sales. In May 1936, *The*

Daily Express ran a series of articles following the fortunes of an investigation on the white slave traffic by one of their reporters. The first article, on the 21st, was headlined Mystery of Britain's Vanished Girls. The following day the headline ran Vanished Girl. Clues Lead Nowhere, but the article still remarked that 'every young woman one meets believes in the story of the theatre ticket and the White Slave Traffic behind it. Talk to wives, sisters, mothers, waitresses, schoolmistresses, the girl in the bus – they all apparently, have a secret dread of this traffic. They may of course be right'.[20] By 25 May the reporter had sought the advice of the 'experts'. The headline ran Detectives Say Girls Vanish Because They 'Tire of Home' (Man's View), Are Trapped (Women's View). The 'man's view' given was that of a 'Scotland-yard man' and the 'woman's view' was from a Miss Storey who was described as a 'criminologist'. Her opinion that white slavery was real but not as prevalent as supposed was accepted and it was questioned, in the form of a letter from the public, whether the police were not playing 'straight into the gangsters' hands by keeping it [white slavery] a secret?'. The popular press clearly exploited the fact that in a complex urban society it was virtually impossible to disprove the practice of white slavery in England, particularly when the targets for accusations of white slavery mirrored the prejudices and fears of that society; Communists and non-white foreigners especially.

Discussion of the drugging and abduction of girls for white slavery also made it to the *Times* correspondence section. In reply to two letters of 25th and 26th May 1932, a letter from Dr Letitia Fairfield on the 30th tried to insert a note of pragmatism and questioned 'of what use to anyone is a semi-conscious girl, under conditions prevailing anywhere in the British Isles?', 'who is going to pay the money for the appalling risk of misusing her while in a drugged condition?'. 'Older readers will remember a similar outcrop of stories in 1912 and 1913 – and not a single case of this alleged drugging by hypodermics was ever substantiated by the police'. Another letter of denial of the white slave traffic in England by F. Sempkins, the Secretary of the NVA, was refused publication. However, Sempkins published denials elsewhere, in national newspapers and journals, and gave them on an individual basis in replies to numerous letters and notes, as well as to people visiting the organisation's offices.

In his writings, Sempkins instead warned against girls accepting a drive in a car from strange men or 'motor cads'.[21] He believed that when girls came 'to a bad end' it was usually attributable to drink, because she mixed with the 'wrong people' or because she wanted to. The best safeguard for any girl or woman, he asserted, was modesty.[22] Sempkins complained that many of the real problems of this kind were being lost in these myth-making stories. The international traffic is a real danger in the world, he affirmed, 'There is human drama in the white slave traffic, plenty of it, but the traffic has none of the gaudy trappings of romance or fiction'. He claimed that in the ranks of missing girls in England few were victims of the white slave traffic although:

> Amongst them are many who are sunk in vicious life and ashamed to go home. But the point is that these girls are not the unwilling victims of cunning agents. They have gone wrong from their own weakness, or force of circumstances. The girls who are absorbed into the white slave market are not all innocent. Some unfortunates are wanton from an early age, for various reasons. Some are selfish, wilful, lazy. The majority are simply weak. Pity most of those victims of circumstances, lacking mental stamina, the products of poverty, slums and disease.[23]

Those women and girls who became involved in prostitution by means other than abduction or who were not innocent before becoming involved in prostitution were therefore to be the subject of condemnation as well as sympathy, shame and the label of psychological weakness. The traffic in women, he asserted, was 'a polite title for a grim and dirty trade. A focus for crime: an incubator for loathsome disease'. Loose morality was, for Sempkins, the first step along the road to prostitution. He warned girls arriving in large cities to 'choose their girl friends carefully, and avoid like the plague those who boast of boy friends, of places they know, and good times they have'. These dangerous girls, although not yet prostitutes, were, he suggested, likely to be gaining something as an amateur. 'Don't worry about druggings, or kidnappings, or mysterious strangers. But beware of mixing drinks; car rides with men you do not know very well; flashy company; unsavoury clubs and drinking places'.[24]

In his writing, Sempkins tried to shift concentration in England away from the naïve romantic associations of 'white slavery' encouraged by literature and cinema films like *The Sheik* (book 1919, film 1921) which starred the archetypal contemporary erotic hero, Rudolph Valentino. Karen Chow has suggested that this genre operated to allow women to exercise economic, in the sense of consuming leisure independently, and sexual freedom in that they confirmed the popular sexual discourses that claimed women's sex drives were autonomous of male sexuality.[25] With regard to New York, it has been suggested, such movies helped young women to construct an erotic, romantic and independent identity to challenge a family-centred identity'.[26] However, such constructions also operated to obscure or conceal the realities of sexual assault and prostitution. Distinctions were made, therefore, between victims of abduction and those who became prostitutes through other less easily definable or understandable routes. Barry has suggested that even into the late twentieth century part of the bias that has made the issue of forced prostitution invisible as a form of slavery originates in concentration on how the girl gets into that position. She states that, if the girl is 'kidnapped, purchased, fraudulently contracted through an agency or organised crime, it is easy to recognise her victimisation. But if she enters slavery having been procured through love and befriending tactics, then few, including herself, are willing to recognise her victimisation'.[27] Of course, the circumstances which have made individual girls (or boys) vulnerable to the effective, albeit sometimes less overtly coercive, tactics of those posing as her friends or lovers, or even through pressures by families, complicate this further.

The romanticism that surrounded stories about the white slave trade could only endure because of the virtual lack of experience of this, at least in its stereotypical form, in twentieth-century English society and this distance served to make such stories socially safe. Sempkins aimed to expose the very real problem of young girls becoming involved in domestic prostitution, albeit from a moral purity stance which tended towards its own kind of scare-mongering. Hence, he associated public socialising, especially at night, with sexual impropriety leading almost inevitably, if gradually, to prostitution. The emphasis upon personality as well as environment in the construction of immoral girls 'from an early age' meant that, according to Sempkins, the girls themselves bore some or all of the responsibility for their moral decline.

Child abuse and prostitution

Paradoxically, during the same period in which the white slave traffic was often prominent in the popular press, other forms of sexual abuse of women and children were rarely broached, although it continued to figure in the literature of feminist or purity groups such as the AMSH and the NVA. Jeffreys remarks that the wave of indignation felt by women against the sexual abuse of women and children, which had previously been instrumental in bringing about discussion of the subject in Parliament, had died away by the 1930s. This is not to say that there was no action. In November 1932 a Joint Committee on Sexual Offences Against Children was established, representing fourteen national organisations (including the NVA, the AMSH and the British Social Hygiene Council). The aim of this Committee was to promote the implementation of recommendations from the Departmental Committee on Sexual Offences (1925) that were not incorporated in the Children's Bill. However, the achievements of the Committee were disappointing, in 1935 it was dissolved 'having published a brief report and two leaflets and little further campaigning occurred on the problem of child sexual abuse'.[28] The 1922 Criminal Law Amendment Act, which succeeded in extending to prostitutes legal protection from abduction, was the last major piece of legislation on sexual offences until the 1950s.

Sheila Jeffreys links the decline of militant feminism and the medicalisation of abuse to a dissipation of indignation. She states that 'women's anger against men was deflated when responsibility was taken away from the male offender and attributed to "his disease". "Sick" offenders could be seen as exceptions whose behaviour had little relevance to that of men in general'. Because of this, it became more difficult for women to approach the issue of sexual abuse from their own experience and using feminist theory.[29] These 'sick' men were, and continue to be seen as, an abnormal minority that was and is overtly condemned, thus framing the stereotypical sexual abuser as an outsider with an abnormal attraction for the pre-pubescent. This raises the important issue of the lack of social, legal and economic empowerment for the women and, more especially, child subjects of sexual abuse and the role of abuse within the family. Furthermore, this image of an abuser reaffirms the problematic nature of the older child, the adolescent, under the age of consent, particularly if it appears that they have some sexual knowledge and/or experience. In many legal cases, young girls who were believed to have played an assertive sexual role received the worst of the judges' criticism. For many of the children's charities that ran homes, the issue of the depth of contamination affecting young girls remained important. In a review of the Barnardo's rules and policy governing the admission of children of February 1933 it was explained that:

we have to draw the line when girls of an age of discretion have become acquainted with much evil, and have, perhaps, already fallen. We would generally refer cases of this type to the Rescue Societies which exist to deal with them. We would not refuse a younger girl who has been morally wronged, provided we were satisfied that she was still innocent-minded, and that by careful treatment we could erase the whole thing from her memory, but she would need careful watch for a long time.[30]

Strategies varied between those organisations that were attempting to change attitudes regarding the abuse of young girls and to press for changes to legislation. Conflicts over such strategies were inconclusive and were terminated by the war. Carol Smart suggests that such differing strategies were divisive between organisations striving broadly for a similar objective, to redefine the sexual abuse of children as harmful.[31] However, the strategies of the NVA and the Association for Moral and Social Hygiene (AMSH), for example, were actually dealing with two different social problems; the sexual abuse of prepubescent children and the sexual activity or even promiscuity, and responsibility for such behaviour, of older girls. The NVA concentrated their campaigning upon girls under about ten years of age, reasoning that there was a significant difference in offence between 'tampering with a child of seven or eight and premature sex relation with a girl nearing 16 with a young man of her acquaintance'.[32] This, however, did not address the issue of the sexuality of adolescent girls under 16 who were, if anything, more vulnerable to older men and so neatly side-stepped the difficult problem of responsibility in these circumstances. It also highlights the social difficulties in defining the point at which the transition from childhood to adulthood has been completed and the confused meaning around what has been termed the 'no-man's-land of adolescence'.[33]

The AMSH concentrated upon redefining the abuser of older girls, constructing an image of them as predatory rather than as being seduced, in order to reduce sympathy for them, particularly among the legal professions. The Association highlighted the need for a balanced view of responsibilities and a realistic acceptance that with greater maturity should come greater blame. Age itself was a crucial factor, although at the base of this was also a vehement denial of the concept that male sexual instinct was uncontrollable in the face of temptation. The following is a long paragraph but worth quoting in full for its explanation of the Association's standpoint regarding the court proceedings in cases regarding the sexual assault of under-age girls. It should be remembered that at this time the defence that the man had reasonable cause to believe the girl was under 16 was valid only for men under 23 years of age.

There is no doubt that some of the girls involved in these cases have encouraged and, perhaps, initiated the conduct which resulted in the ultimate offence, but surely when the girl is only 15 and the man is 29 or 35 years of age, some emphasis might be laid on the responsibility of the man as well as on the girl. It seems strange that men who are 15 or 20 years older than the girl concerned … should be told by the judge that they are more sinned against than sinning, or that he should say that the girl is a danger to all young men, or that she is of such immorality that every decent man and woman is shocked. In several of these cases the girl gets three years detention in a Home, and the man is acquitted or bound over. That is of course, a matter for the judge to decide, and it may be that the girl is the worse of the two, but we wish judges would not encourage people to think that decent men are morally defenceless creatures against the wiles of unscrupulous girls under 16, and that their seduction by the girl, even if they themselves are over 30, is mainly the girl's iniquity.[34]

In 1938, an extract from the *Report of the Children's Branch of the Home Office on the Protection of Children and Young Persons* of that year was quoted in *The Shield*. This refers to female juvenile offenders and although the definition of prostitution is not clear, the questioning of the spiral of cause and effect in underage sexual behaviour is clear.

> Of the girls of 15 to 17 years the offences are mostly theft and prostitution. Quite a large number of these girls have become infected with venereal disease and this fact should be born in mind when so much stress is laid by some of our judges on the 'wickedness' of girls under 16 in seducing men twice as old as themselves! Very little comment is made of the venereal danger to girls and yet many under 16 have been already infected by men.[35]

As well as attempting to redefine the sexual abuse of children, therefore, the AMSH aimed to reconstruct, or at least soften, the popular image of young prostitutes and sexually active young girls in a similar tradition to feminists of the late nineteenth century. These girls, it was contended, had been introduced to sex at an early age by those who bore considerable responsibility for their later behaviour.

From her investigations into prostitution, Gladys Hall had found evidence that sex for payment could begin from a very early age. 'I have evidence of its [prostitution] practice in England for pennies or small sums by children of seven' she observed.[36] She recognised the existence 'for certain men [of] a special attractiveness in youth and inexperience' yet found it difficult to believe that this was motivated by genuine sexual desire. She asserted that:

> Whether it is in part due to some relic of the idea which promoted the custom of the *jus primae noctis*, or to the hope of security from infection or whatever the reason may be, it is exceedingly important to recognise the fact and its possible share in the promotion of early prostitution. Undoubtedly it is an important element in the traffic in very young girls for the supply of licensed houses.[37]

Reflecting the contemporary moral associations made between un-married mothers and prostitution, Hall cited the number of child-mothers in support of her argument. One 'Home' in England was said, in 1930, to have had seven unmarried mothers under 16 years of age in their care.[38] As part of her, now extremely contentious, assumption regarding unmarried mothers, Hall implied a direct relationship between early promiscuity and later prostitution. At a time when access to birth-control information remained restricted and legal abortions could he performed only if failure to perform it would result in the mother's death, the choices for young girls who became pregnant were limited, especially for those without a mother or other relative who might take on the child as her own. The worst case scenario was confinement in an asylum under the 1913 Mental Deficiency Act. Indeed, the association of women who bore illegitimate children with mental deficiency remained until after World War Two. A legal test case in 1938 in which Dr Alex Bourne performed an abortion on a 14 year-old girl, who had been gang raped by soldiers, was won by him on the grounds that the pregnancy would be psychologically damaging and that the decision to perform an abortion should be subject to medical judgement. However, the doctors involved had made certain that there was no suggestion of any sexual immorality on the part of the girl who came from a respectable family.[39]

Social and moral standing were important aspects of judgements in legal cases, especially given the extent to which definitions of, for example, child sexual abuse and child prostitution were contended and blurred and could even be used interchangeably according to social context. When charges were brought against a 57 year-old man in 1935 for his regular sexual relations with a girl of 12 years old, the *Holborn Guardian* termed his activities 'abuse'. The man, had known the girl for about two years and he had, according to the newspaper article, 'abused' her 'quite constantly' in exchange for payment. The mother of the girl had been questioned regarding the money he was giving to the girl, but he had claimed that he was paying her well for errands as he knew that the family was short of money. The girl stated that she received about eight shillings per week, some of which went to her mother, and some she kept.[40] Whether any underlying arrangements had been made with the mother cannot be determined. A case such as this raises some questions. Had the girl in this instance been 15 years old, and from what may have been considered to be a less than respectable family, would different judgements have been made regarding the roles of those involved? If abuse suffered during childhood had led to later resort to prostitution, would later judgements made of the initial abuse have been clouded by its consequences? The context of the circumstances of a case and not only the action involved can be decisive in this respect.

In another case to be found in the records of the NVA, one which never came to the attention of the police, the girl involved perceived the abuse she experienced as a child to have been directly responsible for her resort to prostitution. A young woman gave a disturbing, if brief, account to an NVA worker in 1933. According to the woman, who stated that she was then working as a prostitute, she had been 'sold' at 14 years of age to a man by her mother. She did not leave home until she was 16 years old but visits by the man continued and every time he gave money to her mother. At the age of 21 she had a child by the man, but the baby later died. The man also gave the girl drugs and she became, and was still, an addict. The Secretary to the NVA, Sempkins, was sceptical, although the NVA worker to whom the account was given appeared to believe it. The advice given to the NVA worker was limited to the assertion that the woman ought to be persuaded to state the facts to the authorities. The woman declined and the file ends inconclusively with the worker stating that she was hoping to persuade the woman to trust the organisation before long.[41]

The relevance of definitional issues for historical cases will, unfortunately, not be more clearly discernible until a greater time lapse allows the opening of more twentieth-century records. For example, the records of the Central Criminal Court hold evidence of the rare cases of child prostitution that were brought before it, but the records of the court proceedings are closed for 75 years. The Public Record Office catalogue lists, for example, in one case a charge of 'Cruelty to a child, encouraging the seduction or prostitution of a girl under 16', in the session of 6 December 1938. Another similar case is listed for 1966.[42]

The role that an early introduction to sex was assumed to have in later promiscuity was highlighted in contemporary research into prostitution. The most well-known of such work was Gladys Hall's *Prostitution: A Survey and a Challenge*. This publication attempted to assess the changing social and economic climate and the effects of this upon prostitution. Its main contentions were that social change was 'altering the extent and character of the evil; that many factors, the economic independence of women, the freedom of association between the sexes, the knowledge of contraceptives, and the breakdown of taboos, tend to replace the professional (prostitute) by the amateur, and to substitute temporary liaisons for cash transactions'.[43] One of the dangers of youthful amateurism, it was believed, was that for some it might result in a full-time career as a professional prostitute. Because of the difficulties in establishing where commercial forms of sex began, Hall's definition of the amateur was so loose as to encompass any girls or women (not boys or men) who engaged in sexual relations before marriage. Amateur prostitutes were girls or women who were 'ready to have promiscuous relations for gifts or pleasures, or even for no external reward'.[44] Through her interviews with prostitutes, Hall concluded that certain conditions influenced their choice. Her list included: poverty; loneliness and monotony; alcohol (usually as an accompaniment to prostitution); sexual assault during childhood and emotional instability (although she denied there was such a thing as a 'natural prostitute'). However, in the same way that the author denied the existence of any uncontrollable male sexual urge, the path to prostitution was not an inevitable consequence of some or all of these conditions.[45]

The autobiography of a prostitute, although the provenance of this cannot be confirmed, who was in the trade during this period, claimed that she had been born 'a lady' and asserted that 'I came to be a prostitute for may reasons, but in the end because I deliberately chose to be'.[46] Yet behind this assertiveness lay a life in which she experienced an unstable childhood, including a period in an industrial school and sexual abuse and rape as an adult, so that prostitution for her endowed a certain independence. Thus she maintained, 'I have escaped from emotional sponging. I cannot be put upon. If you want my body, you must pay for it' and observed that there was something 'clean' about that.[47]

Perhaps the greatest criticism was, however, reserved for the prostitutes' *souteneur* or pimp but the prostitutes' client also became an increasingly discussed figure. The AMSH continued to emphasise the role that client demand in the context of public toleration had in encouraging prostitution. In an article in *The Shield* (March 1938) it was claimed that prostitution was not an isolated phenomenon caused by stupidity or laziness but rather it was 'so subtly and deeply rooted that it can only be affected by influences which bear on all our methods of thought and feeling and all our social custom'.

An NVA report for the British National Committee for the Berlin Congress on the Economic Conditions in Relation to Prostitution (1933) also considered the effects of the Depression on prostitution. This report concluded that professional prostitution was declining in Britain and cited the fall in levels of recorded sexual offences since 1914. The factors given as mediating against the increase in prostitution during the Depression were that most women aged 16 to 21 were either employed or on unemployment pay, and so were under some official direction, and also higher educational standards among women. It was also assumed that the Depression had reduced the purchasing power of men, although this was felt to have increased the mobility of prostitutes. In the opinion of the report, the major factors which led women into prostitution were instability of social environment, physiological or psychological abnormality, weakness of character and lack of tradition, but 'non-professional' promiscuity was also cited as a factor which in the longer-term would lead to increased commercial prostitution. The belief that instability of social environment was an important causal factor in leading girls into prostitution was one of the motivations behind the centres that the NVA maintained, and had done so since before the War, at major railway stations and bus terminals in London. During the Depression, large numbers of young people travelled from Wales and the north and also from Ireland in search of work, or even to give birth.[48] Certainly, the NVA seemed to have helped some young people by this means, including runaways of only 14 or 15 years of age, although their assistance was sometimes construed as unwanted interference and received short shrift.[49] Perhaps uniquely at this time, the NVA also operated to try to locate young girls whose families had lost touch with them and were concerned about them. In the major of cases in which the girls were found no mishap or disaster had befallen them. However, on some occasions girls resorted to prostitution and a few letters tell of their being stranded in London, operating at nights from cafes and walking about during the day.[50]

Prostitution, delinquency and psychology

The multi-causal explanations given for young girls turning to prostitution reflect the more complex analysis of delinquency developing during the 1930s, but they also reflect the persistence of older rationales. The literature and records of the NVA and the AMSH emphasised socio-economic causality and were also beginning to integrate the arguments of emerging, more psychologically oriented explanations of delinquency and crime. Both lines of arguments were rooted in the interest in the behavioural problems of children and juveniles which originated before the First World War. Victor Bailey explains that:

> A gradual shift in approach to the explanation of juvenile delin-quency took place in the 1920s. The original emphasis on social and economic factors on the effects of unemployment, and on the material conditions of the home, was slowly replaced by a modified environmental approach in which the psychological conditions obtaining in the home and family were given greater prominence.[51]

Throughout the 1920s, for example, pressure had been building for the government to introduce legislation which would ensure that the sentencing decisions of the juvenile courts were based on detailed inquiry into the circumstances of the offence and offender.

Among a number of studies into juvenile delinquency, the most influential single publication was Cecil Burt's *The Young Delinquent* (1925). Burt was a psychologist in the Education Department of London County Council. His contention was that delinquency in the young was actually an 'extreme of common childish naughtiness'. He also emphasised his belief that the young were easier to analyse and easier to reclaim than adults, a belief that had been institutionalised in the Borstals set up by Ruggles-Brise, Chairman of the Prison Commission. 'In childhood the mind is more easily analysed. Character is less complex; motives simpler to unravel'.[52]

Burt attempted to weigh the influences of inheritance as opposed to environment while affirming that nothing could 'root out an inherited tendency'.[53] Indeed, Burt divided the causality of delinquency into four sections: hereditary conditions; environmental conditions; physical conditions and psychological conditions. But these categories were prioritised. As Bailey has pointed out, for Burt the decisive factor in the creation of delinquency was not poverty or bad surroundings, although he did emphasise 'defective family relationships', but the effects of these on a susceptible mind, thus essentialising the individual and conceiving of environmental factors as fundamentally 'external to the personality'.[54]

One aspect of the more psychological approach to the delinquent behaviour of children was that it was increasingly not accepted that children would grow out of problems or trauma if they were removed from their environment. Previously, the long-term harm of child abuse had been denied, unless it was allowed to lead to a pattern of behaviour which persisted into adulthood. The concentration, certainly for children's homes, was then upon the surveillance of the child. Such a belief had underpinned the 'rescue and removal' strategies of the children's charities since the mid-nineteenth century. Furthermore, the long-term damaging effects of maltreatment or abuse during childhood were being exposed and were blurring the distinctions between the young victim and the young offender. Notions of crime and punishment were becoming more sophisticated as were notions of welfare. Parental, and predominantly maternal, neglect and mental maladjustment were increasingly cited as sources of juvenile crime and delinquency along with poverty, unemployment, and overcrowding; the conjunction of 'depravation and deprivation' in a 'social problem group'.[55] Thus, in Hall's investigation into prostitution she maintained that one of the important causal factors was sexual abuse as a child, often committed by the father.[56] Children in trouble, therefore, were displaying symptoms of maladjustment in a part of society. These children required treatment in order for them to work through psychological or other problems. This approach was inherent in the work of the Child Guidance Clinics that were established in the inter-war period. By 1938 there were 54 of these clinics and by 1944 there were over 70.

These conceptual changes were evident in the Departmental Committee on Young Offenders 1927 and in the Children and Young Persons Act (1933). The former of these interpreted its terms of reference 'to enquire into the treatment of young offenders and young people who, owing to bad associations or surroundings require protection or training' as including 'young people who are the victims of cruelty and other offences committed by adults and whose natural guardianship having proved insufficient or unworthy of trust must be replaced'.[57] The Children and Young Persons Act was a fundamentally important piece of child welfare legislation, it was not radical but has been described as 'a memorial to limited changes justified by experience'.[58] Although the focus was on delinquency and control, which reflected a shift in the construction of the juvenile 'problem' from that of offences, especially sexual offences, against them, the Act grouped together children 'in need of care or protection' whether they were offenders or not. As Thomas has pointed out, this Act introduced the phrase 'Schedule One Offenders' into the language of child protection workers for the remainder of the century, as it composed in its Schedule One a list of offences it was considered possible to commit against a child.[59] The old separation of the Reformatory for young offenders and the Industrial School for those who were neglected, was abolished and took the form of one institution; the Approved School. This was in part to reduce the stigma attached to the older juvenile institutions and to encourage the use of them, in the form of Approved Schools, relative to probation. Significantly, this was a period in which some families were experiencing severe economic strain as a result of the Depression; an increased level of violence towards children was referred to in the NSPCC annual report of 1935. According to the report, 'the inspectors are in agreement that practically half the cases of ill-treatment spring from quarrels between parents. Enforced idleness and lack of means result in frayed nerves. Nagging ensues, quick tempers are roused and children are struck'.[60]

The 1933 Act also gave increased power to the children's charities by widening the definition of neglect to include any omission by the parent or guardian to make proper provision for the maintenance and welfare of a child as well as a failure to supply medical aid or allow a necessary surgical operation to be performed. In the past the NSPCC had, in practice, been inhibited from acting to help a child in moral danger, for example, if the child was not also found wandering or was subject to serious neglect or cruelty. One benefit of this from the perspective of the NSPCC was that, as was stated in the *Child's Guardian*, 'when, we find a child belonging to a prostitute in a house not inhabited by other women of that class, we shall now be able to deal with that, whereas in the past we have been prevented unless it was neglected physically or allowed to be found wandering'.[61] On the grounds of suffering within a potentially damaging environment, the child could be taken away from its mother.

According to Pam Cox, the Children Act of 1933 broadened both 'definitions of neglect and definitions of girlhood. Adolescents up to the age of 17 were now considered 'young persons' and subject to the protection of the Act'. This led to a large increase in the numbers of girls aged between 14 and 17 appearing in court, although as Cox points out, only those under 17 years of age and the mentally defective could be deemed to be 'beyond control' or 'in need of care or protection'. She concludes, however, that in general these 'wider legal categories worked against girls because they encouraged less specific definitions of challenging behaviour and vulnerability' and made young girls who were believed to be behaving 'inappropriately' into a new target for regulation.[62]

Despite its gradual withdrawal from prosecution of sexual offences against children, the NSPCC continued to publish accounts of such cases in the *Child's Guardian*, although without the kind of detail included in coverage of cruelty and neglect against children. One account made it clear that instances of child prostitution within the family were occurring. In the March 1937 edition of the *Child's Guardian* it was noted that a 'sordid, and really unusual case ended up at the Old Bailey'. A sentence of four years' penal servitude each was passed on a man and woman who pleaded guilty to a 'serious offence in respect of the woman's daughter, aged 12'. The judge castigated the couple saying that 'you are two of the vilest people who have ever come before me. You, a mother, stood by and watched and took money for what was happening to your little girl'.

Conclusions

During the inter-war period it was increasingly accepted that children who experienced abuse, trauma or neglect would not necessarily be able to grow out of the effects of that experience. With regard to adult sex offenders the emergence of psychological approaches brought with it the construction of such offenders as maladjusted rather than evil, shifting attention away from their victims. The emergence of psychological methods and theories in child welfare brought with it a more complex understanding of the causality of delinquency, but combined with the increases in juvenile crime during the 1930s brought a more inter-ventionist and controlling aspect to legislation in this area. Juvenile delinquency became more likely to be perceived as a symptom of the psychological effect of the child's upbringing among what was in-creasingly referred to as a 'social problem group'. Outside of the related professions and political circles, and a small number of feminist and purity organisations, issues of child abuse and the prostitution of children remained a taboo subject. Indeed, discussions of abuse and prostitution were often publicised in the form of sensationalised stories about the white slave trade, which in fact served to sideline and obscure the real circumstances that some young girls found themselves in. If anything, the melodramatic accounts of the white shave traders distanced the public from the realities of commercial sex.

The explanations for these phenomena must be sought in the wider social and economic context. The Depression, and the debates surrounding the extent to which this affected child welfare, brought to light the real poverty being experienced by some sections of the population, although this was not fully recognised until evacuation during the Second World War brought the children of such families into the homes of the middle classes. Those young women from areas suffering from the worst effects of the Depression became more mobile in their search for employment. Increased choice of employment and leisure brought young, single women more into the public sphere, which raised fears about the consequences of such freedom.

References

1 *Child's Guardian* 1932 XLII (7), p. 57.
2 C. Hooper, 'Child sexual abuse and the regulation of women, variations on a theme', in C. Smart (ed.) *Regulating Womanhood: Historical Essays on Marriage, Motherhood and Sexuality* (London: Routledge, 1992), pp. 64–5.
3 R. M. Alexander, *The 'Girl Problem': Female Sexual Delinquency in New York, 1900–1930* (New York: Cornel University Press, 1995), Ch. 2.
4 O. Banks, *Faces of Feminism: a Study of Feminism as a Social Movement* (Oxford: Blackwell, 1986).

5 S. Jeffreys, *The Spinster and her Enemies: Feminism and Sexuality 1880–1930* (London: Pandora, 1985), p. 152.
6 K. Chow, 'Popular sexual knowledges and women's agency in 1920s England: Marie Stopes' Married Love and E. M. Hull's The Sheik', *Feminist Review* 63, 1999, p. 68; M. Stopes, *Married Love* (London: Fifield, 1918).
7 S. Alexander, 'Men's fears and women's work: responses to unemployment in London between the Wars', *Gender and Society* 10 (3), 2000, p. 408.
8 T. Hatton, 'Unemployment and the labour market in inter–war Britain', in R. Floud and D. McCloskey (eds) *The Economic History of Britain since 1700* (2nd ed.) (Cambridge: Cambridge University Press, 1994), p. 360.
9 Ibid, p. 374.
10 J. Weeks, *Sex, Politics and Society: The Regulation of Sexuality since 1800* (Harlow: Longman, 1989), p. 202.
11 Ibid, p. 204.
12 S. Bruley, *Women in Britain since 1900* (London: Macmillan, 1999), pp. 73–4.
13 S. Humphries, *A Secret World of Sex: Forbidden Fruit, the British Experience 1900–1950* (London: Sedgwick and Jackson, 1988).
14 G. M. Hall, *Prostitution: a Survey and a Challenge* (London: Williams and Northgate, 1933), p. 107.
15 R. Porter and L. Hall, *The Facts of Life: The Creation of Sexual Knowledge in Britain 1650–1950* (New Haven: Yale University Press, 1995), p. 264.
16 PRO HO45 25404/11. See this file for controversy regarding the consorting of white girls with coloured men.
17 PRO MePol3/758. Police had been informed about this club by a letter from 'ratepayer' in the street in which the club was located.
18 4/Box 110 and 127.
19 NVA 4/Box 110.
20 *Daily Express* 22 May 1936.
21 *Tit Bits* 2 March 1935.
22 Letter to South London Press 4 November 1936.
23 *Sunday Pictorial* 3 July 1935.
24 *Sunday Pictorial* 3 July 1938.
25 K. Chow, 'Popular Sexual Knowledge', p. 72–3 and 81.
26 R. M. Alexander, *The 'Girl Problem'*, p. 18.
27 K. Barry, *Sexual Slavery* (New York: New York University Press, 1979), p. 12.
28 C. Hooper, 'Child sexual abuse', p. 58.
29 S. Jeffreys, *The Spinster and her Enemies*, p. 85.
30 D239/D1/1b/3.
31 C. Smart, 'A history of ambivalence and conflict in the discursive construction of the 'child victim' of sexual abuse', *Social and Legal Studies* 8, 1999, pp. 405–6.
32 4/BVN Box 199, 47th Annual Report 1932, p. 11.
33 A. Davin, in Fletcher, 1999, p. 32.
34 *The Shield* V (3) December 1937.
35 Cited in *The Shield* VI (I) May 1938.
36 G. M. Hall, *Prostitution*, p. 26.
37 Ibid.

38 Ibid, pp. 26–7.
39 *Times* 2, 19 and 29 July 1938.
40 *Holborn Guardian* I 2 July 1935, NVA Archive.
41 NVA 4/Box 110/127.
42 PRO CRIM 1/1056 and PRO CRIM 1/4503.
43 G. M. Hall, *Prostitution*, p. 10.
44 Ibid, p. 17.
45 Ibid, pp. 42–96.
46 S. Cousins, *To Beg I am Ashamed* (London: George Routledge and Sons Ltd, 1938), p. 1.
47 Ibid, p. 2.
48 See L. Marks, 'The luckless waifs and strays of humanity', Irish and Jewish immigrant unwed mothers in London, 1870–1939', *Twentieth Century British History* 3 (2) 1992.
49 4/Box 199.
50 4/Box 119.
51 V. Bailey, *Delinquency and Citizenship: Reclaiming the Young Offender, 1914–1948* (Oxford: Clarendon Press, 1987), p. 12.
52 C. Burt, *The Young Delinquent,* Vol.1 (London: University of London Press, 1925), p. 19.
53 C. Burt, *The Young Delinquent*, p. 604.
54 V. Bailey, *Delinquency and Citizenship*, p. 13.
55 H. Hendrick, *Child Welfare*, pp. 187–8.
56 G. M. Hall, *Prostitution*, p. 90.
57 Cited in R. Dingwall, J. M. Eekelaar and T. Murray, 'Childhood as a social problem: A survey of the history of legal regulation', *Journal of Law and Society* 11 (2), p. 223.
58 V. Bailey, *Delinquency and Citizenship*, p. 84.
59 T. Thomas, *Sex Crime, Sex Offending and Society* (Devon: Willan Publishing, 2000), p. 51.
60 *Child's Guardian* 1935 XLV (2), p. 9.
61 1932 XLII (7), p. 57.
62 P. Cox, 'Rescue and reform: Girls, delinquency and industrial schools, 1908–1933', Ph.D, Cambridge University 1996, pp. 155.

Chapter 6

Reconstruction and a new society

The failure is, to a large extent, the responsibility of society. It is for all of us to see what measure of blame we bear, and what measure of help we can give.[1]

One of the most important engines of social and cultural change during the 1940s and 1950s was the experience and effects of war. Not only did the social dislocations brought about by the war highlight the inadequacies of social provision, but they also exposed the extent to which poverty and its associated problems remained. For many years after the war, even when the country began to experience greater economic prosperity, the consequences of the war continued to be raised as a factor in discussions relating to a wide range of issues, including juvenile delinquency, the perceived relaxation of moral standards, concerns about the wellbeing of the family and also the causation of prostitution.

In 1943 a League of Nations report on the subject of prostitution stated that the demand for commercial sex only called into being an answering supply in circumstances where women were subordinate 'socially, intellectually, and above all, economically, to men'.[2] Thus, in concise terms, did the report cite what were seen as the fundamental mechanisms, which led women and girls into prostitution. Still notable by its absence was any reference to male prostitution, although during the 1950s this was to receive greater attention. Other factors that promoted the supply of commercial sex were, according to the report, the large number of middle-men who lived off the trade: *souteneurs*; touts; brothel-keepers; owners of bars, night clubs and dance-halls, and also public opinion which blamed the prostitute as much or more than her client and which continued to applaud virginity in young women but deride it in young men. Alongside such assertions, the report adhered to the long-standing view of prostitutes as being of low intelligence, lazy, materially self-indulgent and even as representing a distinct and possibly even an atavistic social class. With this was combined a more psychologising Freudian perspective which suggested that prostitutes were the product of abnormal or repressed sexual development and/or were emotionally unstable, nervous and ill-adjusted to society.[3]

The immediate and more environmental reasons for turning to prostitution were seen to be financial, or the result of wearisome employment or ill-health, while some, it was claimed, were introduced to selling their bodies by other prostitutes or by the bribes, love or threats of procurers or *souteneurs*. Indeed it appeared to this League of Nations Advisory Committee that 'as a rising standard of living and improved measures of social welfare help to counteract those causes of prostitution which are external – bad living and working conditions and so on – the relative importance of the physical and psychological causes increases'.[4] Thus the primacy of poverty as an explanation for prostitution was, in a period of expanding social provision and, during the 1950s in England, rising economic prosperity, increasingly questioned. For some observers who did not see prostitution as a consequence of psychological repression or illness, the undermining of the poverty argument resulted in a less sympathetic view of prostitutes and a belief that there was a higher degree of choice in the resort to prostitution in post war Britain.

Other significant changes during the 1940s and 1950s exacerbated the social distancing of the prostitute. The shift to social problems being seen as located in particular families, as opposed to groups within the population, and the spread of a psychological approach to the analysis of such families, was more positive in the sense that problem families were, at least, felt to be redeemable. Yet this shift also intensified the perception that the individual either had more choice, in the context of the expansion of welfare provision and state intervention in the family, or represented the problem family or individual as more abnormal than evident in previous conceptions of those on the margins of society. Thus one contemporary stated that 'I see the typical fifties mentality as "There is a right way to live and a wrong way to live"; you know, all "black" and "white"'.[5] The legislative response to prostitution, in the context of the renewed strength of domestic ideologies, reasserted and reinforced a rigorous and stigmatising face against commercial sex.

War, juveniles and commercial sex

During the 1940s, the dislocations and confusions of war and its effects upon children made the vulnerability of their circumstances more visible, and open to an exceptional level of comment. More than any other single phenomenon, mass evacuation was a means by which the country had come to know itself more fully and had gained insight into the true extent of the deprivation which still existed. During the first wave of evacuations, 827,000 school children and 524,000 children under school age were transferred from the major cities.[6] By January 1940, when the expected devastation had not occurred, three-quarters had drifted back only to be uprooted again by the Blitz. During the evacuation process there were indications that judgements regarding distinctions between the deserving and the undeserving remained popular. For example, the National Council for the Unmarried Mother and Her Child objected to pregnant women being evacuated with 'mothers of five or more illegitimate children and with prostitutes'.[7] Self-knowledge included the exposing of prejudice and hostility towards other extant social differences; to evacuated children who wet the bed, had hair lice or lacked table manners. Such knowledge was to form the vanguard of the conceptual shift in analysis from the 'social problem group' of the inter-war years to the 'problem family' of the 1940s and 50s by which environmental rather than hereditary factors were emphasised, and 'problem families' perceived as redeemable.

War was also a time of strain for children's charities. In a rapidly changing social context, heralding the expansion of state provision, Barnardo's reaffirmed its traditional values but also declared its ability to adapt. Barnardo's 75th annual report of 1940 recounted:

> how an old-established charity, rich in tradition and practical experience of constructive social endeavour, is adapting itself to the overwhelming needs of modern times and, amid all the difficulties, anxieties and strain of war, remains staunch to the Charter, 'No Destitute Child Ever Refused Admission'.[8]

Children's charities were, they maintained, working for a better future and not waiting for a period of reconstruction to be initiated, indeed this was the major source of legitimation for the continuation of their work during wartime. The 1940 Winter edition of the NSPCC supporters' magazine, the *Child's Guardian*, asserted that the Society was 'doing something *now* to bring a better world into being ... to maim them [children's charities] at this moment, and then express vague aspirations regarding the better world we may build in some future year seems to us to be futility at its worst'.

The NSPCC in particular was heavily involved in the welfare of children during and following evacuation and deplored ill-treatment or cruelty to young evacuees. Concern was also raised about the effects of wartime disruption upon children who stayed with their families. The great moral fear was that, in the absence of patriarchal direction, the wives of men serving in the military overseas would abandon their maternal responsibilities for the enjoyment of greater independence and freedom. It was maintained that:

> The lack of control in respect to the wife and mother has been the cause of practically complete loss of interest in children and home, both are gravely neglected. Time which should be spent in the home and for the children is wasted in public-houses, dance-halls and cinemas; not only is time wasted in folly and worse than folly, but so also is the family income, to the extreme detriment of the children.[9]

The absence of paternal influence in the home was perceived to be a direct root of increases in juvenile delinquency, exacerbated if the mother was also working, a part of which involved fears over the morality of young pleasure-seeking girls. The *Quarterly Review* (October 1944) of the Medical Women's Federation (established 1917), associated the social disorder of the war with a breakdown in standards of conduct and a failure to learn and practice an 'ideal of conduct'.

The war was certainly disruptive for juveniles and the increased rates of offending were attributed, amongst other things, to the interruption of schooling, shelter life, the black-out, the break-up of families, high wages for boys, the closing of clubs for young people and the ample opportunities for looting supplied by bombing. To a conference in May 1941, the Chair of Stamford Hill Juvenile Court, Eileen Younghusband, stated that children and young people had more temptations and fewer safeguards during the war. She also remarked that:

> It may be said against shelters that they encourage a new type of vagrancy since boys and girls who kick over the traces need not be deterred from leaving home by the fact that they are not earning enough for board and lodging elsewhere. They can sleep every night at some shelter or other, getting some meals there and dinner at a café, and doing without any regular headquarters for a considerable time.[10]

Young people, especially young women, frequenting public houses and drinking alcohol was one prominent area of concern, which instigated investigation by the Home Office. A Home Office memorandum suggested that it was 'probably no exaggeration to say that half the girls admitted to the London Remand Homes (which would, of course, include those in need of care or protection as well as those committed for offences), have in fact been frequenting and drinking in public places'. However, it was concluded that these girls were 'of a type which would in any case have got into trouble through their associating with American, Canadian or other soldiers and that drinking has been an incident in the course of their downfall rather than a cause of it'.[11]

Mass Observation, an organisation founded in 1937 to carry out detailed empirical research into ordinary people's lives, also investigated juvenile drinking. They concluded that drinking in pubs by those under 18 years of age was not widespread. Nevertheless, there were some areas and specific establishments that were, it was claimed, notorious for this, particularly in association with 'picking up acquaintance with Allied Troops'. In one pub in Sheffield, the observer counted at least seventeen girls present who appeared to be under 18 years old, some of them considerably younger, which it was claimed represented 'an environment in which young girls drink considerably in an unusually sensual atmosphere'.[12] Although such Mass Observation comment revealed the middle-class values of the observer, the survey also suggested that other drinkers were not always disposed towards young people, especially girls, in pubs. During an observation in a 'dock area in a northern port' a man was overheard fulminating with reference to two girls of about 16 to 18 years old:

> Look at those bloody little bitches over there, they want their bloody arses smacked, don't know what things are coming to, they drink like fish, and they take the sailors, asking for trouble, and when they're left in the cart they wail about it, serves them bloody well right if they're left to stew in their own juice.[13]

In another pub a drunken girl of about 17 was heard to offer a night with her to a rating, the rating replied 'How much money will you want from me if I come?'[14]

Perceived challenges to older standards of social and sexual propriety, also represented by the women's uniformed services, produced alarmist articles in the press. In part, these exaggerations were indications of greater social and economic independence being exercised by young single women. Many commentators made little distinction between greater social independence, promiscuity and prostitution, so that the image of the prostitute became representative of social fears in a period of severe disruption in most aspects of life. Indeed, prostitution did increase during wartime, but to a much lesser extent than the alarmist comment would suggest. Thus, among the repercussions of the fragmentation of community and family controls for many young working girls were seen by the NSPCC to be 'sexual incontinence, promiscuity, an increase in soliciting, and a consequent rise in the incidence of venereal disease'.[15] Under-age prostitution came to the fore of public consciousness as though it was an entirely new phenomenon. As one medical contemporary wrote:

> we had thought it [under-age prostitution] couldn't happen here – so it was a lesson to the over-complacent that eternal vigilance is needed to maintain a decent standard of conduct in any State. For the first time, the London authorities had to open a unit of 50 beds for girls under 16 with venereal disease.[16]

Certainly, the strong public association of venereal disease with prostitution and the persistent use of blurred and imprecise definitions of amateur prostitution enabled the continued effectiveness of the label of prostitute as a stigmatising and powerful means of controlling female behaviour and makes the deciphering of the evidence regarding child prostitution, in particular, difficult for historians. Nevertheless some evidence, albeit limited, is convincing.

The small minority of young girls whose behaviour resulted in a court appearance was severely and sometimes colourfully condemned. A speech made in December 1943 by Basil Henriques, Chairman of the East London Juvenile Court in Hackney, regarding the young girls who appeared before him, attracted considerable newspaper coverage and was commented upon in Parliament. Henriques asserted that young girls were attracted to anybody in uniform, 'particularly a soldier who can afford to give them a good time'. He also criticised American films, specifically one called *Stage-door Canteen*, in which a serviceman on leave tries to find a girl, for inciting 'the promiscuous intercourse and even prostitution of girls from 14 to 17'.[17] As evidence, Henriques gave the case of a girl of 15 who had frankly admitted to the police that she had been going to the West End and sleeping with soldiers, and had in court asserted that she chose a life of prostitution. A Ministry of Health memorandum referring to Henriques' speech accepted that such a 'very grave social evil' existed and questioned whether 'some central authority should undertake the task of stimulating the activities of the police, local education authorities and voluntary bodies in preventive work amongst under 17 [sic], who can be brought before the juvenile courts as being in need of care or protection or beyond control'.[18] Following communications with the Ministry of Health Committee on Venereal Disease Control and with regional police commissioners, it was concluded that the difficulties of state intervention were too great, for example the shortage of women power prevented the formation of a female police force. The difficulty of distinguishing 'these days' between 'good time girls of 15 and a wife of 25' was also noted.[19]

The issue of the sexual activity of those under the age of consent had also been raised during the war in relation to Regulation 33B of the Defence of the Realm Act, designed to curtail the spread of venereal disease. The Association of Moral and Social Hygiene (AMSH) complained that the Regulation gave no definition of a 'contact' so that this could result in a child being subjected to the same compulsory treatment as an adult, although there is no suggestion that this ever happened. Under Regulation 33B, if two persons who had contracted a venereal disease named the same person as the contact, that is the source of infection, that person would be required to submit to compulsory examination and treatment. If, or once deemed to be, not or no longer suffering from venereal disease in a communicable form, or to be cleared of infection, the contact would be issued with a 'certificate of clearance'. The informants, as the AMSH pointed out, were not to be compulsorily treated and it was doubted whether proceedings would be taken against malicious informants. In addition, the Association felt that compulsory treatment might discourage people from coming forward voluntarily, and also pointed out that compulsory treatment itself did not ensure less promiscuous conduct in future.[20]

Emphasis was upon contact rather than conduct and, as during the First World War, upon the assumption that venereal disease could be tackled by penalising a small group of persons. Penalties for non-submission to treatment were three months imprisonment or £100 fine or both. Certainly, the 'contacts' informed upon were predominantly female. Between 8 January and 30 September 1943, 3,344 women were informed on, compared with 213 men. Most took treatment willingly; however, the Regulation was legally enforced in the case of only one man compared to 95 women.[21] As during the First World War, there was controversy regarding the access of British troops to licensed brothels abroad, especially the French *Maisons Tolerées*, and the increase in prostitutes servicing domestic and overseas troops in Britain. There were, after all, over a quarter of a million overseas troops stationed in Britain by the spring of 1944. The National Vigilance Association (NVA) was critical of military and government authorities which saw these brothels as a necessary evil without regard for the conditions under which the women themselves lived.[22]

The dislocations and confusions of war brought a greater knowledge and appreciation of children and increased public concern about the morality and delinquency of the young. This could be seen in investigations into public drinking and in the coverage given to the concern of magistrates about the extent of prostitution and the youth of some of those involved. Mass evacuation highlighted the extent of social deprivation that still existed and which had been persistently denied by government health and education departments during the Depression of the 1930s. The tensions caused by mass evacuation exposed class hostilities and misunderstandings. But the intermixing of adults and children from different backgrounds and environments – urban and rural, poorer and richer, educated and ill educated – also encouraged greater understanding and a shift in perceptions regarding the part of society from which social problems were seen to derive, from the social group to the family.

Post-War social change and social policy

The experience of economic depression during the 1930s and of six years of 'total' war brought about a shift in opinion with regard to the role of the state in the maintenance of society, and particularly with regard to that most fundamental of social institutions – the family. A primary consideration for government was the reconstruction not only of the economy but also of society. Even before the end of the war, consideration was being given and research conducted into the implications and effects upon children of the destabilisation or destruction of their families.[23] Hence, the post war years saw the 'rise of the family as an object of positive social policy'.[24] Therefore, as well as being a centralising piece of legislation, the Children's Act of 1948 focused primarily upon the interests of children as opposed to the punishing of inadequate parenting. It established Children's Departments in local authorities imbued with a philosophy placing greater emphasis upon prevention and upon voluntary agreements between families and child care departments.

Following extensive legislation aimed at reconstruction and at establishing the pillars of a new socialist mixed economy, attention focused increasingly upon the maintenance and organisation of that which had already been put in place. Children's charities, in common with many in the voluntary sector, were increasingly concerned about the centralising moves of government, but sought out their role in relation to the extended state. In 1950 the NSPCC supporters' magazine quoted positive statements made by the Home Secretary, James Chuter Ede, urging co-operation between local state and voluntary agencies. In 1950 the *Child's Guardian* quoted him saying that the 'Government have reached the conclusion that the present need is not for an extension of statutory powers or for inquiry by a Departmental Committee, but for the fully co-ordinated use of the local authority and other statutory and voluntary services available'. Ede was referring in particular to the appointment of child welfare officers in each county and borough to co-ordinate local services for children, both state and voluntary, with emphasis, under the 1948 Children Act, being placed upon the care of children in their own homes.[25] In this way casework was encouraged and the social work professions expanded, partly to operate as a mechanism to reinforce and encourage what were seen as natural and moral forms of family life.

The Beveridge Report on *Social Insurance and Allied Services*, the 'blueprint of the welfare state' was predominantly a moderate liberal document which targeted the five 'giants' that Beveridge asserted were at the root of the ills of British society: want, disease, ignorance, squalor and idleness. Traditional liberal perspectives on society and social problems could be seen, for example, in the inclusion of idleness in the five giants and in the reliance upon principles of self-help and independence though contributory benefit and pension systems.[26] However, more radical was the assertion that the state should play a prominent role in maintaining minimum standards of living and in some cases optimum universal provision, such as the National Health Service. As the 'third principle' of the Beveridge Report stated:

> Social security must be achieved by co-operation between the State and the individual. The State should offer security for service and contribution. The State in organising security should not stifle incentive, opportunity, responsibility; in establishing a national minimum, it should leave room and encouragement for voluntary action by each individual to provide more than that minimum for himself and his family.[27]

Thus an old *laissez-faire* stance that had viewed public provision as inimical to incentive had been largely put aside following a war which had proved the potential of collective effort within public direction and provision.

The Beveridge Report built not only upon pre-existing structures and practices but also upon pre-existing moral philosophies. This related not only to self-help principles but also to a depiction of the nuclear family, with the male breadwinner and dependent housewife and mother, as the normal and proper 'bedrock' of society.[28] Beveridge aimed to give wives a separate insurance status and referred to their 'vital work in ensuring the adequate continuance of the British race and British ideals in the world'.[29] Indeed, during the 1950s the family was increasingly represented by functionalists as having a strategic importance in mediating between the needs of wider society and the needs of the individual, particularly children.[30] Marriage and fidelity were therefore encouraged so that unmarried mothers were given no state benefits other than means-tested national assistance, albeit without having to make themselves available for work. In the event of co-habitation, benefit would be withdrawn in line with assumptions about the 'family bread winner model'. Nor did most unmarried mothers benefit from the introduction of family allowances since they were not initially awarded to the first child. However, it was the changing circumstances of the married woman/ mother within the nuclear family that dominated public attention. Financially and ideologically, the tax system, benefit rates and the organisation of national insurance operated primarily to support the nuclear family and discriminated against those outside of this structure, although discrimination was less evident in the new National Health Service.

In the early post-war years the government, anticipating a labour shortage, had encouraged women to stay in employment, yet state nursery provision was withdrawn and little progress was made on equal pay. To a large extent, it was women with older rather than younger children who tended to stay in work and the government increasingly targeted those over 35 years of age. The ideal of complementary roles for the partners within a marriage promoted during the 1920s and reinforced during the 1950s occurred, therefore, at a time when greater strains were being placed on this ideal through the, by then, slowly expanding participation rates among married women. As an idea it promoted mutuality but covered over the persistence of deep inequalities, not only within married relationships but also regarding economic and social structures. As Davidoff *et al* observe, it was 'a powerful ideal, which stressed the importance of romantic love, sexual attraction and mutual interests, while disguising realities of gendered inequalities of power and access to resources. Yet, it set a standard by which it was believed all marriages would ultimately stand or fall'.[31]

The role of the mother was scrutinised with regard to the welfare of children and the issue of full-time working mothers was discussed extensively, especially those with young children. A series of radio broadcasts during the late 1940s by Winnicott used popularised psychoanalytical theory to stress the natural character of maternity.[32] The work of John Bowlby, Director of the Tavistock Clinic, and his theories on maternal deprivation, were extraordinarily significant, in part due to the use of his work by the government, Children's Officers and social workers in attempts to maintain family life. Such ideas were also evident in prominent professional organisations like the BMA and the Magistrates Association (for example, see the BMA, 1956). Deprived children were depicted by Bowlby as a 'source of infection as real and as serious as are carriers of diphtheria and typhoid' and maternal deprivation was directly related to juvenile delinquency.[33]

Marriage and maternity were perceived as the right and proper purpose of women, a purpose which no other pursuit by women could or should fulfil. Furthermore, women who rejected marriage and maternity were viewed in some cases not only as unfulfilled but also as emotionally and sexually abnormal.[34] Hence the prostitute's supposed rejection of marriage and maternity was perceived by some as a source of guilt and of her kindness to other prostitutes.[35] This is not to say that such views represented the only discourse on motherhood, another weaker discourse defended the right of mothers to work, albeit with stipulations which often revealed the class-dominated perspectives of their authors. An article entitled 'Modern Mothers', in *Medical World* June 1956, disagreed that full-time working by mothers had ill-effects on children but emphasised the need for proper, stable alternative childcare provision.[36] Similarly, the Chair of the Executive Committee of the National Baby Welfare Council, Gladys Saunders, stated, in an article in *Nursery World* (29 June 1957), that there were no hard and fast rules, but concluded that 'If the parents are educated people with a reasonable sense of duty it may be safely left to them to make their own decision in this matter'.

Increased state intervention in the maintenance of the family and, following the establishment of the Children's Department under the 1948 Act, the expansion of the social work professions brought the family ever more into the public arena. The new psychoanalytical writings of social workers were influenced by the work of writers such as Bowlby, but were often mixed with older individualist traditions.[37] Such influences could be seen in attitudes towards a broad range of socially marginalised groups including unmarried mothers, prostitutes and sexual offenders. In practice the advice and provision made for such groups altered little, for example, help for unmarried mothers was still very much dominated by voluntary and often religious societies with all the moral implications that entailed. Help for prostitutes took the form either of homes designed to rehabilitate, again administered by voluntary and religious groups, or inadequate numbers of state hostels, remand homes or approved schools for offenders or those deemed to be in need of care and protection. Thus while state intervention and support for the family increased, this was very much within a particular moral philosophy which emphasised what was seen as the 'traditional' family as the bulwark of society. Provision and facilities for those outside the boundary of the nuclear family and conventional social morality were less well developed and to a great extent remained in the hands of the voluntary sector. Thus for two groups firmly outside of the nuclear family, unmarried mothers and prostitutes, groups which had long and erroneously been associated with one another due to the use of vague and flexible concepts regarding promiscuity and the amateur and profession prostitute, little changed in terms of social provision.

Delinquency and sexuality

Juvenile delinquency was the subject of considerable research and debate during the 1950s which included and expanded from discussion of the effects of maternal deprivation. Contemporary studies of juvenile delinquency examined, for example, possible relations between juvenile crime and broken homes, illegitimacy and dead-end employment (Mannheim, 1948) or inter-generational transmission (Mays, 1954), or the contrast between the values of the new acquisitive society and those of working class boys.[38] By the 1950s, consumerism was increasingly part of the explanatory rhetoric around juvenile delinquency, reflecting the relative strength of the economy and the improved financial circumstances of many young people. Between 1938 and 1958 average real incomes increased by 25 per cent, but the average real income of adolescents increased by around 50 per cent.[39] The image of young people having a distinct sexuality and culture, or sub-culture, was encouraged by the media and by industries (music, fashion and leisure) eager to capture their growing incomes.

Parallel and over-lapping with these images of youth subcultures were continued concerns, and even moral panic, over juvenile delinquency, seen most prominently in the media coverage of cinema disturbances by 'Teddy' boys in the mid-1950s.[40] Fears about promiscuity and vice also overlapped and intertwined with concerns about juvenile delinquency, both areas being seen as evidence of social and moral deterioration. While it was generally conceded that sexual pleasure was desirable between husband and wife there were concerns that, when claimed by other groups, sexuality would be a socially disruptive force, shown for example

125

in debates over the dangers of 'petting', which referred to various non-coital sexual activities.[41] Young people figured prominently in a series of moral panics, particularly in London, which were fuelled by local representations made to the government. Young people also figured prominently in public and political debate about the extent to which the State could and should intervene with private sexual morality.

The climate of public discussion of sexuality received great impetus from the publication of Alfred Kinsey's two surveys on male and female behaviour in America, *Sexual Behaviour in the Human Male* (1948) and *Sexual Behaviour in the Human Female* (1953). Importantly, Kinsey worked not within assumptions about a concept of 'normality' but with a broader reference to nature-given variations in sexual behaviour, 'a framework in which sexual behaviour and sexual conventions are treated as malleable, as the products of culture and history and circumstance; that is, Kinsey worked within what would now be termed a 'social constructionist' approach.[42] These surveys also revealed the extent to which domestic and social ideologies regarding sexual behaviour could part from the realities. He revealed that about half of married women in his survey had had sex before marriage. Also, of the thousands of men in America surveyed by Kinsey, 37 per cent stated that they had climaxed with another male. However, Kinsey did not maintain that over a third of the male population was homosexual, instead he suggested a notion of a 'sexual continuum' with a scale from 0 (those men with no homosexual experience, about 50 per cent) to 6 (those men who had same-sex relations throughout their life, about four per cent).[43]

Kinsey's work inspired the first national random survey to be carried out on this subject in Britain, Mass Observation's 'Little Kinsey' (1949), in connection with which over 2,000 people were spoken to. 'Little Kinsey' confirmed earlier research about the dissatisfaction of married women with their sex lives. As Liz Stanley has pointed out, 'marriage for many women brought with it sex of a kind all too often unwanted, not enjoyed and merely endured, but at the same time marriage also meant public acceptability, a division of labour ensuring women's economic survival, and, above all else, children'.[44] In 'Little Kinsey', Mass Observation was predominantly concerned with sexual attitudes. However, an observational methodology, in which all observers were 'subjective cameras', and which focused, therefore, upon behaviour rather than attitude, was also utilised, although this was often interpreted through the theorising of the observer.[45]

The surveys for 'Little Kinsey' were conducted in two very different towns, Worcester (Churchtown) and Middlesborough (Steeltown).[46] Chapter 8 of the unpublished (until Stanley, 1995) manuscript concerns the subject of prostitution and this is concentrated upon here. From the public survey it was concluded that, although the subject of prostitution elicited some 'verbal horror and disgust', outside of particular 'black spots' it played a 'slighter part in our national life than is often imagined'.[47] This was stated even though one in four of Mass Observation's national panel admitted to experience of sexual relations with prostitutes. The number on the national panel during this period is believed to be a 1,000, of which, in 1947, 72 per cent were male.[48]

A Mass Observation observer suggested in Chapter 8 of 'Little Kinsey' that prostitution was not perceived as a threat to the family, unlike extra-marital sex, but rather as a 'blot' which it was 'possible to shut one's eyes to. Except for a minority who regard her as unfortunate, the prostitute is generally felt by the morally disapproving to be hard, bad and degraded'. The man's need for a prostitute was more accepted than the prostitute's need to go on the streets, in which case prostitutes were perceived as keeping the streets safe for 'decent' women. However, respondents were in some ways sympathetic to prostitutes. Thus:

> It is felt that present-day conditions provide plenty of legitimate work for everyone and the prostitute could keep out of prostitution if she really wished. But more often, if people think in economic terms at all, it is to excuse the prostitute rather than to blame her for her profession, but both attitudes imply disapproval of prostitution itself.[49]

The 'blackspots' for prostitution in this study were found in urban, industrial Middlesborough rather than Worcester, although some reference was made to wartime prostitution in the latter town. There was a certain amount of fatalism with regard to the existence of prostitution in Middlesborough. The Church of England parson commented that 'where there is a port there is almost inevitably a fairly flourishing 'red light' business', the physician at the VD clinic concurred and the probation officer further explained that the younger prostitutes, under 21, went on the vessels in the docks as there was 'no demand for the older ones on the boats'.[50]

The depiction of prostitutes as mentally disadvantaged was still common, although this was described in rather vague psychological terms. The probation officer in Worcester felt that this 'low mentality' was largely due to young girls never having had any affection shown to them. Sometimes, he stated, 'they are illegitimate children who have never had a proper home, as children of forced marriages seeking the affection they never got from their parents. They think they have found it when they meet a man who likes them and they begin to go wrong'. With regard to under-age prostitution, a caseworker for the Diocesan Association for Moral Welfare Work in Worcester stated that 'We get very little trouble with girls under 16 years of age'.[51]

Direct observation suggested the involvement of some young girls in prostitution, albeit that the moral lens of the Mass Observation observer blurs the evidence for the historian. One observer working in March 1949 in the Francis Drake pub, in Middlesborough, on the edge of the dock area, commented that 'I feel sure that no other pub anywhere in the county could be much worse as regards standards of sex morality. Everything is so open, there is no beating about the bush'. His observation of the clearly quite relaxed and even intimate social behaviour going on in the pub was blunted by his belief that, while he recognised that some of the girls in the pub were merely out to have a good time, or 'to get a sex contact just for the duration of their stay in the pub. They would permit petting etc in the pub… But discontinued the relationship on their leaving as on this evening. They are of course the prostitutes of tomorrow – well on the way'.[52] The observer also felt secure in his abilities to distinguish a prostitute, thus it was noted that three different Swedish seamen come into the pub, 'each with a prostitute, female aged between 17 and 25'. Yet he decides that others in the pub are not prostitutes as a result of the following recorded observation of three girls of, he surmises, between 15 and 19 years of age, invited to sit down by a prostitute.

> They [two Swedish seamen] stand over two of these girls ruffling their hair and caressing their faces, [one] lets his hand wander once on one of the girl's breasts and then he kissed her neck … He speaks to them softly (apparently asking them to go with him). The two girls look at each other, giggle, and shake their heads. 'No' they say.

Wolfenden and the Street Offences Act 1959

The legal pillars of state intervention in female prostitution for the second half of the twentieth century were established by the Sexual Offences Act 1956 and particularly by the Street Offences Act 1959. The Sexual Offences Act 1956 was predominantly a consolidating measure, although one MP did voice doubt at the usefulness of consolidating what he considered to be 'bad law'. The same MP, Lieutenant-Colonel Marcus Lipton, also objected to the movement to consolidate the law when a Departmental Committee had been appointed in 1954 to look into the whole legal area of homosexuality and prostitution and had not yet reported.[53] What the Sexual Offences Act (1956, 4 and 5 Eliz, C.69) established was an organised and clear structure of association, and penalties for sexual offences: rape; under-age sex; sex with those deemed mentally incapable of giving consent; incest; unnatural offences (buggery); sexual assault; abduction with intent to marry or have unlawful sexual intercourse; procuration; soliciting; and brothel-keeping. Furthermore, the Act maintained the differing levels of penalties meted out for sexual intercourse with under age girls. Intercourse with a girl under 13 years of age could be punished with life imprisonment, whereas if the girl was between 13 and 16 years of age the penalty was two years imprisonment. Other moral calculations were also evident in the schedules to the act. The offence of solicitation (on indictment) by a man could receive the same punishment (two years imprisonment) as causing or encouraging the prostitution of a girl under 16.

The Departmental Committee on Homosexual Offences and Prostitution (Wolfenden Committee) reported in 1957 and its recommendations regarding prostitution were incorporated into the Street Offences Act 1959. As a new measure, and one which dealt with a controversial subject, it was this piece of legislation, and the enquiry that preceded it, that attracted the most critical attention. Parliamentary and public conflict centred on the rights and wrongs of state intervention into the sex lives of individuals. The Wolfenden Committee has been seen as 'the period's most influential liberal statement' and as providing the 'pragmatic basis for the limited, but symbolically significant, social reforms of the 1960s, and the framework for all the major "official" proposals on morality throughout the 1970s as well'.[54] Regarding some issues, however, the Wolfenden Committee Report elucidated long-standing principles and confirmed them for the rest of the century. This is the case with the issue of privacy, which has been a primary consideration for British governments in matters of sexuality and sexual offending throughout the twentieth century. In 1984 the Criminal Law Committee quoted verbatim from the Wolfenden Report:

> ... the criminal law should not intervene in the private lives of citizens or seek to enforce any particular pattern of sexual behaviour further than is necessary 'to preserve public order and decency to protect the citizens from what is offensive or injurious and to provide sufficient safeguards against exploitation and corruption of others'.[55]

Thus, importance was given to the privacy of individuals subject to the overriding interests of protecting children and young people, the mentally ill and others considered to be vulnerable or weak.[56] A more rigid distinction was made between 'law and morality, crime and sin' so that while prostitution might be immoral it was 'not the law's business'.[57]

Despite the importance of the Wolfenden Committee's recommendations on legislation no prostitute, and indeed only three avowed homosexuals, were interviewed. This was pointed out by one writer as evidence of one of the main obstacles to rational reform, 'the prostitute remains an isolated figure, known only in highly specialised relations with clients, *souteneurs*, her colleagues, landladies, a few social workers and the police'.[58] Indeed, Sir John Wolfenden noted in the forward to an autobiography of a prostitute published in 1959 that 'one of the main difficulties we had while the Departmental Committee was sitting was to get a first-hand account of the life and attitude of the prostitute herself'.[59]

In the name of cleaning up the streets, and despite the avowed desire of the Wolfenden Committee to protect young people, the Street Offences Act 1959 legitimated the harassment of female prostitutes of all ages. The need for the police to prove annoyance was removed, no age distinction was made with reference to cautioning and conviction for the offence of soliciting and the term 'common prostitute' was retained. Parliamentary debate suggested that the cautioning system was expected to identify and divert those under-age to the welfare system but it also served to increase the discretionary powers of the police. Furthermore, women could be arrested on suspicion of committing an offence under this Act. By not criminalising the client of commercial sex, curb crawling was not made illegal until 1985, the Act ensured moreover the maintenance of the moral double standard.

Smart has convincingly suggested that such 'repressive' means of regulating prostitutes have been culturally acceptable because the discourses that have constructed the prostitute have placed her outside the boundaries of decent treatment. Indeed, the Street Offences Act actually reversed an amendment of 1951 which secured for prostitutes certain rights against abduction and procuration that had been denied them under the 1885 Criminal Law Amendment Act. Smart also asserts that the narrowness of the dividing line between prostitutes and other women makes the discourses represented by this legislation into a 'coded warning' to all women[60] in a similar way to the historical use of terms such as 'amateur' or 'clandestine' prostitute. During the 1960s, and some historians and criminologists have since concurred, it was widely believed that one of the effects of the Street Offences Act was to encourage a restructuring of the organisation of prostitution towards the use of third parties and 'call girl rackets', increasing the vulnerability of prostitutes themselves.[61]

In relation to such issues, the shocking image of the under-age prostitute plying her (still presumed to be female) trade in public areas was used in the limited opposition to the Street Offences Bill in Parliament to emphasise the worst scenarios which it might fail to prevent and might even exacerbate. Supporters of the Bill emphasised the preservation of the young from the moral contamination represented by the streetwalker, the use of cautioning as a means of early intervention and also the existence of child welfare legislation enabling the police and social services to deal with young people under 17 years old in need of care and protection. This view was maintained despite the fact that a cautioning system was already in use that had proved less than effective in preventing entry into prostitution. Furthermore, MPs accepted that there were little or no alternatives being offered by way of accommodation and, as was pointed out, 'What is the good of saying that they do this deliberately [prostitute themselves] unless somewhere is provided for them to go'. The shortage of hostel accommodation, particularly in London, was recognised but this was put aside as being an administrative rather than a legislative problem.[62]

The attempt to introduce a clause that prohibited the conviction of any person below the age of 18 under this Act was unsuccessful. Leslie Hale, MP for Oldham West, the proposer of the clause, had stated, 'I have great objection to young girls hawking their bodies about Hyde Park, often being compelled to grant their sexual favours against a tree, and then drifting home with what they can get to try to pay the rent'. The image given was of:

> the sort of bad girl of 15 who has got into trouble at home, quarrelled with her parents, committed a criminal offence and gone to an approved school. That is the background – and one knows the trouble that the approved schools have in dealing with these girls, and it is no criticism of the schools to speak of their failures.[63]

Faith in the police as a conduit through which to siphon and segregate young girls into either the criminal justice or the child welfare system was implicit, albeit that some mistakes were accepted, including those brought about by the difficulties in establishing age. Leslie Hale referred to the role of the police:

> Where they find a young girl on the streets they [the police] try not to arrest, and, considering the number of these youngsters one sees

> about the streets, the number who are arrested early in their career is remarkably small. That is a decent thing, and it is something for which we can admire the police.[64]

The belief in targeting the very young for intervention through the cautioning system of the Street Offences Act was combined with resignation towards those who became established in the sex trade. Hale accused the government of hypocrisy, asserting that the 'aim of the Bill is not to make prostitution illegal. The aim of the Bill is to shove this ugly thing aside. If only we can produce a situation in which nobody sees it and the white sepulchre can hide this thing, then there can be all the corruption anyone likes'.[65]

Specifically with regard to young women of 17 who were not dealt with under child welfare legislation, Sydney Silverman (MP Nelson and Colne) begged the government, 'For heaven's sake, if you must do this thing [remove the need to prove annoyance and continue with the label 'common prostitute'], and you think that you will do any good by it, do not do it to children'.[66]

In a reference to male prostitution the Church of England Moral Welfare Council suggested that it was more of a problem than that of women and was part of the general cheapening and commercialisation of sex.[67] Indeed, the Wolfenden Committee had recommended that the term 'brothel' include premises used for homosexual sex. While the Committee had rejected the idea that someone could be 'converted' to homosexuality, it endorsed the possibility of corruption of the young through bribery. It was stated that a 'boy or youth… is induced by means of gifts whether in money or in kind to participate in homosexual behaviour as a source of easy money or as a means of enjoying material comforts or other pleasures beyond those which he could expect by decent behaviour'.[68]

Several organisations campaigned against or denounced the discriminatory aspects of the Bill, including the AMSH, The National Association of Probation Officers, the Central After-Care Association and the British Vigilance Association (renamed from the National Vigilance Association in 1953),[69] which claimed that vice would only be driven underground by the change in the legislation and that younger prostitutes would then not be seen by the police at all. The recommendation of the Wolfenden Committee that was supported by many of these groups was that calling for heavier penalties (maximum five years) for those living off immoral earnings.

Following Wolfenden and the Street Offences Act, convictions for soliciting fell from nearly 17,000 in 1958 to 1,100 in 1962, although few would argue that prostitution itself had declined significantly in such a sort space of time, even within an improving economy. However, this may well have been an indication that prostitution was becoming more organised in answer to legislative changes and to the increase of alternative venues enabling them to ply their trade off the streets. T.N.C.Gibbens, a prominent psychiatrist, voiced his concern about the effects of the Act upon the structure of prostitution, fearing that if 'threatened with imprisonment, it seems reasonable to fear that they will be particularly easy to organise and exploit in ways which are not so clearly in their interests as at present'. Parliament, he also suggested, had not fully considered the effects of imprisoning prostitutes at a time when efforts were being made to reduce the numbers of short sentences imposed to allow for more rehabilitative regimes.[70] According to Gibbens, the 'modern view' of how to deal with prostitution and waywardness among young people was to 'emphasise their need for some extended system of help, guidance and persuasion, rather than have a system based on sharp distinction between freedom and compulsion'.[71]

Contemporary attitudes and research on prostitution

During the 1950s, research and writing on the subject of prostitution increased considerably, although in many respects this was still a research area that was seen as less than respectable. Much of the research and public discussion of the subject revolved around, or was instigated by, the processes connected with the Parliamentary debates on the changes in legislation, which in themselves were expressions of moral anxiety. Certainly, the improving economy, full employment and the establishment of the welfare state undermined in many eyes the older explanations and justifications of prostitution. This led on the one hand to a greater tendency by, for example, the NVA to target groups seen as particularly vulnerable. Thus a sub-committee was established to address the problem of young Irish girls entering the country sometimes without money, employment or friends. Though in relatively small numbers, girls from the age of 14 entering the country alone were vulnerable. The AMSH concurred, and published figures which showed, for example, that in 1953 the NVA dealt with 13 Irish girls of 15 years of age, 27 of 16 and 60 girls of 17 years of age.[72]

Writers like George Ryley Scott asserted that 'No girl is driven into a life of prostitution through inability to secure a job. There is a bigger demand for domestic servants than there is a supply'.[73] He placed the force of his argument upon a kind of pragmatic cynicism couched in underclass terms. He claimed that the 'drudgery and monotony' experienced in employment by young working-class women, as well as conditions of marriage involving 'mental cruelty and degradation' meant that, despite the rhetoric of its 'dour' and 'ugly' Puritan critics, professional prostitution was 'not more degrading, sinful or immoral than the role of wife or mistress. Both in marriage and in prostitution, sex is the bait which woman offers to man'. Focusing upon cultural socialisation, Scott's attitude placed the prostitute firmly in a deviant familial context in which inter-generational prostitution was accepted. Thus he maintained that in many cases, 'the mother is a prostitute herself, the father is a pimp, and they send their daughter on the streets without the slightest compunction, often themselves initiating her in sexual intercourse'.[74]

A publication which offered a more research-oriented perspective on the subject of prostitution during this period, and which attracted controversy both in government circles and in the media, was *Women of the Streets, A Sociological Study of the Common Prostitute* (1955). This study was conducted for the British Social Biology Council (BSBC) and was supported initially by both the Metropolitan Police and the Home Office. Rosalind Wilkinson, the researcher who later gave evidence to the Wolfenden Committee, interviewed 150 prostitutes from the West End and Stepney. The sensitivity of the subject was indicated by the belief of the researcher that due to the subject matter it was unsuitable to publish, although she also maintained that if published in a censored form it would damage her academic standing as a social worker.[75] In actual fact the final published version was subject to some censorship by the Home Office[76] and official resistance may also have curtailed future intended research by the BSBC into male prostitution. *Women of the Streets* depicted a society of prostitutes as a kind of 'ancient counter-culture' in which, often after a period of drifting, the girl or young woman openly renounced ordinary social standards. So, 'she has acquired a profession where she is needed, and needed by men, where she has regular hours and colleagues, and most important of all, where she finds herself in the company of people who are like herself in personality and outlook'.[77] Prostitution was perceived as a choice albeit within particular unfavourable circumstances that often originated within the family.

Women of the Streets offers a kind of geographical and social mapping of the areas of London in which prostitution was practised, especially Soho, Mayfair, Hyde Park, Paddington and Victoria, and the different classes and ages of prostitutes that worked in these areas, as well as the strategies they employed. Behind the geo-spacial and broad social perspectives given of the trade in commercial sex, *Women of the Streets* details 69 case histories of prostitutes which bear witness to their often unstable or neglected childhoods. Some began in prostitution at a young age, sometimes as 'part of the process of settling down after [leaving] approved school' at 16 years old. Of the eighteen cases who were under 21 when they began selling sex, ten had been dealt with by the courts as juveniles (six were care and protection cases and four had been dealt with for larceny), six were ex-approved schoolgirls and four were ex-Borstal. According to Wilkinson, the younger prostitutes predominated in Stepney, which was 'one of the most popular resorts for absconders from schools, and girls who, having left their home towns, have come to London not knowing where to go'. Few, it was believed, resorted to the trade through dire necessity or were coerced into it, although most were exploited.[78]

Prostitutes were perceived as being perfectly capable of seeking out help from existing social provision should they want it.[79] It was asserted that while the 'reception or the help they receive may not always be encouraging or constructive the reason for failure often lies with the character of the woman herself' since rehabilitation demanded more stability than they were generally capable of.[80] Yet the circumstances of a minority of the women who were interviewed was plainly necessitous, in particular that of Nancy who was referred to as being 'spastic'. Nancy was unable to button her own clothes or light a cigarette herself and had been certified under the Mental Deficiency Acts when still a child. The situation of such women was, Wilkinson admitted, unsatisfactory. She concluded that the lifestyle that Nancy managed to provide for herself after absconding from supervision, living in a bombed-out squat in Stepney, was preferable, certainly in the eyes of Nancy herself, to that meted out to her six months later when she was arrested for soliciting and was institutionalised.[81]

The BSBC published other work on the subject of prostitution. In *Prostitution* by Eleanor Frank (1955) associations with other marginal social groups, the feeble-minded and the criminal were made, along with assumptions about the inevitability of the trade, 'the man in the street must have the woman of the streets'. In common with *Women of the Streets* and also Scott's publication, the prostitute was no longer perceived to have the same economic justifications as her counter-parts of a century before and therefore was less deserving, the prostitute 'driven by no economic compulsion, preys upon the community. Why then should we not make the conditions of her profession as difficult for her as possible?'[82]

The concentration of prostitution in some areas of London both reflected and exacerbated existing regional economic and social patterns. But it was the presence of prostitutes and the signs of their trade that attracted much of the indignation of local residents. This was most evident and most vocal in the campaigning of residents, headed by local religious leaders, in Stepney. The social changes that occurred in Stepney during the late 1940s and 1950s included the fresh influx of immigrants, the degrading of the housing stock, partly as consequence of wartime bombing and lack of investment, the breaking down of local communities and groups, and the expansion of cafés and clubs in line with increases in youth incomes.[83] The decline in the proportion of Jewish to non-Jewish residents was also a cause for concern for some.[84]

Attention, however, nevertheless focused upon an increase in prostitution in the area, although the dockside area had long attracted them. It was even stated in 1957 that 'other forms of indecency, including male prostitution, are not uncommon'. Prostitutes and pimps brought with them increased rents on property, public displays of sexual behaviour and the discarding in the streets of condoms, a busier and later night-life and also the creation of what was considered by local religious leaders to be a promiscuous environment for local young people to grow up in. Local teenagers were 'attracted by noisy Juke Boxes, bright lights and the forbidden entertainment and company of the cafés'. Prostitute-society was referred to as a kind of threatening mobile counter-community 'many spent some of their early years in Homes and Institutions. They are idle, homeless, the rejects of stable society, and in the community of prostitutes they enjoy a fellowship they have failed to find in other social groupings'.[85]

Child and youth prostitution

Primary sources infer that under-aged prostitution composed a small proportion of the commercial sex trade. During the 1940s and 1950s those writers who commented on the issue tended to concentrate upon girls under 17, although the youth of 17 year-olds in the trade, who were legally treated as adults, was frequently highlighted. In *Women of the Streets* it was pointed out that the 'case of juvenile prostitutes or potential prostitutes under 17 is one where the state can and does interfere for the girl's own welfare'.[86] Reference was also made to one 'Hyde Park girl' who had begun in prostitution at 16 in the north of England, almost as soon as she was licensed from approved school, and who, with other prostitutes, was smuggled onto the ships, away from the river police, dock police and watchmen. Another prostitute, Jenny, had begun at 17.[87]

Magistrates were occasionally reported as being exasperated by their limited powers in relation to 17 year-old prostitutes, or to quote Mr.E.R.Guest of the West London Court, 'these baby prostitutes who are flooding the place', other than treating them as adults.[88] There was also a certain amount of resignation with regard to 16 year-olds however, on 9 August 1957, the *Westminster and Pimlico News* reported on a case that appeared at the Chelsea Juvenile Court. In order to escape from a remand home in which she was being held, a 16 year-old girl had hit the principal over the head with an iron bar. The chair of the bench, Barbara Wootton, was quoted as saying that if 'you are determined to be a prostitute that will be your kind of life. If you are determined to go your own way you will, but if you go on this way I think you will regret it'. Another newspaper covering the same case noted that, a few days, earlier the girl had been fined at Marlborough Street magistrates court for insulting behaviour in Hyde Park, where she had given a false name and her age as 21. The girl had already been under a supervision order, but had left home because things 'weren't working out'.[89]

Medical staff in remand homes were clearly not unfamiliar with young girls involved in prostitution. As part of the information gathered for the BMA evidence to the Wolfenden Committee, a report was submitted to the Medical Women's Federation on a remand home in Manchester.[90] The home detained girls aged 14 to 16 with around half being 16. Of 126 cases in 1952, about half were from broken homes and 64 had experienced sexual intercourse; six of the girls were pregnant. According to the doctor at the home:

> Many pick up or are picked up by men in the streets of Manchester and then go to houses which are being used as brothels. Many are initiated by older women perhaps between 20 and 30 who have degenerated into prostitutes. There are usually about one or two a year who have been definitely procured by some woman – in some cases the girl's own mother – who owns the house in conjunction with a man and they come to court, the man for living on the immoral earning of the woman and both for keeping a house for immoral purposes. Many houses are known to the police, or suspected by them and the girls are found actually with men during the raid on the premises.[91]

The remand home was the site of specific research on under-aged prostitution. In the context of general anxiety over prostitution, psychiatrist T.N.C.Gibbens went through the records of 400 girls in remand homes whom he had examined during 1953 and published his conclusions in the *British Journal of Criminology* (1957). Eighteen of the girls had been living by prostitution at the time of their arrest and about the same number were arrested in the company of prostitutes.

With the help of the probation service, Gibbens followed up 185 girls placed under supervision and a further 57 who were put on probation for offences against property. Of these, 17 had a period of probable or certain prostitution while under supervision. He was first anxious to correct the conception that all wayward girls were virtually all actual or potential prostitutes. He asserted that, 'these girls have a fairly clear idea of what they mean by being a prostitute, and their definition will do for us. It means to have sexual intercourse indiscriminately for payment, recognising that this is what is being paid for. Apart from a very few cases in which juveniles are arrested in brothels, it means street prostitution'.[92]

> In the social strata from which wayward girls usually come, prostitution is a familiar thing and is accepted as part of the social order. These girls are not so shocked and scandalized as the middle class; they seem to look on prostitution rather as the middle class look upon chronic alcoholism – that it is disgraceful but that some people may have rather compelling reasons for taking to it for a time, and that it does not involve complete social ostracism.[93]

Gibbens' approach was psychological and categorising but more subtle than that of, for example, Glover. Of his primary group of girls who had been living by prostitution, he described four as 'uncivilised', aggressive, partly as a result of their exasperation at being uncared for. 'The moral and material hygiene of [their] home is extremely low and an aunt or sister is perhaps also a prostitute'. Gibbens implies that these girls were examples of a declining, almost atavistic type and that prostitution represented a kind of sexual backwardness (also see Glover, 1957 second edition: 9, 'almost 86 per cent of prostitutes exhibit some degree of intellectual and emotional backwardness'). Eight girls in this group he categorised as intelligent and unstable, three of them had attempted suicide at some time. Their intelligence was, Gibben felt, important because 'these girls have a clear conception of what prostitution is; they plunge into it quite intentionally as a form of moral suicide as if to say "This is how low I can go" ' (1957: 6). In agreement with Edward Glover's publication, *The Psychopathology of Prostitution* (1957 second edition), Gibbens asserted that unconscious 'homosexuality' was an important feature in his third group of girls who were more normal, but this was also a factor in his second group, four of whom he noted were overtly homosexual. One girl in Gibbens' third group had become a prostitute at

15 and had two convictions in an adult court before it was realised she was a juvenile. On the surface, he asserted, unconscious homosexuality expressed itself in a 'thinly disguised' hostility towards, and possibly a desire to degrade, men. Thus erroneously making a direct association between lesbianism and hostility towards men. Chief among the factors Gibbens identified as leading to under-age prostitution were, inadequate parenting, with particular emphasis upon the father, money, indolence or depression and also a fascination with prostitutes, usually by middle class girls. However, he also suggested that juvenile prostitution was inherently much more of a transitory phenomenon than adult prostitution.[94]

Around the same time, a joint report by the BMA and the Magistrates Association asserted that a child 'Suffering, due to poverty, ignorance, or exploitation for financial gain is no longer socially tolerated'. The report provides a comprehensive overview of the different agencies which were then employed to deal with cases of children in trouble showing that, unless reported directly by relatives or neighbours, this would only be detected where children touched institutional structures, predominantly the school or the local doctor. The problem of co-ordinating, and increasingly the effectiveness of such complex structures was, like much research since, cited as a cause of failures to detect cases of neglect, abuse or cruelty; early identification of 'problem families', it was asserted, would increase prevention.[95]

A book published in 1960 affords a further overview of public discussion on the subject of prostitution and the effects of the legislative changes of the 1950s. Also emphasised is the extent to which it was believed that adult prostitutes had, in their younger lives, been mistreated. *The Shame of the City, An Inquiry into the Vice of London*, one of whose authors was an ex-Detective Superintendent in the CID, is a subjective and experiential approach to the perceived problems of vice in the capital. It asserted that there had been a clear increase in prostitution during the 1950s, following a decline from about 1885 to 1945, a point upon which the Wolfenden Committee had stated there was no reliable evidence. The publication recognised the complex structure of the prostitute market and divided the trade into twelve separate types, not including 'part-time' or 'amateur' prostitutes, seven of which did not work the streets. The authors perceived the fundamental reasons for women resorting to prostitution to be 'failure of mental adjustment to the problems of civilised life in terms of the personal needs of the individual' or 'indifference to sexual intercourse which amounts to a-morality' and which extracted the meaning from sex and heightened the lure of money.[96] In part, this was seen to be the consequence of early and excessive experience or knowledge of sex from a young age, poor family backgrounds, and violent fathers who inured women to violence from their pimps.[97]

For example, Edie, from a poor background in the East End who saw her parents having fights and sex and whose father was a violent drunkard. At ten years old, a 13 year-old boy tried to rape her; she resisted fiercely but finally agreed to have sex for a shilling. Thereafter she took to prostitution until she was taken into the charge of the London County Council as in need of care or protection. After running away from homes and foster-parents she returned to streets, where, shortly after puberty, she had a miscarriage. At 17 years of age, and past the age when she could be subject to attempts by social workers to control her, she took to the streets full-time. This, Gosling and Warner maintained, was a classic tale. Even though such desperate stories were not as common among prostitutes as they had been in the past, prostitutes were easy victims both in their youth and in their adulthood.[98]

Significantly, Gosling and Warner made considerable reference to male prostitutes catering for homosexuals and also to police methods in dealing with the illegal trade which they believed had increased after the war and particularly after 1956 as a result of large numbers of Hungarian refugees who found the easy money attractive. Police activity concentrated on public or semi-public places which homosexuals were known to frequent, public conveniences and also certain known pubs and clubs; 'special watch is also kept at certain events to which people go in large numbers, particularly public exhibitions which attract boys'.[99]

Conclusions

As Macnicol has suggested, after the Second World War problem groups, such as the sections of society from which prostitutes were believed to be derived, were increasingly 'reconstructed in the form of the problem family approach, retaining many of the earlier features but replacing the pessimistic hereditarian analysis with a "socialisation" model of transmission which was more in keeping with the interventionism of the 1940s'.[100] Such concepts, however, continued to concentrate on the way in which sections of the population, sometimes referred to as the 'underclass', were defined in large part by their contact with social institutions, such as the prison, mental hospital, remand home, approved school and also social benefits agencies. This is certainly a problem with the evidence available for historical research into issues such as prostitution. However, this kind of perspective does reveal the extent to which life for some people was dominated by contact with welfare and criminal justice institutions. For some, these institutions represented a kind of continuum throughout their lives. Nevertheless, the predominance of this form of evidence can result in concentration upon the poorest, most vulnerable but at the same time most obvious, through the very operation of institutions, and this must be accepted. The circumstances of under-aged prostitutes subject to the workings of unequal power, gender and age relations were among the least empowered, if they worked the streets they may have been visible but as prostitutes and not as children.

Macnicol has also suggested that the use of the concept of an underclass has actually obscured the extent to which those being referred to actually composed those at the bottom of the pile at any given time.[101] Thus, analysis has taken into account the wider changes of the period which, like any other person, prostitutes experienced and responded to. Certainly, changing attitudes towards prostitutes were inextricably linked to the broader social, political and economic context. Rising disposable incomes and standards of living as well as the establishment of the welfare state brought about a shift in perceptions regarding the causality of prostitution. Poverty had long been seen as predominant in the aetiology of prostitution but, when the economic climate improved, observers and commentators began to modify their theoretical stance in the light of the spread in popularity of psychology, strongly influenced by Freud. The 'discovery of poverty' in the 1960s was to reassert economic necessity in the causality of prostitution. Other factors which increased the social distance of the prostitute from mainstream society were the way in which the values of the nuclear family were reinforced as the bulwark of society and the disapproval of those who fell outside of this construction.

The position of young, single people, and the possibility that they might not conform to social conventions, thus raised fears and even moral panic that future social stability would be undermined. Despite the climate of public discussion of sexuality, given impetus by changes in legislation, most young people during the 1940s and 1950s continued to be morally conservative. However, a minority of young people were involved in crime and in prostitution. While direct evidence for under-age prostitution is limited, it remains clear that the trade was carried on, indeed Gibbens claimed that about five per cent of the 14 to 16 year-old girls he interviewed had been involved in the sex trade and the publication *Women of the Streets* was able to map the areas of London in which very young prostitutes worked. Legislation that claimed to deal punitively with habitual prostitutes, but to intercept the young at an early stage, was to prove ineffective when under-age prostitutes continued to lie about their age, when they were resistant to the work of probation and social workers and when they did not work the streets.

References

1 *Hansard* 5th series, 22 April 1959 vol.604, col.450.
2 League of Nations Advisory Committee on Social Questions C.26.M.26.1943.IV p.26.
3 Ibid, pp.27–30; also see, for example, Glover, 1957 (2nd edn).
4 League of Nations Advisory Committee on Social Questions C.26.M.26.1943.IV, p.40 and pp.27–32.
5 T. Jordan, *Growing Up in the 50s* (London: Optima, 1990), p. 28.
6 C. Haste, *Rules of Desire, Sex in Britain: World War I to the Present* (London: Chatto and Windus Ltd, 1992), p. 99.
7 Annual Report 1941 cited in C. Haste, *Rules of Desire*, p. 130.
8 The Barnardos Archive, The University of Liverpool D239/A3/1/75.
9 *Child's Guardian* Winter 1942–3, p. 1.
10 *Shield* IX (1) Feb 1942, p. 31.
11 PRO HO45/25144.
12 PRO HO 45/25144, Mass-Observation Report on Juvenile Drinking, n.d, p. 31.
13 Ibid, p. 33.
14 Ibid.
15 *Child's Guardian* Spring 1944, p. 8.
16 L. Fairfield, 'Notes on prostitution', *British Journal of Criminology* 9, 1959, p. 170.
17 See, for example, *News Chronicle, Daily Telegraph, Daily Herald,* 8 December 1943.
18 PRO MH102/1150.
19 Ibid.
20 *Shield* IX No. 3/4/1943, pp. 116–9.
21 C. Haste, *Rules of Desire,* p. 134.
22 NVA 4/BVA/Box 115 – minutes of meeting 8 May 1940.
23 For examples see, D. Burlingham and A. Freud, *Young Children in Wartime* (London: Allen and Unwin, 1942); B. Holman, 'Fifty years ago: the Curtis and Clyde Reports', *Children and Society* 10, 1996; Ministry of Health, 'The break-up of the Poor Law and the care of children and old people' cited in R. A. Parker, 'The gestation of reform: the Children Act 1948', in *Approaches to Welfare* (London: Routledge and Kegan Paul, 1983); *Picture Post* 1941 vol.10 (1).
24 N. Parton, *The Politics of Child Abuse* (Basingstoke: Macmillan, 1985), p. 42.
25 *Child's Guardian* Autumn 1955, LXV (13), p. 13.
26 D. Fraser, *The Evolution of the Welfare State* (Basingstoke: Macmillan, 1986);

E. Midwinter, *Development of Social Welfare in Britain* (Buckinghamshire: Open University Press, 1994).

27 Social Insurance and Allied Services, PP 1942 (Cmnd.6404), pp. 6–7.

28 J. Lewis, 'Anxieties about the family and the relationships between parents, children and the state in twentieth century England', in M.Richards and P. Light (eds), *Children of Social Worlds: Development in a Social Context* (Cambridge Mass: Harvard University Press, 1986).

29 *Social Insurance and Allied Services*, PP 1942 (Cmnd.6404), p. 53; J. Lewis, 'Welfare States: gender, the family and women', *Social History* 19 (1), 1994, p. 42.

30 J. Lewis, 'Anxieties about the family', p. 32; T. Parsons and R.F. Bales, *Family Socialization and Interaction Process* (Glencoe, III: Free Press, 1955).

31 L.Davidoff *et al*, *The Family Story: Blood, Contract and Intimacy, 1830–1960* (London: Longman, 1999), p. 190.

32 P. Thane, 'Towards equal opportunities? Women in Britain since 1945', in T.R. Gourvish and A. O'Day (eds) *Britain since 1945* (Basingstoke: Macmillan, 1991); J. Lewis, *Women in Britain since 1945* (Oxford: Blackwell, 1992).

33 J. Bowlby, *Maternal Care and Mental Health* (Geneva: W.H.O, 1951), p. 412; also see J. Bowlby, *Child Care and the Growth of Love* (Harmondsworth: Penguin, 1953).

34 J. Weeks, *Sex, Politics and Society: The Regulation of Sexuality since 1800* (Harlow: Longman, 1989), p. 237; J. Bowlby, *Child Care and the Growth of Love*.

35 E. Frank, *Prostitution* (London: BSBC, 1955), p. 6.

36 J.K. Aitken, 'Modern mothers', *Medical World*, June 1956, p. 522.

37 J. Lewis and J. Welshman, 'The issue of the never-married mother in Britain, 1920-70', *Social History of Medicine* 19, 1997, p. 404.

38 J. Springhall, *Coming of Age: Adolescence in England 1860–1960* (Dublin: Gill and Macmillan, 1986), pp. 193–5.

39 J. Weeks, *Sex, Politics and Society*, p. 253.

40 S. Cohen, *Folks Devils and Moral Panics: The Creation of the Mods and Rockers* (London: MacGibbon and Kee, 1972); J. Clarke, S. Hall, T, Jefferson and B. Roberts, 'Subcultures, cultures and class', in *Resistance Through Ritials: Youth Subcultures in Post War Britain* (London: Hutchinson, 1976).

41 L. A. Hall, *Sex, Gender and Social Change in Britain since 1880,* European Culture and Society Series (Basingstoke: Macmillan, 2000), pp. 156–7.

42 L. Stanley, *Sex Surveyed 1949–1994: From Mass Observation's 'Little Kinsey' to the National Survey and the Hite Reports* (London: Taylor and Francis, 1995), p. 37.

43 A. McLaren, *Twentieth–Century Sexuality: A History* (Oxford: Blackwell, 1999), pp. 145–7.

44 L. Stanley, *Sex Surveyed*, p. 6.

45 Ibid, p. 29.

46 Mass Observation Archive (MO) TC12, Box 2–15.

47 Ibid, Box 4 12/4/B, p. 3.

48 Communication with Joy Eldridge, Mass-Observation Archive; L. Stanley,

Sex Surveyed, p. 194; MO FR 2479, May 1947.
49 MO TC 12, Box 4 12/4/B, pp. 14–5.
50 Ibid, p. 8.
51 MO TC 12 Box 4 12/4B and 15F.
52 MO TC 12 Box 4 12/4F.
53 *Hansard* 5th series, 6 July 1955 vol.555, col.1751.
54 J. Weeks, *Sex, Politics and Society*, p. 239; also see R. Matthews, 'Beyond Wolfenden? Prostitution, politics and the law', in R. Matthews and J. Young (eds), *Confronting Crime* (London: Sage, 1986).
55 Cited in T. Thomas, *Sex Crime: Sex Offending and Society* (Devon: Willan Publishing, 2000), p. 11.
56 J.E. Hall-Williams, 'The Wolfenden Report – An appraisal', *Political Quarterly* 29, 1958, p. 134; also see Q. Edwards, *What is Lawful? Does Innocence Begin Where Crime Ends? Afterthought on the Wolfenden Report* (Westminster: Church Information Office, 1959).
57 Wolfenden Committee Report, p.142; Matthews, 'Beyond Wolfenden', p. 188; also see T. Newburn, *Permission and Regulation, Law and Morals in Post-War Britain*, (London: Routledge, 1992), ch. 3.
58 L. Fairfield, 'Notes on prostitution', p. 164
59 Anon, *Streetwalker* (London: Bodley Head, 1959).
60 'Legal subjects and subject objects: Ideology, law and female sexuality', in C.Smart (ed.) *Law, Crime and Sexuality: Essays in Feminism* (London: Sage, 1995), p. 49.
61 J. Weeks, *Sex, Politics and Society*, p. 244; Matthews, 'Beyond Wolfenden'; T. Newburn, *Permission and Regulation*, p. 52.
62 *Hansard* fifth series 22 April 1959 vol.604, col.462.
63 L. Hale, fifth series 22 April *Hansard* 1959 vol.604, cols.445–6.
64 *Hansard* fifth series 22 April 1959 vol.604, col.446.
65 Ibid, col.447.
66 Ibid, col.468
67 *Times* 25 May 1956, 6f.
68 Wolfenden Committee, para 97.
69 The first report of the British Vigilance Association was also issued in 1953 following the amalgamation of the National and International Committee, the Bureau for the Suppression of Traffic in Persons and the NVA.
70 Also see, for example, Hall-Williams, 'The Wolfenden Report', pp. 139–140.
71 'The Wolfenden Report, Prostitution', *Howard Journal* X (1) 1958, p.29.
72 *Shield,* December 1954 and June 1955 XII (6), pp. 35–6.
73 G. R. Scott, *A History of Prostitution from Antiquity to the Present Day* (London: Torchstream Books, 1954), p. 22.
74 Ibid, pp. 24–30.
75 *Daily Express* 29 September 1954; *Sunday Express* 3 October 1954.
76 PRO MEPO 3/2907.
77 C.H. Rolph, *Women of the Streets: A Sociological Study of the Common Prostitute* (London: Secker and Warburg, 1955), p. 135.
78 Ibid, pp 46–51.

79 Also see for example, Fairfield, 'Notes on Prostitution', p. 171.
80 C. H. Rolph, *Women of the Streets*, p. 101.
81 Ibid, pp. 101–4.
82 Wellcome Archive SA/MWF/Box 81/H.9/3.
83 R. Hood and K. Joyce, 'Three generations, oral testimony on crime and social change in London's East End', *British Journal of Criminology* 1999, 39 (1), pp. 151–2; P. Willmott, *Adolescent Boys in East London* (London: Routledge and Kegan Paul, 1966); *Jewish Chronicle* 6 September 1957; *Woman's Sunday Mirror* 28 July 1957.
84 L. L. Loewe, *Basil Henriques: A portrait based on his diaries, letters and speeches as collated by his widow, Rose Henriques* (London: Routledge and Kegan Paul, 1976), p. 152.
85 Rev. E. Young *et al*, Vice increase in Stepney', 1957 report in NVA Archives; *Times* 5 June 1957, 1e.
86 C. H. Rolph, *Women of the Streets*, p. 105.
87 Ibid, pp. 59 and 84.
88 *Times* 3 October 1958, 15d.
89 *Daily Express* 9 August 1957.
90 Wellcome Archive, SA/WMF/Box 9 and 81.
91 Ibid, Box 81.
92 T. N. C. Gibbens, 'Juvenile prostitution', *British Journal of Criminology* 8, 1957, pp. 3–4.
93 Ibid, p. 3.
94 Ibid, pp. 6–8.
95 BMA, *Cruelty to and Neglect of Children, Report of a Joint Committee of the British Medical Association and the Magistrates Association* (London: BMA, 1856), pp. 8 and 17–9.
96 J. Gosling and D. Warner, *The Shame of the City: An Inquiry into the Vice of London* (London: W.H.Allen, 1960), p. 26 and 45.
97 Ibid, pp. 70 and 117.
98 Ibid, pp. 52–4.
99 Ibid, pp. 181–3.
100 J. Macnicol, 'In pursuit of an underclass', *Journal of Social Policy* 16 (3), 1987, p. 313.
101 Ibid, p. 315.

Chapter 7

The rediscovery of child prostitution during the 1960s and 1970s

This is the real world and not the fantasy world ... where all children are bright, clean, and honest as the day is long.[1]

The 1960s and 1970s were marked by the implementation of several significant pieces of liberalising legislation concerning divorce, birth control, abortion and homosexuality, which reflected and reinforced changing social attitudes and behaviour. A loosening of moral restraint and an increased politicisation of sexual activity, in part through the campaigning of feminist groups, undoubtedly also marked the 1960s and 1970s, and the Profumo Affair (1963) exposed the extent to which private sexual behaviour could be not only politicised, but also newsworthy.

Fears for the family in the context of increasing employment participation rates among women and, especially during the early 1970s, a crucial deterioration in national economic fortunes heightened public anxiety about economic and social change. Yet, research on the behaviour of young people tended to indicate a continued conservatism in sexual activity. Michael Schofield's *The Sexual Behaviour of Young People* (1965) asserted that only a minority of young people were engaging in sexual intercourse before marriage, although sexual behaviour, such as petting, was widespread.[2] While Gorer's later study of sex and marriage (1971), noted that only 26 per cent of men and 63 per cent of women in his sample (aged 16 to 45 years old) were virgins when they married,[3] an additional fifth of the men and a quarter of the women stated that the person they later married was the first person they had sex with.[4] However, during the 1970s a more pluralist morality was increasingly evident, in which premarital sexual experience was more acceptable, although less reform-minded opinion remained opposed to what was criticised as permissive and deteriorating in social and moral standards.

Increased public discussion of sexual matters had received a kind of sanction as a result of the investigations and debate surrounding the Wolfenden Committee and the passage of the Sexual Offences Act (1956) and the Street Offences Act (1959). Extensive media coverage of these important legislative changes brought about a conspicuous, but until the 1960s and 1970s still limited, shift in the more up market press towards coverage of sensitive issues, such as homosexuality, prostitution and child sexual abuse. Such subjects had been largely absent, or received a very subdued coverage in the national press, with the notable exception of the *News of the World*, for much of the twentieth century, although the war years and the attendant concerns over venereal disease tended to disrupt this pattern. By the 1960s, the national press generally was much more willing to cover and speculate upon sexual issues, and especially upon sexual crimes. In part this was due to the emergence, or rather re-emergence in public debate of the complex social problems of poverty and child battery which increased anxiety about child welfare in many circles during the 1960s. Thus, when serious cases of child prostitution were revealed during the 1970s, the media coverage was extensive and, in conjunction with other crimes against children, served to seriously expose the fault lines in the ideal of childhood as protected, innocent and passive. The plurality of the experience of childhood, and the existence of such disturbing social problems, also challenged the universalist claims and attainments of public provision.

The print media, social problems and child prostitution

An article in the *Sunday Times* in 1978, entitled 'The sour side of sixteen schoolgirls on the streets', asserted that prostitution among schoolgirls was increasing, largely due to marital breakdown, family instability and to increased sexual activity among the young. It was estimated that the number of cases had doubled in the previous five years, and the Head of Scotland Yard's juvenile affairs bureau stated that there had been a marked increase in prostitution by young people under 17 years old.[5] The article used the example of the case of a 14 year-old girl who had run away from home and was found by police working in a massage parlour.[6]

Much contemporary opinion seemed to confirm that the Street Offences Act of 1959 had, despite Parliamentary rhetoric at the time, done little to deal with the problem of very young prostitutes. Some maintained that the Act had served to increase organised prostitution from cafés, clubs and massage parlours and exacerbate the invisibility of child prostitution.[7] One of the conclusions of the Working Party on the Street Offences Act of the Josephine Butler Society, the successor to the Association for Moral and Social Hygiene, was that *'The Cautioning System* which was intended to prevent young girls from adopting a life of prostitution has failed in this purpose, partly because the Act itself has driven them off the streets'.[8]

> Social workers report that the application of *Preventive Methods* has become more difficult, and that the homeless girl is more quickly waylaid by ponces and swept into club life and the call-girl system. The more widespread sale of the more easily obtainable drugs also tends to condition them to a prostitute's life.[9]

Under the cautioning system, the young person did not have to go back to the police station and so her true age might not be discovered until she was, following two cautions, actually arrested. This system was also likely to encourage individuals to give a false identity and also to increase the geographical mobility of prostitutes. Furthermore, as the article in the *Sunday Times* in 1978 pointed out, even after the police located an under-aged girl or boy working as a prostitute, the only provision usually available was a local authority residential home from which absconding was common. Therefore, the article concluded, 'until we understand why girls feel the need to run away – from home or from these residential homes – under age prostitution seems set to increase'.[10]

During the 1970s, the *Times* and the *Sunday Times* campaigned for an emphasis on the child as opposed to the parents in social support; the *Times* alone covered at least eight major news stories on children involved in prostitution, a marginal issue within child welfare concerns. Indeed, media coverage of legal cases concerning two major stories of child prostitution in the mid-1970s finally and irrevocably brought the practice and existence of under-aged commercial sex into the public eye. Questions were also asked in Parliament about these cases.[11] The first case concerned the procurement of young boys from the Playland amusement arcade, Piccadilly Circus in London, and the second concerned the involvement of under-age girls in prostitution while in council care. Both of these cases not only presented firm evidence that child prostitution existed but also illustrated some of the forms this took. These cases also suggest that the attention given, even to serious social problems, is dependent upon how effectively they are linked to wider issues and the influence of the agencies expressing concern about them.

Much of the analysis in this chapter about these cases uses information that has been pieced together using contemporary newspapers, especially the *Times*, the *Daily Mail* and the *Daily Telegraph*. Two local newspapers, one weekly (*EPE*) and one daily (*LN*), whose circulation covered the geographical area in which the girls in the legal cases were prostituting themselves while in care, were also consulted. Although the area in which these girls lived will be clear to anyone who follows up the references given for the national papers, the titles of the local newspapers have been abbreviated to enable some obscuring of the area concerned. Research conducted during the 1980s and 1990s has shown that child prostitution is a national issue. The references in national newspapers are given as they and the relevant dates are easily located through the index of the *Times*. Although newspapers provide a wealth of information regarding not only the events but also media response and social attitudes to contemporary issues, they are in some senses a limited primary source. Because of the limitations of newspapers, other sources were sought. Unfortunately, the British Association of Social Workers was unable to supply any relevant material and the regional social services department in which the case of the girls involved in prostitution while in local authority care occurred were unable to locate a copy of the inquiry report into the case.

The amount of time that journalists have been able to devote to researching stories has historically been constrained by the publishing process. Thus journalists have tended to rely on interviews with 'experts', such as professionals and politicians, and/or with people involved directly or indirectly with the events concerned. Print space constraints also demand that journalists bring a high level of selectivity to their work and also formulate powerful messages using well-established images. Such short cuts often result in a simplified, and sometimes misleading, coverage of the issue and the linking or categorising together of issues that are discreet phenomena. Hence, newspapers have played an important, if relatively recent, role in confirming the perception of child commercial sex primarily as prostitution rather than child abuse. It is the journalistic construction that shapes the basis of the news story, reflecting and influencing social knowledge and opinion. As has been pointed out elsewhere:

> the original information exists in society but the news process causes its information meaning structure to be altered. This 'news' or new information state has become more accessible to wider readership or audience, thereby implying that the information is 'real', that is, it may be used to direct society.[12]

Furthermore, because of the peculiar position of the newspaper media as being able not only to represent public opinion but also to be part of public opinion, they can campaign on issues on that basis.[13] In this way the newspaper media can influence which issues are seen as social problems requiring a resolution of some kind, and also impacts upon the length of time that an issue remains in the news. Thus, Nigel Parton has observed that the media can be seen:

> not just to reproduce the definitions of primary definers [those interviewed or quoted as experts] but to produce independently the news, and in the process transform and objectify the issue into a real social problem that the general public is concerned about and demands action.[14]

However, it is necessary to qualify this in the light of more recent research which emphasises the level of contestation in the defining of issues as journalists balance access to 'experts', other sources, organisational and specifically editorial constraints.[15]

In their survey of newspapers, Soothill and Walby observed that the coverage of sex crime expanded significantly during the 1970s in both the popular and 'quality' press, particularly between 1971 and 1978.[16] Between 1951 and the 1970s, they assert, the only newspaper which consistently reported on rape cases was the *News of the World* and these reports were much less explicit than those to be found during and after the 1970s. Furthermore, it was clear from their study, and also a study by Walby, Hay and Soothill, that many newspapers during the 1970s began intentionally to use reports of sex crimes as a mechanism to maintain or increase sales.[17] Local papers, however, were felt to have 'a more restrained and factual mode of reporting' despite facing similar pressures for survival.[18] In reported cases of underage sex by girls in 1985, Soothill and Walby maintain that consent was not an issue as in the case with adult women. Girls were either portrayed as virgins which implied victim status or 'Lolitas', in which case reports highlighted the dangers of teenage temptresses and portrayed men as powerless.[19]

Newspaper coverage of the two main incidents of under-age prostitution dealt with in this chapter tended to present this phenomenon in ways which heavily focused upon the involvement of girls rather than boys. Furthermore, although the standard of coverage varied considerably between newspapers, the girls involved in these cases were often presented in a similar victim/threat framework, albeit often in a more complex and socially aware manner, to that suggested by the work of Soothill and Walby. This is, however, partly a reflection of the differing nature of the crimes being considered and the greater use of local newspaper reports. The 'expert' opinion consulted was usually that of social services, the police and/or politicians. The difficulties of writing about what were clearly troubled children led some journalists into considerations of the family and psychological backgrounds of such children. The nature of the cases themselves and the media necessity to simplify complex social phenomena resulted in two main representations of child prostitution. The first was that young girls were manipulated and coerced into the trade by an older man who then lived off her earnings. The second was that girls entered prostitution through peer pressure and the desire for money to pay for a way of life that she would otherwise be unable to afford.

These representations can be seen as being founded partly on existing and long-standing attitudes regarding prostitution and youth delinquency and as such persisted with some of the defects of these arguments. The primary inadequacy of the often simplistic models constructed by the press at this time was that they maintained to a considerable degree the victim/threat dichotomy; the coercive model represented the girl as a victim while the peer pressure and desire for money model represented the girl as delinquent. Thus, for example, the coercive model, with its implied state of previous innocence, did not allow analytically for cases in which the girl involved seemed willingly to defend or protect the individual who coerced her into prostitution. Indeed, this stance penalised the child who had some prior sexual knowledge and/or experience.[20]

Nevertheless, the roots of these models can be identified in a much more sophisticated and research-based form in studies on child prostitution that have been undertaken during the 1990s. However, research into child prostitution during the late twentieth century has, in its attention to life chances and to the realities of the choices available to some young people, critically problematised the historical links made between passivity and innocence, active participation and guilt.[21] This approach has encouraged a greater subjective stance which enables a fuller appreciation of the individual feelings and rationales of child prostitutes, in line with the paradigm promoted by Allison James and Alan Prout (see introduction).[22]

Issues that are deemed to be worthy of extensive newspaper space, and hence believed to elicit public interest, change over time and are affected by the economic, social and political context. Thus, it was not until the mid-1970s that the issue of child prostitution received extensive newspaper attention. Indeed, the 1970s proved to be a watershed in the widespread recognition that children were involved in prostitution. This issue emerged as a social problem in the light of a combination of several contemporary factors. One factor was the concern over the rise in juvenile crime and delinquency and the resurgence in the search for the root of this behaviour. Another factor was the recent extensive publicity given to child welfare professionals as a result of their failure to prevent the death of Maria Colwell in 1974 at the hands of her stepfather. This tragic event was important in bringing about increased pressure for a re-orientation towards child protection and child centred care. The issue of child physical abuse and the Maria Colwell case has been amply examined by Nigel Parton in his publication *The Politics of Child Abuse* (1985) and his analysis allows some comparisons to be made here between the media treatment of child abuse and that of child prostitution. The third important contextual factor was the changes in the organisation of the social services during the early 1970s. The final factor was a political climate which had seen the decline of consensus by the end of the 1960s and then the increasing strength of New Right ideology, which focused debate upon perceived failures in the Welfare State. The combination of these elements was instrumental in focusing media attention upon child prostitution in the mid-1970s.

Children and commercial sex

One of the most immediate characteristics of the child sex trade revealed during the mid-1970s was the small rewards that the children received. Apparent in the paltry value placed on the bodies of these children was the often dislocated and precarious state of their economic and social circumstances. One publication later referred to boy prostitutes as 'troubled, defiant, lost, confused, belligerent and unhappy'.[23] Thus in the Playland amusement arcade in Piccadilly, boys as young as ten years old who had run away from their homes were procured by offers of money but also of food, drink and/or shelter. In describing the activities involved, newspaper articles used older, familiar language, such as 'rent-boys' being 'procured' or 'lured into vice' but also language that, although relatively new to the media, was used by those involved in, or aware of, the trade, especially in the United States. The court heard that the Playland arcade was the centre of a 'male prostitution ring' and, according to the men on trial, the boys had been referred to as 'fresh bunnys' or chickens with the analogy being that the clients were 'chicken hawks'.[24] Journalist Robin Lloyd published an international study of boy prostitution entitled *Playland: a Study of Boy Prostitutes* in which this trade was referred to rather sensationally as 'Great Britain and America's best-kept secret'.[25]

In this case adult male visitors, knowing the reputation of the arcade as a place which attracted young boys who could, by arrangement, be obtained for sexual purposes, would pick out a boy and pay up to £5 for an introduction. The boys were also on occasion involved in photography sessions. The arcade, which was open sometimes until 3 am, had become a centre for runaway boys, often with no money and nowhere to sleep for the night who had, according to one report, travelled to London 'to start a new life'.[26]

This story broke into the national press following the sentencing of a number of men in June 1975. Four men were convicted on a range of charges in association with these activities: 'plotting to procure the commission of acts of gross indecency'; 'gross indecency'; 'indecent assault'; 'living on immoral earnings of prostitution' and 'buggery'. Those convicted were claimed in court to be agents of wealthier clients who would pay them £10 for each new boy procured.[27] According to Robin Lloyd, this amusement arcade was not the only location in Piccadilly popular for such purposes; the underground station and surrounding area were, at the time, a well-established area for underage male prostitutes to trade. In four hours spent in this area, Lloyd claimed to have spoken to fourteen boys under 16 years of age who were involved in commercial sex; he gives the names of their home towns in Britain, and for a few, how much they had asked for. Lloyd also asserted that each of the boys he spoke to, except one, knew at least six other boys on the game either in London or in their hometown.[28]

Like the Playland case, the matter of young girls involved in prostitution while in local authority care appeared in the press following a court appearance and conviction (in April 1976). However, the coverage given to this, and related cases, was more extensive and was said by one paper to have produced a 'public outcry'.[29] The core of the legal case was the arrest and later conviction of an adult man to six years in prison for actual bodily harm against a 15 year-old girl, having unlawful intercourse with her and for living on her immoral earnings. According to a local paper, he had previous convictions for living on immoral earnings.[30] The girl had first met this man when she ran away from home early in 1975. When she was found a juvenile court order put her into a children's home. However, while there she again met up with the man and began, for two months, to work as a prostitute, passing all of the money she made on to him. It was reported that she stated to the court, 'he invited me to his home and was nice to me. He told me he wanted money to buy a car and asked me to help him, I agreed'.[31] Soon after she was sent home under supervision and was then able to earn at least £100 a week, working every evening and weekends, again passing the money on to him, for a total of five months. She continued working as a prostitute despite being arrested by the police with a client, cautioned under the Street Offences Act and the social services being informed. The court was told that the girl was savagely thrashed if she disobeyed him, was late or tried to keep money back. The girl told the court 'I lied to the police to protect him as much as possible. I don't know why he had such a hold on me. He could be nice but he was horrible when he was angry'.[32] A local paper quoted the girl as saying that 'another time I left him a note saying I wasn't going to work for him any more but he came and found me at the corner of my road and told me if I ever stopped working for him he would run me over with his car'.[33]

The element of manipulation and violence used to drive this young girl into prostitution was one of the most offensive aspects of the case. By the late 1970s, this picture appears to have been accepted as the most common way in which children became involved in prostitution. For example, a social worker in Birmingham was quoted in a *Sunday Times* article suggesting that the 'pattern of recruitment here [with runaways] is that a girl gets picked up by a man who gives her somewhere to stay… He wins her affection, then persuades her first to oblige his friends, and then puts her into prostitution proper'.[34] The Josephine Butler Society still utilised the power of the language and images of the past in its campaigning against prostitution, and usually presented this in terms of the coercive pattern or model. It was asserted with reference to a claimed international traffic that 'girls are still tricked, betrayed and broken in the classic manner. There is nothing new in this… Certain things escape notice because we refuse to acknowledge their existence'.[35] Predictably, there was some sensationalisation in the tabloids as well as an element of salaciousness as the case was described, for example, as a 'sex scandal' or a 'sex case' involving a 'sex slave girl'.[36]

Once investigations into the case of this girl were underway, the police uncovered other related cases. Investigations and interviews by journalists with people associated with the first case, and with professionals with knowledge about the subject, directly or indirectly, fed a print media eager to follow up the sensationalist ground already laid by the first courtroom revelations. Two other girls in local authority care in the same children's home had, it was alleged, also worked as prostitutes, although this was not known to social workers at the time. The activities of one of these girls became known because of her association with the girl whose case had already gone to court. According to a local newspaper, this second girl had run away from the children's home in 1975.[37] This girl, aged 17, was later located and gave evidence to the independent regional inquiry into child prostitution in local authority care that followed the uncovering of these cases. The investigative tribunal concluded that there was no evidence that the second girl was involved in prostitution. The third girl included in the press coverage was, it was claimed, only 14 years of age when she was involved in the sex trade.[38] The *Daily Telegraph* asserted that social workers had no idea what the 14 year-old was doing until she was arrested for soliciting and found to be three months pregnant.[39]

The story of the 14 year-old girl who had been found working as a prostitute, although it was suggested that she had only just begun in the trade, had not been revealed at the time because her case had been heard in a juvenile court. One of the reasons for this was that no adult had been convicted in relation to her prostitution and the juvenile court was a more protected arena as it heard 'care and protection' cases as well as criminal cases. A local paper saw in this case not just as the behavioural problems of one young person but as an increasing trend among pleasure-seeking girls.

> It was easy to dismiss the whole sordid business as the behaviour of a young tart, a rotten apple already well rooted in the shady underworld. But the girl is not like that. Her mother says she is a girl who 'likes a good time' and who was prepared to sell herself to pay for it. She is not the only one. A policewoman told me she had seen many 13, 14 and 15-year-olds on the streets of Manchester, trying to undercut the older girls by only charging 50p instead of the usual £5. 'In general prostitutes are younger than they were'.[40]

Shortly after these cases were brought to light, the *Times* claimed that a further alleged case involving a boy aged 13 (or 14 in the *Daily Telegraph*, 21 April 1976, p.3) had been uncovered in the same area. 'It is understood that the boy was placed in a children's home… after he had been caught stealing. Last November he was found loitering near public lavatories. After a similar occurrence in March he told the police that he had been paid 50p by men for sexual acts. He was cautioned and returned to council care'.[41] Newspaper reports late in 1976 also disclosed that a social worker in the same region had attempted to have intercourse with a girl of 15 years old who was in local authority care, although the social worker had been unaware the girl was in care at the time. This was the girl whose prostitution had first hit the headlines. The social worker was convicted and fined £100, his defence had asserted that it was 'clear that no harm was done to the girl herself. She was already a hardened prostitute'.[42]

This series of related cases prompted the press to speculate about the causes of child prostitution. An article in the *Sunday Times* in 1978 offered a general analysis of under-age prostitution and emphasised the overlap between young people who ran away from care or home and child prostitution. It was felt that older girls on the run would be less likely to be caught because they could provide for themselves relatively invisibly through prostitution compared to boys who, it was felt, would be more likely to resort to theft.[43] Apart from the lack of recognition of prostitution among boys under the age of 16, despite the publicity which had been given to the Playland case, the article implied that the numbers of children involved in commercial sex was more widespread than previously believed. Runaways, whether from care or from home, were felt to be unlikely to go to the official agencies or the projects emerging to help young people in trouble, such as the Soho Project, unless they were prepared to go back into care. A spokesperson from the Soho Project qualified the activities of some of these girls, 'You can't call it prostitution … Some of these girls will sleep with people just for a meal, for a bed, or just some warmth'.[44] Again, the focus remained upon girls, not boys, and the prostitute rather than the client, a stance which was facilitated by the historical linkages made between the delinquency and criminality of girls and women and their sexuality and sexual activities. In the context of a recognition of the emotional and/or physical need which often played a part in the resort to prostitution by young girls, this behaviour was also conceived of in terms of two models which highlighted gender and power inequalities: one in which older men coerced the girls and the other in which the girls were influenced by peer pressure and the desire for money for a lifestyle they would otherwise be unable to afford.

Studies of delinquency

Child care legislation was influenced by rising juvenile crime rates from the mid-1950s to the mid-1960s. In 1954 the total number of persons under 17 years old found guilty of indictable offences was 34,829, by 1963 this had risen to 67,784; of this figure 6,644 offences were committed by girls, with shop lifting constituting over half of the offences involved. However, because adult offences also tended to increase over the period, and indeed since 1938, the number of indictable offences by juveniles actually remained a fairly constant proportion of all indictable offences, between about 32 and 35 per cent.[45] Also after 1963, this proportion dropped due partly to the increased use of police cautioning and the raising of the criminal age of responsibility from eight to ten years of age. Nevertheless, public and political concern about the absolute rises in the numbers of offences committed by young people focused upon youth sub-cultural groups, rising incomes, lack of parental discipline and the influence of films and television.

During the 1960s and 1970s, there were numerous studies on the delinquency of young girls.[46] At the same time, the issues of male prostitution and the involvement of young boys in the trade were beginning to appear in academic publications, literature and the media in Britain, when prior concentration had been almost wholly upon the non-sexual delinquency and/or criminality of young boys and men. Professional investigation into boy prostitution had occurred earlier in the United States, for example William Harlin Butt's psychopathological study of New York, 'Boy Prostitutes of the Metropolis' (1947) in the *Journal of Clinical Psychology*, although academic research into adult male prostitution had already been published, for example, Werner Picton's 'Male Prostitution in Berlin' (1931).[47] The greater concentration upon female under-age prostitution was based upon the framing of female deviance as being either the product of maladjusted sexuality or a rejection of their biologically ordained passivity and conservatism; as against the depiction of male deviance as being in part a reflection of natural assertion and aggression.[48]

In many cases, research into female juvenile delinquency remained attached to such older conceptions and, as Carlen has observed, it was not until the 1970s that old explanations for female crime and delinquency began to be displaced.[49] Thus, one of the most prominent studies during this period *Delinquency in Girls* produced by Cowie, Cowie and Slater asserted that 'Not only is the delinquent girl less common [than the delinquent boy], but her offences are almost entirely limited to sexual behaviour and such simple forms of stealing as shoplifting'.[50] This publication, the research for which was conducted in an approved school for girls in the south of England, concluded that delinquency among girls was often the consequence of domestic instability and economic and emotional deprivation which was productive of greater 'mental abnormality'. But it also suggested that female delinquency could, in part, be the product of biological factors, such as hormone imbalance.[51]

During this period, images of both girl and boy under-age prostitution continued to be used as exemplars of the dangers of social and moral change. Boy prostitution was linked to homosexuality, which was perceived by some to be increasing due to the emasculation of the male in modern society. According to one American analysis, 'Men stand alone now; class, rank, family, even the fundamental sex rule no longer props them up'.[52] The same account offered a very broad and morally conservative consideration of the social context that presided over the general loosening of moral standards and the increase of homosexuality.

> The beats, the juvenile delinquents, the rebellious young protesting, often in noisy silence … the confusion of role and the absence of goals and expectations – all these have led some young people to question all current moral values and standards of behaviour. This crumbling of barriers has brought sex deviation into focus and consequently has affected sexual behaviour among youths and young women too.[53]

Literature on the subject of prostitution remained limited, and that on under-age boy prostitution scarce, with much of it based on research in America. Among the oldest of the studies in which boy prostitution emerged as an issue was a follow-up by Doshay (1943) of 256 boys who appeared in a New York court for various sex offences. Most of these boys came from poverty-stricken backgrounds with few life chances. In England, a study of 16 boys under 16 years of age who 'persistently prostituted themselves in the community, and seventeen whose main activities were in an institution' was published in 1966. This referred to work already published on psychopathic and 'sex-deviated' adolescents (1964, 1965a, 1965b) and defined a boy prostitute as 'one under 16 years old who repeatedly performs sexual acts for other males for reward, and is known for this service by his community'.[54] These 33 boys were aged between 12 and 22 years. Only one of these boys, according to the article, had actually been convicted for prostitution and it was stated that by the age of 13 the boy had 'seduced some fifty men, and caused the suicide of one'. Twenty-six of the others had convictions for a variety of, mainly property, offences.[55]

According to the article, eight of the boys who had prostituted themselves in the community started before puberty, and three had prostitute mothers (and absent fathers) whose clients also used the boys. Those boys who had been involved in prostitution only while in care tended, according to the report, to be less disturbed and to have parents who were 'less adverse to them. Some at least only accepted rewards for services rendered within institutions to selected older males. Two community boys were admitted from approved schools where they were successfully seducing prefects and one master'.[56] What is important here is that, despite the young age of the boys, the responsibility for their prostitution was seen to be their own, which reflected the individualistic tendency of contemporary psychiatry. Little consideration was made of the pressures or even violence that may have resulted in their prostitution in institutions, nor of the complexities of power and/or victim relations. Comment regarding the users of these boys was also limited, although some quite specific observations were made, such as, 'cinema prostitution seemed to be a common way of earning extra cash among Nottingham boys. It seemed to be regarded somewhat like masturbation, discussed among boys, and strenuously denied by all to adults'.[57] Much of the scant literature on boy prostitution highlighted the extent to which boys and young men could participate in homosexual activity without developing a self-conception of themselves as a homosexual precisely because the material reward was seen to be the sole motivation.[58] This was an important factor in the power relations between the boy and his client and the moral distinctions made by the boys, but also operated to reduce the psychological obstacles to the continuance of boy prostitution.

In October and November 1969 the *People* ran a series of stories on vice. The research for these articles had been conducted at the request of the Josephine Butler Society, which had done this after having failed to raise money to finance independent research. As the society's magazine stated 'when all attempts in this direction failed, it was decided to approach a responsible newspaper to see whether they would undertake research in a less academic way than the Society had intended'.[59] On 26 October an article in this series was published entitled 'Schoolgirls on the game'. According to the article, 'The worst aspect of prostitution in Britain' was the growing numbers of younger teenagers it attracted, some as young as 13 years old. The reasons cited for this supposed increase were broken homes and insecurity as well as the need for money and/or drugs.

> One girl interviewed by a *People* investigator was just 15 and still at school, but played truant two or three afternoons a week to pick up clients … She first slept with a man when she was 13. The man was aged about 40, and they met in a café. She asked, and was paid, £3. 'My friends were doing it,' she said. 'They thought I was "chicken" because I had no experience. So I went with the man to prove I was their equal. I went to school the next day to tell them all about it'.[60]

It was claimed that under-aged girls, dressed to look older, were commonly involved in prostitution in Soho and in 'almost every city in Britain' and conducted themselves with a casual indifference born from the pill and the permissive society and spirit of rebellion. Once caught, the article complained, those under 17 could be sent to a children's home or approved school, but 'Too often at such institutions the not-so-intelligent young girls are influenced by the old hands and there is no saving them'.[61]

Aside from the cynicism regarding local authority care, the most pertinent aspect of this article is that it illustrates a model of under-aged prostitution which differs from that based on coercion by an older, usually male, figure. Rather, peer influence, immorality and an individual desire for money are cited as the primary causal agents, although in both models a background of social and economic instability was usually accepted. This latter model suggests an element of empowerment and a challenge to authority in the prostitution of the young. Youth prostitution was depicted here as a purely female phenomenon. The boy prostitution reported in the Playland case was depicted as more exceptional and perverse in addition to the immorality of prostitution. For example, one newspaper story on the Playland prostitution stated that only those 'with strong characters realised that they had been ensnared and thumbed a lift home. The weaker ones became more and more ensnared until they became so used to their new life of perversion that they began to telephone their wealthy "friends" like prostitutes touting for business'.[62]

In the context of wider concerns for the wellbeing of the family, it was broken homes, not specifically inadequate or abusive homes, that were often highlighted in the press. However, one of the local newspapers in the town in which the girl prostitution cases had emerged in 1976 examined the issues in some detail and emphasised the emotional deprivation resulting from specifically inadequate or abusive families. The deputy director of a regional social services department was quoted saying, 'many of them [child prostitutes] want somebody to care about them. The hardened pro knows very well the client doesn't care at all but the young girl is likely to be looking for affection'.[63] The parents of the 14 year-old girl in this case had separated when she was seven months old, and she afterwards had an unstable home life, and, with her mother, moved house frequently. 'At eight she was playing truant regularly from school, at nine she ran away from home and at twelve she was found guilty of theft. A year later she was in court again on a shoplifting charge'.[64] Her mother also claimed that as her daughter grew older she became physically violent.

Child prostitution, the social services and the media

Despite the proven involvement of a larger number of children in the Playland case, the circumstances in which girls prostituted themselves while in local authority care provoked greater and more sustained media attention and for this reason will be the focus of the remainder of this chapter. Explanations for this can largely be found in the wider associations and repercussions of the revelations concerning the girl prostitutes in care. The judge in the case was, for instance, quoted as saying that he was 'exceedingly disturbed at what [he had] heard in connection with the social services'.[65] Right wing political rhetoric around the case went so far as to challenge the legitimacy of the social services and the 'misplaced liberalism, of democratic welfarism'.[66] This series of related cases regarding prostitution while in care was not only a watershed in the wider recognition that child prostitution existed, but was also one of a small number of cases during the mid-1970s where the competence of social workers, and specifically young women social workers, was publicly questioned in the media.[67]

In common with the coverage of the Maria Colwell tragedy, the role and capabilities of the social workers involved received considerable attention, so linking the cases through informal and very public inquiries into social work and extending to issues around the priorities, resourcing and operation of social services departments. The girl prostitute case occurred in the aftermath of the inquiry and report into the tragic death of Maria Colwell and the more child-centred approach it recommended. As has been remarked by Olive Stevenson, who was a member of the official inquiry team, 'that report has come to symbolise a sea change in British child welfare practice and public attitudes to it'.[68] The wider cultural and political significance of the Maria Colwell case has been aptly summarised by Hendrick:

> she seemed to personify the 'innocent' victim, to represent that which was being destroyed by alien forces. The child's death pointed the finger at the range of groups allegedly threatening 'the British way of life' – social workers, feminists, Marxists, radical students and teachers, divorcees – and at the equally threatening trends: criminality, pro-abortion, anti-authoritarianism, pop culture, drugs, and lack of self-reliance, each of which was seen as the product of 'permissiveness' in all its forms, especially the sexual, the social and the cultural.[69]

While several of these contextual elements remained true for the girl prostitutes case, the girls themselves could not so easily be depicted as innocent victims unless violently coerced into it, which complicated the linkages that could be made by the press. Thus, child prostitution became much more associated by the press with delinquency and the search for its causality rather than direct abuse by adults. There was, however a similar concentration upon the role and responsibilities of the social workers involved in the cases. With regard to coverage of under-aged prostitution this also extended to a serious questioning of the nature and effects of local authority residential care.

A week after the first case of the girl in local authority care being coerced into prostitution appeared in court and in the press, the setting up of an independent local inquiry team to examine the events was announced. According to the *Times* the inquiry was to be held in private as the best way to obtain the truth, with a public statement to be issued afterwards.[70] Demands for an inquiry had begun after the county director of social services had been quoted as admitting in court that social workers had known that the girl was working as a prostitute and had allowed her to continue. This was a decision that was criticised by the judge and also by the girl's mother.[71] Indeed the mother of the oldest of the three girls considered by the inquiry stated that her daughter 'became a prostitute because she went into care. Other girls at the home told me later that … [she] was soliciting, kept running away and the social workers seemed powerless to stop her'.[72]

The decision to allow the girl to continue in prostitution caused a furore which questioned the judgement of the social workers involved, but also the efficacy of local authority care, sometimes almost to the exclusion of the abuse of young girls which was actually at the heart of the case. A ruling by the delegates at the annual conference of the British Association of Social Workers in 1976 also implied criticism of this decision and ruled that one of the factors that social workers should consider before taking 'appropriate' action was that they 'should exercise a clear responsibility to act in the interests of children they were supervising which involved setting limits on behaviour, and the protection of children from exploitation'.[73] The Association 'denounced and rejected the silly assertion' that social workers were 'weirdies swayed by way-out ideas'. Indeed, the British Association of Social Workers had been among those who had called for an inquiry because of what it claimed was 'social work battering' and 'scapegoating'. Local Labour MPs also attempted to support the region's social workers, commenting upon their difficult work and heavy caseloads.[74] A defence of the social workers' position noted that they had few practical alternatives when dealing with children running away from care, particularly in the context of a shortage of residential accommodation.[75] Indeed, for social services the real issue was the problems caused by repeat absconders from care and the consequences of this for the children. The Assistant General Secretary for the British Association of Social Workers stated that it was:

> impossible – and undesirable – to monitor girls in care every minute of the day ... Many girls in care are sexually active, and in their own time it is likely they will make undesirable contacts. This could lead them to prostitute themselves for money. This situation will be true of children in the care of local authorities all over.[76]

The official inquiry did not place the blame on any individual social worker but concluded that social workers faced problems with regard to the lack of suitable homes, and adequate regional assessment places, for teenage girls as well as from the arbitrary decisions of some heads of homes about which children they would accept. The lack of trained social workers was also pointed out. This had become a particular problem following the large-scale reorganisation of social services in 1970. Those social workers who were qualified, and many were not, had usually specialised in a particular field. According to Olive Stevenson, they were not prepared for the generic social work that was now required of them and many 'clung to old roles and tasks'.[77] At the time, Packman suspected that the demand for generic social work might lead to a lowering of standards and that the creation of large departments would increase the distance, and possible sense of alienation, between managers and practitioners at field level.[78] Although it was not clear whether this was a specific problem in this case, a local newspaper did report that the inquiry had been critical of team decisions and found room for improvement in some procedures. Area directors, it was suggested, should be personally responsible for case reviews and also liaison between social workers, the police and school teachers should be improved.[79]

The inquiry recommendation which gained the most media attention, however, was that local authorities should provide special intensive-care units called 'safety suites' each comprising bedrooms, kitchens, bathrooms and accommodation for staff and in which girls would be locked for short periods. The recommendations of the inquiry were accepted by the county council's social services committee which also pointed out that work was already underway on two assessment centres in the area which were to have secure units. In fact, this recommendation and action was following upon the provision made for such secure units under Section 71 of the Children Act of 1975. By the 1 February 1978, 31 units were in use, 26 in England and Wales, and more were under construction.[80]

This case attracted extensive media attention because it raised wider political issues and not just because it highlighted the existence of child prostitution. As in the past, child prostitution was taken as an indictment of broader social problems, however, the particular social problems emphasised in media and political discussion were very much directed by the social, economic and political context of the period. Within a maturing Welfare State and the revival of a political camp opposed to state provision, child prostitution became used as a symbol of the deficiencies of left liberal attitudes and permissiveness that had blossomed during the 1960s. This was reflected in the development of a public and media receptive to, and willing to discuss, issues of sexuality, sexual abuse and sexual crime.

In 1967, the then Labour Government Cabinet expressed concerns about the repercussions of the increased openness about sexual activity, and also about drugs among young people. In the same year that Mick Jagger and Keith Richards were convicted of drug-taking (1967), and in which the *Observer* referred to the growth of a youthful 'culture of defiance and rejection' (2 July 1967), a survey was instigated by the Cabinet into the prevalence of drunkenness, drug-taking and prostitution among young people.[81] No specific age band was stipulated, however, some urban centres reported on local incidents occurring during 1967. In Manchester, two men had been prosecuted for procuring a 16 year-old girl and living off her earnings. In Bristol, from 1 January to 26 September 1967, there were 98 arrests at the central police station for prostitution, and 78 for possession of dangerous drugs and permitting premises to be used for smoking dangerous drugs. Of these figures, 24 persons were of the age of 17 or under and 96 were under the age of 21. According to the social services in Leeds, prostitution in young persons sometimes occurred 'in the case of young mentally sub-normal girls with personality disorders'.[82]

Concepts of delinquency and the structure of social services for children

The organisational changes occurring within social services at this time profoundly influenced not only the way in which social workers dealt with children in trouble but also the powers they were given to do this. The focus and methods of social services childcare policy was also to reflect upon the treatment of child prostitutes. The importance and priority accorded to children in trouble had been emphasised in the Ingleby Report (1960). This was, however, firmly linked to the child within the family and within their own homes. The report also re-emphasised the stance of the Children and Young Persons Act (1933) in making the connection between neglect and delinquency. The primary responsibility for the effective socialisation and care of children lay with the family. Thus prevention by intervening in the family was more explicitly asserted, carrying with it implications of discipline and legalism as well as welfare.

Hendrick has pointed out, 'Ingleby was the first of a series of documents reiterating the view that forms of moral and physical neglect were the antecedents of criminal delinquency'.[83] The emphasis was followed on, for example, in the Labour Party's *Crime: A Challenge to Us All* (1964), and in two important White Papers: *The Child, the Family, and the Young Offender* (1965) and in *Children in Trouble* (1968).[84] In the former White Paper it was asserted that 'much delinquency – and indeed many other social problems – can be traced back to inadequacy or breakdown in the family. The right place to begin, therefore, is with the family'.[85] However, the paper also maintained that 'there is no intention to deal lightly with young offenders quite the contrary. What is needed is firm discipline and constructive treatment directed to the welfare or rehabilitation of the individual or young person',[86] thus legitimating measures like the later introduction of secure units for children. *Children in Trouble* asserted that 'social control of harmful behaviour by the young, and social measures to help and protect the young, are not distinct and separate processes' but complementary ones.[87] Preventive social work, not just with the child in trouble but with the family as a whole, was advocated and then enabled by the Children and Young Persons Acts that were passed in 1963 and 1969. The welfare of the child was inextricably linked to that of the family, aside from institutional care little state provision was made for those children who had run away or who had been thrown out of their parental home. This was to be an area of expanding provision and care by children's voluntary societies, although, in fact, throughout the twentieth century the juvenile justice system had been dependent on voluntary sector accommodation for girls variously described as, for example, difficult, immoral or troublesome and even for those accused of criminal offences.[88]

Even though the 1969 Act was not implemented in its entirety due to the incoming Conservative Government of 1970 having more justice oriented priorities, new procedures were implemented which would reduce the numbers of children appearing in court. For example, in addition to an offence, it had to be shown that the child was 'in need of care or control which he is unlikely to receive [in his own home] unless the court makes an order under this section'.[89] The court was to be a place of last resort for the chronic delinquent and intervention, wherever possible, would be made by other agencies – the police, social workers or teachers. However, while other agencies, particularly the police, worked predominantly to keep children out of court, the role of social workers was to keep them out of trouble, hence the emphasis was often more upon control than upon care. The latter task, as has been shown, proved during this period to be the most open to public disagreement and difficulty.

The 1969 Act proved controversial in its shifting of power structures. At the centre of this was the care order, which replaced the previous approved school order and the fit persons order. This gave social workers the discretion to choose where young offenders would be sent. According to Hendrick (1994) and Packman (1975), this was seen by many magistrates as undermining the judiciary in favour of social workers and resulted in the increased use of Borstals, detention centres, remand centres and prison for young offenders; sentences given directly by the courts. 'The former alleged that the latter ignored their intentions in making care orders by removing any punitive aspects of the order and returning the child to its own home rather than to, say, a community home'.[90] Difficulties in this respect were exacerbated by government failure to provide a sufficient number of alternative forms of residential accommodation to Borstal and remand centres. As Hendrick notes, where appropriate, custodial measures were used more frequently, making them far from the last resort envisaged by 1960s reformers.[91]

In the context of the extended role that local authority social work was taking in the family, the nature of social work itself was being debated around this time. Within the childcare service there were increasing calls for greater co-ordination between different departments with the general aim of marshalling resources to forestall delinquency by every means available. Research during the 1960s was beginning to reveal that, in urban areas at least, a high proportion of young delinquents were not from broken homes. Also some researchers were disputing the orthodoxy that the family was necessarily the best location for childcare. As was noted in 1968 in a study on female juvenile delinquency, 'The belief, widely held as an article of faith, that it is prejudicial to the child to remove it from its natural home, even when that home is a bad one, and from its natural mother, even when she is neglectful, has come under severe criticism'.[92] This questioned the prior emphasis upon family-centred care, which had been most evident in the tendency of social workers to pass the 'straightforward' cases, exhibiting no family problems, back to the police for action.[93]

The idea of a new family service also appeared in evidence to the Ingleby Committee and the Labour Party's *Crime: A Challenge to Us All* (1964) and was re-iterated in the White Paper *The Child, the Family and the Young Offender* (1965). This latter report announced the intention to set up an independent committee to review the organisation and responsibilities of the local authority personal social services and consider what changes were required to ensure an effective family service.[94] A few months later the Seebohm Committee was appointed to suggest changes desirable to bringing about a 'family service' and in its report of July 1968 recommended the establishment of a new local authority Social Services Department which, though 'family oriented', was to be 'community based'. The community was to include the many isolated people living outside of families and who were in need of help. Social service departments would include responsibility for children's departments and services, mental health social work services, welfare services for the elderly, handicapped and homeless.[95] However, far from actively intervening to help those children on the social margins, the establishment of social services departments, according to Hendrick, kept the family partly in focus but resulted in the child being 'virtually subsumed'.[96] In practice these recommendations, which were incorporated in the Local Authority Social Services Act 1970 (in effect April 1971), signalled the disbanding of a specific childcare service, with little or no objections from the professions involved, and brought about the hesitant beginnings of generic social work practice.

The reorganisation created a much more complex and bureaucratic structure and gradually disquiet grew regarding a perceived decline in the quality of childcare within the Welfare State. This was particularly highlighted in the political rationale of the emerging New Right, although unease was also expressed by many public and voluntary organisation. This New Right ideology criticised the very foundations of the Welfare State and claimed that it resulted in wasted resources and higher taxation. Liberal social workers were accused of encouraging soft attitudes towards deviance and irresponsible behaviour as well as welfare dependency. As Parton has observed:

The establishment of social work and social service departments could thus be seen as the most recent and obvious manifestations of the post-war social democratic welfare state and its adjunct the 'rehabilitative ideal', just at the time when such developments were being subjected to growing social and critical scrutiny which were focused in the rise of the New Right.[97]

In October 1972, the Conservative Secretary of State for the Social Services, Sir Keith Joseph, asserted that 'despite all that has been done to improve and extend the social services since the war, the country now faces an unprecedented explosion of identified need'.[98] In this article, Keith Joseph maintained the importance of child welfare within his analysis of inter-generationally transmitted social problems, or the 'cycle of deprivation', and his belief in a social service which would target such need more effectively.[99] This was an argument he repeated several times between 1972 and 1974, and, as Macnicol has suggested, was a variant on long-standing underclass debates in which the deprivation and inadequacies of one generation are, without adequate intervention, passed on to the next generation as a function of intergenerational socialisation.[100] Thus, Parton argues, the abuse of children within the family was perceived as a characteristic of 'an underlyng pathology'.[101] Despite criticism of this underclass type of analysis and the gradual unfolding of the inadequacies of the 'cycle of deprivation' approach in subsequent research, the concept had considerable impact upon social thinking of the time.[102] Such questioning of the role and responsibilities of the Welfare State reached into the fundamental rationale of child welfare provision since the Second World War and increasingly exposed the new social work professions to public and parliamentary obloquy.

The cycle of deprivation thesis was resorted to as providing an explanation why, despite the relative economic prosperity and significantly expanded welfare services of the 1950s and 1960s, severe social problems persisted. Issues of child abuse and child prostitution received such attention at the time in part because concentration upon morality, upon behaviour and values, could divert attention from the social, economic and political causes of deprivation.[103] An editorial regarding the girl prostitution case in the *Daily Telegraph* in 1976 nicely illustrates this stance:

> The fashionable notion that more expenditure is the only way to improve social services took a hard knock last week from those extraordinary stories of young girls who were alleged to have been allowed to work as prostitutes while in the care of council social workers. What is needed in such cases, clearly, is not more money but more sense – and better values. To dismiss such episodes as 'errors of judgement' is wholly inadequate. No social service with the right values could possibly perpetuate such a travesty of welfare.[104]

Statements by Dr Rhodes Boyson, Conservative MP for North Brent, reiterated such moral assertions. When the case first appeared in the headlines he demanded an immediate ministerial inquiry into the case maintaining that:

> Too many people in charge of the morals of our young have been brainwashed by mindless sociologists. They give no guidance, no standards, no discipline ... We need more policemen and fewer social workers. Social workers are becoming part of the trouble with Britain. If this is an example of what they do we need to get back towards the Victorian days of discipline.[105]

Christopher Jenks has remarked that such debates are actually referring to three distinct kinds of underclass: an economic one related to unemployment; a moral one relating to those displaying deviant behaviour and an educational one referring to those lacking cultural and social skills.[106] These three kinds of underclass are, of course, often interrelated in discussions on the subjects of, for example, poverty, promiscuity, delinquency and crime, and unemployment. The linkages made in this respect were evident in the newspaper reporting of the girl prostitution case. Also evident was the concentration upon the individual in representations of how and why girls became involved in commercial sex; through coercion by an older man or through peer pressure and pleasure-seeking. Both of these kinds of accounts tended also to refer to background factors such as family dislocation but not to the extent evident in the use of the more 1990s and less pejorative term social exclusion, which focuses upon processes and structures as opposed to individuals.[107]

In the light of the political contention of the 1970s, disagreement regarding the role and appropriate methods of social workers left the profession vulnerable to attack in instances where they appeared to have failed their clients. As Parton has suggested, concerns about child abuse have been 'inextricably interrelated with debates about the nature and direction of social work and the accountability of social workers'.[108] Chris Andrews, then Secretary of the British Association of Social Workers, affirmed this point at the time. He stated that if:

> society is seeking a scapegoat, the vulnerable position of the social worker has been all too apparent ... social work itself has at times appeared to be on trial. Basic assumptions have been questioned, as has the legal and judicial framework in which much social work is practised.[109]

David Walker, a social science correspondent for the *Times Higher Education Supplement*, noted the nature of the media treatment of social workers. In an examination of stories referring to social work in one week of the main national dailies he commented that in some papers 'allegations of negligence got the big headline treatment, contributing to a real feeling of persecution'.[110] When the news broke with regard to the case of girls involved in prostitution while in local authority care, it almost immediately became the centre of conflict and was referred to as causing a 'political storm'.[111] Indeed, a local MP observed that 'some people are genuinely concerned that wrong decisions may have been taken by social workers … over girls in their charge who have engaged in prostitution. Others, including MPs have simply used recent cases as an excuse to express their prejudices and attack social workers generally'.[112] At its broadest the disagreements and criticisms which followed debated the role of the state in dealing with some of the most profound and long-standing of the country's social problems.

Conclusions

There is little doubt that the political controversy surrounding the case of under-age girls in care involved in prostitution resulted in greater media attention being afforded the subject. The evidence that several children may have been selling their bodies while in care, with or without the knowledge of social workers, placed the unpleasant likelihood that many other children were doing the same indisputably under the noses of the public. Such evidence of child prostitution was much less open to being interpreted as extraordinary or rare occurrences and indeed statements in the press from social work spokespersons muted the possibility that it may have been systemic.

Much less media and political attention was given to other individual cases of child prostitution that came to light as a result of appearances in the courts. For instance, the case revealed in 1970 of a brothel in Brixton being staffed and worked entirely by children,[113] or a case in Birmingham in 1979 in which a couple were prosecuted in connection with the prostitution of an eleven year-old girl.[114] Nor did the experiences of 'Christina' as a child prostitute, later recorded in *Criminal Women* (1985), come to light as a cause for wider concern outside of the police, by whom she was apprehended, or the child care system to which she was returned on more than one occasion.[115] The media attention given to particular child prostitution cases in the mid-1970s signalled only the beginning of the uncovering of this social problem in twentieth-century Britain. In the United States, however, research on youth prostitution and also public concern had been increasing since the late 1960s. In 1979, Brown noted, for example, that 43 per cent of the runaways going to New York were between the ages of 11 and 14, and that the average runaway has enough money for three days.[116] In one disastrous case, a girl who had run away to New York had by the age of 13 become 'a mainlining hooker, working for the street pimps'.[117] It was not until the late 1990s that central government in Britain was to begin to contend with entrenched structural and attitudinal obstacles within the child care and criminal justice systems.

Newspaper coverage of the two main incidents of under-age prostitution referred to in this chapter tended to present this phenomenon in particular ways, both of which heavily focused upon the involvement of girls rather than boys. The first was that young girls were manipulated and coerced into prostitution by an older man who then lived off her earnings. The other was that girls entered prostitution through peer pressure and the desire for money to pay for a way of life that she would otherwise be unable to afford. The former left no space for a understanding of why girls might be unwilling to prosecute those who prostituted them and the latter continued to associate participation with blame in this form of abuse.

The cases involving children in care also made explicit the link between absconders from residential homes and/or family homes, homelessness and child prostitution and were more open to being interpreted as systematic in this respect. The longer-term effects of New Right individualism, which became increasingly vocal throughout the 1970s and which entered the political mainstream at the end of the decade, were to be seen in the increasing numbers of socially excluded in the 1980s. During the 1980s and 1990s, changes to welfare benefits for the young, in the context of increases in single parenthood, divorce and reconstituted families, have exacerbated the precarious social and economic position of those children who experience severe problems within their families and/or who run away from home and/or care. One consequence of this has been an increased resort to informal economic activity, such as begging, drug dealing and prostitution. This is dealt with extensively in the following chapter on child prostitution during the 1980s and 1990s.

References

1 Assistant Secretary of the British Association of Social Workers, *Daily Mail* 21 April 1976.

2 L.A. Hall, *Sex, Gender and Social Change in Britain since 1880* (London: Macmillan, 2000), p. 172.

3 Cited in J. Lewis, 'The boundaries between marriage, non-marriage and parenthood: changes in behaviour and policy in postwar Britain', *Journal of Family History* 21 (3) 1996, p. 375.

4 L. Stanley, *Sex Surveyed 1949–1994: From Mass-Observation's 'Little Kinsey' to the National Survey and the Hite Reports* (London: Taylor and Francis, 1995), p. 48.

5 12 February, p.12.col.a.

6 *Sunday Times* 12 February 1978, p.12.col.a.

7 *Sunday Times* 12 February 1978, p.12, col.a; Report of the After-Care Association 4/BVA/A/1–11; N. Swingler, *New Society* 16 January 1969.

8 *Shield* November 1964, p.p. 15–6 italics as in original.

9 Ibid.

10 *Sunday Times* 12 February, p.12, col.a.

11 *Hansard* vol.923, col.137–8, vol.990, col.14405, 320 and 421, vol.919, col.219.

12 F. Campbell, 'Journalistic construction of the news: information gathering', *New Library World* 98 (1133), 1997, pp. 60–1; also see S. Cohen, *Folk Devils and Moral Panics: The Creation of the Mods and Rockers* (London: MacGibbon and Kee, 1972).

13 N. Parton, *The Politics of Child Abuse* (London: David and Charles, 1985), p. 86.

14 Ibid, pp. 86–7.

15 P. Skidmore, 'Telling tales: media power, ideology and the reporting of child sexual abuse in Britain', in D.Kidd-Hewitt and R.Osbourne (eds) *Crime and the Media: The Post-Modern Spectacle* (London: Pluto Press, 1995).

16 K. Soothill and S. Walby, *Sex Crimes in the News* (London: Routledge, 1991), p.18.

17 Ibid, p. 18; S. Walby, A. Hay and K. Soothill, 'The social construction of rape', *Theory, Culture and Society* 2 (1) 1983.

18 K. Soothill and S. Walby, *Sex Crimes in the News*, p. 156.

19 Ibid, p.82.

20 See for example, J. Kitzinger, 'Who are you kidding? Children, power and the struggle against sexual abuse', in A. James and A. Prout (eds) *Constructing and Reconstructing Childhood*, 2nd ed, (London: Falmer Press, 1997) on child abuse and innocence.

21 See Chapter 8 of this publication, M. Melrose, D. Barrett and I. Brodie, *One Way Street* and also S.M. Edwards, 'Abused and exploited – Young girls in prostitution', *Whose Daughter Next?* (Barnardo's, 1998).

22 A. James and A. Prout (eds) *Constructing and Reconstructing Childhood*, 2nd ed (London: Falmer Press, 1997), ch.1.

23 R. Lloyd, *Playland: A Study of Boy Prostitution* (London: Blond and Briggs, 1977), p. 12.

24 Ibid.

25 Ibid, p. 204.

26 *Times* 20 September 1975, p.2.col.e.

27 *Times* 21 June 1975, p.2.col.c and 20 September 1975, p.2.col.e.
28 R. Lloyd, *Playland*, pp. 202–3.
29 *Times* 26 September 1976, p.5, col.b.
30 *EPE* 1 April 1976.
31 *Daily Mail* 2 April 1976, p.1.
32 *Times* 2 April 1976, p.4.col.e; *Daily Mail* 2 April 1976, p.1.
33 *EPE* 1 April 1976.
34 12 February 1978, p.12.col.a.
35 *Shield* November 1970, p. 14.
36 *Daily Mail* 21 April 1976, p.1 and 22 April 1976, p.1.
37 *LN* 1 April 1976.
38 *Times* 6 April 1976, p.5.col.f.
39 3 April 1976, p.3.
40 *EPE* 2 April 1976.
41 *Times* 21 April 1976, p.4, col.g.
42 *Times* 7 September 1976, p.4.col.f.
43 12 February 1978, p.12.col.a.
44 *Sunday Times* 12 February 1978, p.12.col.a.
45 *Report on the Work of the Children's Department 1964–66*, PP, 1967 (Cmd.603) XXIV, p32.
46 For example, J. Cowie, V. Cowie and E. Slater, *Delinquency in Girls* (London: Heinemann, 1968); P. Epps, 'A preliminary study of 300 female delinquents undergoing Borstal training', *British Journal of Criminology* 4, 1951; M. May, M. Dawkins and M. Kratz, 'Comments on special problems of delinquent and maladjusted girls', *British Journal of Criminology* 11 (3) 1964; A. Walker, 'Special problems of delinquent and maladjusted girls', *British Journal of Criminology* 11 (2), 1963.
47 *Howard Journal* 3 (2).
48 P. Carlen *et al*, *Criminal Women* (Cambridge: Polity Press, 1985), introduction.
49 Ibid, p. 6.
50 J. Cowie, V. Cowie and E. Slater, *Delinquency in Girls*, introduction.
51 Ibid, pp. 166–7.
52 H. M. Ruitenbeek, 'Men alone: The male homosexual and the disintegrated family', in H. M. Ruitenbeek (ed.) *The Problem of Homosexuality in Modern Society* (New York: E. P. Dutton and Co, 1963), p. 93.
53 Ibid, p. 93.
54 M. Craft, 'Boy prostitutes and their fate', *British Journal of Psychiatry* 112, 1966, p. 1111.
55 Ibid.
56 Ibid, pp.1112 and 1113.
57 Ibid, p. 1113.
58 For example, S. Raven, 'Boys will be boys: the male prostitute in London' and A. J. Reiss Jr, 'The social integration of queers and peers' both in H. M. Ruitenbeek (ed.) *The Problem of Homosexuality*.
59 *Shield* November 1970, p. 5.
60 *People* 26 October 1969, p.19.

61 Ibid.

62 *Times* 20 September 1975, p.2.col.e.

63 *EPE* 2 April 1976.

64 Ibid.

65 *LN* 1 April 1976.

66 H. Hendrick, *Child Welfare: England 1872–1989* (London: Routledge, 1994), p. 248.

67 D. Walker, 'Are social workers badly treated by the newspapers?' *Social Work Today* 7 (9) 5 August 1976, p. 292.

68 'It was more difficult than we thought: a reflection on 50 years of child welfare practice', *Child and Family Social Work* 3, 1998, p. 159.

69 H. Hendrick, *Child Welfare*, p. 253.

70 13 April 1976, p.4, col.b.

71 *Times* 2 April 1976, p.4, col.e.

72 *Daily Telegraph* 3 April 1976, p.4, col.e.

73 *EPE* 5 April 1976.

74 *LN* 1 and 8 April 1976; *EPE* 2 April 1976.

75 *Times* 2 April 1976, p.4, col.e; see J. Packman, *The Child's Generation: Child Care Policy from Curtis to Houghton* (London: Basil Blackwell, 1975), p. 125 concerning shortages of accommodation.

76 *Sunday Times* 4 April 1976, p.3, col.h.

77 'It was more difficult than we thought', p. 158.

78 J. Packman, *The Child's Generation*, pp. 159 and 173.

79 *LN* 30 September 1976; *Times* 29 September 1976, p.5, col.a.

80 *Hansard* 16 February 1978, vol.944, col.351–2; also see E. Younghusband, *Social Work in Britain: 1950–1975, Vol.1* (London: George Allen and Unwin), pp. 58–9.

81 PRO CAB 153/99.

82 PRO CAB 153/99.

83 H. Hendrick, *Child Welfare*, p. 225.

84 Ibid, p. 225.

85 PP, 1965 (Cmnd.2742) XXIX, p. 3.

86 Ibid, p. 12.

87 PP 1967–8 (Cmd.3601) XXXIX, p. 4.

88 P. Cox, 'Rescue and reform: girls, delinquency and industrial schools, 1908–1933', Ph.D Cambridge University 1996, p. 41.

89 Cited in H. Hendrick, *Child Welfare*, p. 232; also see E. Younghusband, *Social Work in Britain*.

90 Ibid, p. 234.

91 Ibid.

92 J. Cowie, V. Cowie and E. Slater, *Delinquency in Girls*, p. 37.

93 J. Packman, *The Child's Generation*, p. 127; M. J. Power *et al*, 'Delinquency and the Family', *British Journal of Social Work*, 1974.

94 PP, 1965 (Cmnd.2742) XXIX, p.4.

95 J. Packman, *The Child's Generation*, p. 161.

96 H. Hendrick, *Child Welfare*, p. 236.

97 N. Parton, *The Politics of Child Abuse* (London: Macmillan, 1985), p. 83–4.
98 *New Society*, 'The next ten years', p.8.
99 Ibid, p. 9.
100 J. Macnicol, 'In Pursuit of the Underclass', *Journal of Social Policy* 16 (3), p. 293–318.
101 N. Parton, *Politics of Child Abuse*, p. 4.
102 J. Macnicol, 'In Pursuit of the Underclass', pp. 294–6.
103 D. Walker, 'Are social workers badly treated by the newspapers?', p. 292.
104 4 April, p.3.
105 *Daily Mail* 21 April 1976, p.1.
106 Cited in Lister, 1999, p. 3.
107 Ibid, p. 11.
108 N. Parton, *Politics of Child Abuse*, p. 78.
109 *Social Work Today* 4 (12) 1974, p. 637.
110 D. Walker, 'Are social workers badly treated by the newspapers?', p. 292.
111 *EPE* 2 April 1976; *Daily Telegraph* 3 April 1976, p.3.
112 *LN* 8 April 1976.
113 *Times* 21 November 1970, p.2, col.d; 9 October 1971, p.2, col.d.
114 *Times* 11 December 1979, p.2, col.d; *Birmingham Post* 11 December 1979, p.3.
115 P. Carlen *et al*, *Criminal Women*, pp. 60–77.
116 M. E. Brown, 'Teenage prostitution', *Adolescence* 14, 1979, p. 674.
117 K. Wooden cited in M. E. Brown, 'Teenage prostitution', p. 675.

Chapter 8

Child prostitution in the 1980s and 1990s

During the 1980s and 1990s, as a result of increasing globalisation and internationalisation of capital,[1] child prostitution has become an issue of growing concern in many parts of the world.[2] Here, however, we confine the scope of our discussion to the situation in Britain during this period and explore the socio-economic and policy context in which child prostitution occurs, the extent of child prostitution and legal and public service responses to child prostitution. We will draw on evidence from an empirical, retrospective, study of child prostitution, in which one of the authors has recently been involved, and which relied on in-depth interviews with 50 people, from six geographical regions, all of whom had become involved in prostitution as juveniles.[3]

The socio-economic and policy context of child prostitution

In Britain during the 1980s and 1990s increased globalisation, and the welfare retrenchment which followed as its 'logical policy and ideological adjunct',[4] have resulted in levels of poverty and inequality which have been unprecedented in the post-war period.[5] Globalisation (or postmodernity) is characterised by a 'central tension' between 'the cult of the self' and 'new or merely persisting forms of structural exclusion',[6] and in the 1980s income inequality in Britain rose faster than in any other industrialised nation except New Zealand.[7]

In the historical conjuncture of late capitalism there are 'winners' and 'losers' and many people now argue that it is young people who are the 'postmodern losers'.[8] While changes to welfare policies (for example, social security, housing and education) have effectively renegotiated the basis of the social rights of citizenship for everyone[9] there is evidence that young people are now 'significantly structurally disadvantaged' as they attempt to become 'defamiliarised' and make the transition to adulthood.[10]

The removal of rights to welfare benefits for the majority of 16 and 17 year-olds, the introduction of lower benefit levels for those aged under 25, the introduction of youth training schemes and benefit penalties for those who abandon, or refuse, such schemes, changes to arrangements for hostel payments and the introduction of age related housing benefits with reduced rates for single young people under the age of 25[11] means that young people's entitlement to welfare benefits is now primarily determined by age rather than need or financial commitments.[12] As a result there has developed what Carlen[13] has described as 'an asymmetry of citizenship' in relation to young people – whereby the state requires them to fulfil their obligations as 'full', adult, citizens but fails in its duty to care for them as such. This asymmetry means that for a minority of young people unemployment, poverty and homelessness have become 'tragically linked as their rights to independent income and housing benefits have been lost'.[14]

During the 1980s and 1990s young people have experienced twice the average rate of unemployment and those who do work are five times more likely than adult employees to be paid below half of male average earnings. In 1997 three-quarters of 16 and 17 year-olds who were unemployed were without an income.[15] The 1980s and 1990s have also witnessed rising levels of homelessness amongst young people.[16]

During the 1980s, 'citizenship' has been officially disarticulated from the values of post-war 'welfarism' and rearticulated to 'new social values of popular capitalism and individualism'.[17] In relation to young people this has meant transferring responsibility, where possible, from the state to the family.[18] The increased dependency of young people on their families has been brought about in the same period as family structures themselves have become more 'brittle', for example, the growth of single parenthood, divorce and reconstituted families.[19] Coinciding with these processes has been a reduction in the ability of statutory social services to respond effectively to the needs of young people who experience difficulties in their families as a result of procedural complexity and under-resourcing[20] and it has been argued that for young people who are in conflict with their families it is now virtually impossible for them to live independently of their families.[21]

Given the labour market conditions and the reduced social rights with which young people are confronted it is perhaps not surprising that increasing numbers of them appear to be turning to 'informal' or 'street level' forms of economic activity, ranging from working informally, begging, drug dealing and/or prostitution, in order to subsist.[22]

During the 1990s in particular a number of important research studies have established that entry into prostitution is inextricably linked to poverty, sexual abuse, going missing from home and/or care and to educational disaffection.[23] In a recent study one of the current authors found that almost three-quarters of those interviewed had become involved in prostitution as a result of economic deprivation (that is, prostitution had been adopted as a 'survival strategy' or as a means of securing incomes which they would otherwise have been unable to command). The same proportion had experienced conflict or abuse in their families and almost half reported that their first sexual experience had taken place in the context of abuse. Approximately half of those interviewed had experiences of being 'looked after' at some time in their lives and of these over half had histories of going missing. A larger proportion had histories of going missing from home while a fifth had histories of going missing from home and care. Almost three-quarters had interrupted or prematurely terminated educational careers with many reporting that they had 'just stopped going' to school when they were as young as 12 or 13.[24]

The evidence suggests therefore that such young people have already been excluded or excluded themselves from 'other lifestyle sectors' (school, work, family)[25] and as a result of these exclusions tend to live 'an itinerant lifestyle in the spaces between family and state'.[26] In such spaces (on the street) some young people appear to find 'a level of ontological security and trust' which compensates for the anxieties, uncertainties and insecurities of being young 'on the margins of civil society'.[27] In the recent study in which one of the current authors was involved, for example, many young people reported that it was financial hardship combined with their fear of social isolation beyond the world of prostitution which served to keep them involved.[28]

Scale of child prostitution in the 1980s and 1990s

There are of course many difficulties with attempts to estimate the numbers of children and young people involved in prostitution[29] primarily because such young people constitute a 'hidden' population[30] and there are many specific methodological and ethical problems involved in researching this field.[31] Further, estimates of the scale of the problem may be advanced by those concerned to promote 'moral, political and policy claims in contentious areas'[32] and differences in definitions of what constitutes 'prostitution' may be reflected in different estimates of prevalence.[33]

The law in relation to prostitution is discriminatory in that, for example, in 1994 the High Court ruled that *only women* can be charged with loitering under the Street Offences Act 1959',[34] therefore only women can be charged with offences which constitute 'prostitution'. Young men and boys are more likely to be charged, under the Sexual Offences Act 1956, with offences such as 'obstructing the public highway'.[35] Official statistics reveal that in 1995 three boys aged between 10 and 17 were cautioned and four convicted of such offences compared to 263 cautions and 101 convictions for girls of the same age.[36] This legal discrimination means that official statistics are unable to provide us with an accurate picture of the scale of young men's involvement in prostitution. When examining official statistics it is important to bear in mind that they reflect the policies and priorities of local police forces as much as the behaviour they purport to measure[37] and that the relative mobility of the population involved in prostitution[38] might give us some grounds for doubting their reliability. Further, official statistics notoriously underestimate the extent of deviant activities of any given population.[39]

Although estimates of prevalence of young people's involvement in prostitution are disputed[40] and the evidence fragmentary, being based primarily on voluntary sector agencies and small scale research projects,[41] it has been suggested that in Britain up to 5,000 young people may be involved at any one time[42] and that the ratio of girls to boys is four to one.[43]

Although these figures are alarming in fact they compare quite favourably with estimates from other countries, for example, in Asia 650,000 children work as prostitutes,[44] it is thought that 300,000 young people are involved in prostitution in the USA and 200,000 in Thailand while in Paris it is estimated that 5,000 young men and 3,000 young women under the age of 18 are involved in prostitution. Globally it is estimated that over a million children enter the sex trade each year[45] and the role of 'sex tourism' as an aspect of globalisation should not be overlooked.[46]

Despite the paucity of available national or international statistics the consensus suggests that increasing numbers of young people, faced with poverty and social exclusion, in the east and the west, in the 'First World' and the 'Third World', are turning to prostitution as a means of subsistence.[47] Indeed, in the British study on which we are drawing here, a majority of participants had the impression that more and more young people were becoming involved compared to when they had first become involved themselves.[48] Although almost half had become involved in prostitution when they 14 or younger and almost two-thirds when they were 16 or younger, their perceptions tended to be that there were very few other young people involved at the time when they had first become involved in prostitution.[49]

Our participants commented that not only were there more young people involved today but also that the ages at which they were becoming involved appeared to be getting younger. For some this was an issue of concern (many of the older women thought that young girls should 'just not need to be there' while for others it was a matter of annoyance – they were aware of the premium on youth in the sex trade and commented quite matter-of-factly that 'young girls' were always able to 'make a lot of money because punters like fresh meat and they always go for a new face'. We spoke to a young man of 20 who had been involved in prostitution since he was 13. He had noticed that, 'As you get older you seem to get less and less' and told us that when he was 13, 14 and 15 he had earned more than since he was 16.[50]

Our suspicions that more young people are becoming involved at younger ages were borne out for us by the fact that an overwhelming majority of our participants told us they had become involved in prostitution as a result of the peer group networks in which they were involved. This mechanism of entry into prostitution was cited more frequently by our younger participants (under 25) than our older participants. Thirteen interviewees told us they had become involved in-dependently and just ten reported that another had forced them into prostitution.[51] It would seem therefore that the character of child prostitution itself may be changing at the end of the twentieth century and that the role of the 'pimp' is now perhaps less important[52] than previous studies have suggested.[53] We were told more than once by agency workers and older women working in prostitution that 'the drug is the pimp these days'.

Legal and social service responses to young people involved in prostitution

It has been noted elsewhere that social service responses to young people involved in prostitution have in the past often left much to be desired as a result of a combination of competing paradigms through which child prostitution is defined[54] and because 'few childcare workers have experience of developing an understanding of the behaviour of young people involved in prostitution'.[55] In practice, as in research, this area of work probably carries the potential of 'stigma contagion'[56] and may well be one which practitioners would choose to avoid.

As the result of a 'tendency', perhaps, to prefer the 'criminal justice'/ 'villain' model social services departments have often failed to provide young people involved in prostitution with the care and protection they so obviously require and, instead of initiating child protection procedures, have been content for the police to process such vulnerable young people through the criminal justice system[57] despite the fact that legally many are not old enough to consent to sex.

This situation can be partially explained by the failure, in the Street Offences Act 1959, to distinguish the ages at which young women may be charged with offences of 'loitering and soliciting'. Because of this failure it has been, absurdly, possible for young women who cannot legally consent to sex to be prosecuted for attempting to sell it.[58] An additional factor which explains the failure of social care and control agencies to respond to these young people as 'victims of abuse' or 'children in need' is the legacy of the Wolfenden Committee's report (1957) which essentially defined prostitution as a private agreement between the prostitute and her client.[59] The effect of the Wolfenden Report and the legislation which followed it was to treat prostitution as a legitimate object of state intervention only when it affronted 'public decency' and not when those involved in it were damaged or degraded by their involvement.[60]

Another problem has been that young people involved in prostitution may 'defend her man to the hilt' and in these circumstances 'social workers don't always see it [prostitution] as abuse', on the other hand, these young people are not usually 'nice, polite children. They tend to be scruffy and have attitude problems'[61] and in the eyes of care and control agencies may therefore be held to blame for the circumstances in which they find themselves.

Despite the weight of evidence which suggests that some young people are pushed into prostitution as a result of past negative experiences and reduced circumstances[62] and that other, equally desperate and vulnerable young people, are pulled by the perceived positive outcomes their involvement may bring (financial gain, a sense of power over the punters, a sense of belonging)[63] social care and control agencies appear previously to have adopted the view that young people 'freely' choose to be involved in prostitution. Social control agencies appear to have been content to punish them for their 'choice' while social care agencies seem to have been more concerned with controlling 'troublesome' children than caring for and protecting them.

Happily, as a result, primarily, of pressure exerted by agencies in the voluntary sector, this situation looks to be improving. The New Labour government has recently issued guidance in relation to the treatment and management of child and juvenile prostitution.[64] The fact that, at last, the government of the day has 'heard' that there is a 'problem' and has responded to the news is some advance in itself! We have moved from a position of denial by government at the beginning of the 1980s to acknowledgement and positive response by the turn of the century.

The guidance recommends, for the first time, that the 'primary law enforcement effort must be against abusers' and suggests that 'where children are already involved in prostitution, the emphasis must to be to protect them from further abuse and to support them out of prostitution' (Section 2.5). The guidance acknowledges that the involvement of children in prostitution is 'indicative of coercion or desperation rather than choice' (Section 2.1) and goes on to assert that ' the vast majority of children do not voluntarily enter prostitution: they are coerced, enticed or are utterly desperate. It is not a free economic or moral choice' (Section 4.2). However, the same guidance also allows for the provisions of the Street Offences Act 1959 s.1. to be applied, in some circumstances, to girls over the age of 10 and the provisions of the Sexual Offences Act 1956 s.36 to be applied to boys of the same age (Section 3.9).

The guidance describes men who pay for sex with children or juveniles as 'child abusers who are breaking the law' (Section 4.5). What it does not do is clearly define these young people as *victims of abuse* – which they so often are even prior to their abuse through prostitution. Instead it is recommended that they be treated as 'children in need' (Children Act 1989 section 17), 'who may be suffering, or may be likely to suffer, significant harm' (Children Act section 47). Under the terms of the Children Act the local authority then has the power to remove the young person to 'a place of safety' or insist that they remain in one.[65]

The guidance recommends that statutory and voluntary agencies such as the police, social services, education services and youth services work together 'to safeguard and promote the welfare of the child' (Section 3.1). Such an approach was adopted in police pilot studies in Wolverhampton and Nottinghamshire and it was found that not only was the problem in these areas more extensive than had previously been imagined but also that more young people came forward to seek help and were able to be diverted successfully from prostitution.[66] The guidance also acknow-ledges that such young people may 'be fearful of being involved with the police or social services' (Section 5.13) and suggests that greater success may be achieved by using outreach workers and non-statutory agencies. It notes that: 'Area Child Protection Committees (ACPCs) should have in place a local protocol on responding to children about whom there are concerns that they are involved in prostitution' (Section 5.1) and that these protocols should 'clarify the circumstances in which it would be appropriate for non-statutory agencies to engage with a child before involving other statutory agencies' (Section 5.14).

The guidance acknowledges that diversion from prostitution is not a simple process and allows that 'there may be occasions, after all attempts at diversion out of prostitution have failed, when it may be appropriate for those who voluntarily continue in prostitution to enter the criminal justice system in the way that other young offenders do' (Section 2.5). The use of criminal powers against these young people is, however, hedged about with safeguards. It is suggested that 'the initial presumption should always be that a boy or girl is not soliciting voluntarily' and that 'there must be a thorough investigation of all aspects of a case to ensure that there is no evidence of an abusive relationship that could involve physical, mental or emotional coercion'. There must also be 'a shared conviction of those involved in the inter-agency discussion that an individual's return to prostitution is genuinely of their own volition'.

We are, then, left with a legislative framework, which remains highly unsatisfactory (even if improved), and in which there is still space in which contradictions and confusions may occur.[67] It is suggested on the one hand that for care and control agencies working with these young people 'the emphasis must to be to protect them from further abuse and to support them out of prostitution' (Section 2.5), while, on the other, if attempts at diversion have failed 'over a period of time' (unspecified) 'and a judgement is made that it will not prove effective in the foreseeable future' (Section 6.21) they may be processed through the criminal justice system. The authors contend that punishment should not be seen as the only alternative to care and protection and would suggest that it is precisely those who are most 'in need' and most 'at risk' who are most likely to return to prostitution and place themselves in situations where they will suffer further abuse.[68] Although they may 'persistently' return to prostitution, the evidence presented above suggests that this cannot be understood as 'voluntary' in the conventional use of the term.[69] Further, logic would seem to suggest that the more 'persistent' the child is, the more 'at risk of significant harm' the child becomes.

Conclusions

We have seen in this chapter that during the 1990s more young people appear to be becoming involved in prostitution at younger ages and that the debate about child prostitution has been moved forward: at least the existence of the problem has been formally acknowledged. Despite its contradictions the new guidance offered by the government provides some hope that things will improve for young people involved in prostitution and if local agencies can work co-operatively in the interests of the welfare of the child this will undoubtedly make a real difference to the lives of such young people.[70]

However, if, as we suggest at the beginning of this chapter, macro-economic forces are partly responsible for propelling young people into prostitution and trapping them there once they have become involved then in the long term it is only by tackling these forces that we may work towards preventing other young people from becoming involved in prostitution.[71] It is by tackling the causes of poverty rather than its symptoms that we will begin to effect significant differences in terms of the long-terms prospects for children and young people involved in prostitution. What is obviously needed is a micro-social multi-agency approach that adapts to particular local environments and conditions in conjunction with a macro-level approach that will tackle the relative poverty of these young people and the families and communities from which they come.

References

1 B. Jordan, *A Theory of Poverty and Social Exclusion* (Cambridge: Polity, 1996); I. Robinson, 'Globilization: Nine thesis on our epoch', *Race and Class* 38 (2), 1996; A. Sivanandan, 'New circuits of imperialism', in A. Sivanandan (ed.) *Communities of Resistance* (London: Verso, 1990).

2 See for example J. Green, *It's No Game: Responding to the Needs of Young Women at Risk or Involved in Prostitution* (Leicester: National Youth Agency, 1992); R. Barbaret, D. Barrett and M. O'Neill, 'Young people and prostitution: No respecter of boundaries in North Western Europe'. *Social Work in Europe* 2 (2), 1995; S. Kershaw, 'Sex for sale: A profile of young male sex workers' circumstances, choices and risks', *Youth and Policy* 63, 1999; O'Connell-Davidson, 'Sex Tourism in Cuba', *Race and Class* 38 (1), 1996; O. Calcetas-Santos, *Report of the special rapporteur on the sale of children, child prostitution and child pornography*, European Commission of Human Rights 53rd. session, Item 21 (b). 1997; S. Sidorenko-Stephenson, 'Moscow street children and emerging urban marginality', paper presented to panel on Youth and Cultural Globilization in post-Soviet Russia, BASEES Conference, Fitzwilliam College, Cambridge, 27–29 March 1999; M. Melrose and D. Barrett, 'Report on a study of juvenile prostitution', paper presented at National Vice Conference, Portishead 29–30 June 1999.

3 M. Melrose *et al, One Way Street? Retrospectives on Childhood Prostitution* (London: The Children's Society, 1999); M. Melrose, 'Not much juvenile justice in these neighbourhoods: report on a study of juvenile prostitution, paper presented at British Criminology Conference, July 13–15 1999; M. Melrose and D. Barrett, 'Report on a study of juvenile prostitution'.

4 I. Robinson, 'Globilization'.

5 P. Barclay, *Inquiry into Income and Wealth, Vol.1* (York: Joseph Rowntree Foundation, 1995); J. Hills, *Inquiry into Income and Wealth, Vol.2* (York: Joseph Rowntree Foundation, 1995); B. Jordan, *A Theory of Poverty*; H. Dean with M. Melrose, *Poverty, Riches and Social Citizenship* (Basingstoke: Macmillan, 1998).

6 M. Collison, 'In search of the high life: drugs, crime, masculinities and consumption', *British Journal of Criminology* 36 (3), 1996, p. 429.

7 Sir P. Barclay, *Inquiry into Wealth and Income*.

8 M. Collison, 'In search of the high life', in the sense that it is they who have borne the brunt of recent economic changes; J. Bradshaw, *Child Poverty and Deprivation in the UK* (London: National Children's Bureau, 1990); V. Kumar, *Poverty and Inequality in the UK: The Effects on Children* (London: National Children's Bureau, 1993); J. Roche and S. Tucker, *Youth in Society: Contemporary Theory, Policy and Practice* (London: Sage, 1997); H. Dean, 'Underclassed or undermined? Young people and social citizenship', in R. MacDonald (ed.) *Youth, the Underclass and Social Exclusion* (London: Routledge, 1997).

9 See for example B. Jessop, 'The transition to post-Fordism and the Schumpetarian workfare state', R. Burrows and B. Loader (eds) *Towards a Post-Fordist Welfare State?* (London: Routledge, 1994).

10 B. Coles, *Youth and Social Policy: Youth Citizenship and Young Careers* (London: UCL, 1995), p. 79; E. McLaughlin and C. Glendenning, 'Paying for care in Europe: Is there a feminist approach?' in L. Hantrais and S. Mangen (eds) *Family Policy and the Welfare of Women*, Cross-national research papers (Loughborough: The University of Loughborough, 1994); A. France, 'Youth citizenship in the 1990s', *Youth and Policy* 53, 1996; B. Coles and G. Craig, 'Excluded youth and the growth of begging', in H. Dean (ed.) *Begging Questions: Street-Level Economic Activity and Social Policy Failure* (Bristol: The Policy Press, 1999).

11 See J. Allbeson, 'Seen but not heard: young people', in S. Ward (ed.) *DHSS in Crisis: Social Security Under Pressure and Under Review* (London: Child Poverty Action Group, 1985); J. Green, *It's No Game*; J. Green, S. Mulroy and M. O'Neill, 'Young people and prostitution from a Youth Service perspective', in D. Barrett (ed.) *Child Prostitution in Britain: Dilemmas and Practical Responses* (London: Children's Society, 1997); H. Dean, 'Underclassed or undermined'.

12 B. Coles and G. Craig, 'Excluded youth'.

13 P. Carlen, *Jigsaw: A Political Criminology of Youth Homelessness* (Buckingham: Open University Press, 1996), p. 2.

14 K. Andrews and J. Jacobs, *Punishing the Poor: Poverty under Thatcher* (Basingstoke: Macmillan, 1990), p. 74.

15 Joseph Rowntree Foundation, *Findings – Monitoring Poverty and Social Exclusion* (York: Joseph Rowntree Foundation, 1998).
16 A. Douglas and R. Gilroy, 'Young women and homelessness', in R. Gilroy and R. Woods (eds) *Housing Women* (London: Routledge, 1994); P. Carlen, *Jigsaw*; B. Coles and G. Craig, 'Excluded Youth'.
17 A. France, 'Youth citizenship'.
18 V. Bottomley, 'The Government and family policy: background note', *Report of the All Parliamentary Group on Parenting and International Year of the Family UK*, Parliamentary Hearings (London: MHMSO, 1994).
19 B. Coles and G. Craig, 'Excluded Youth', p 68.
20 J. Pitts, 'Causes of youth prostitution, new forms of practice and political responses', in D. Barrett (ed.) *Child Prostitution in Britain*; P. Ayre, 'Child abuse on the front page: learning from the British experience', paper presented at the Fourth International Conference on the Rights of the Child, Laval, Quebec, Canada 13–15 October 1999.
21 B. Coles, *Youth and Youth Policy.*
22 See J. Green, *It's No Game*; H. Dean and M. Melrose, 'Unraveling citizenship: the significance of social security benefit fraud', *Critical Social Policy* issue 48, 16 (3), 1996; H. Dean and M. Melrose 'Manageable discord: Fraud and resistance in the social security system', *Social Policy and Administration* 31 (2), 1997; P. Bourgois, *In Search of Respect: Selling Crack in El Barrio* (Cambridge: Cambridge University Press, 1996); B. Jordan, *A Theory of Poverty*; B. Coles and G. Craig, 'Excluded youth'; M. Melrose *et al*, *One Way Street.*
23 See for example R. Andrieu-Sanz and K. Vasquez-Anton, 'Young women prostitutes in Bilbao', in M. Cain (ed.) *Growing Up Good: Policing the Behaviour of Girls in Europe* (London: Sage, 1989); H. Kinnell, *Prostitutes' Experiences of Being in Care: Results of a Safe Project Investigation* (Birmingham: Birmingham Community Health Trust, 1991); J. Jesson, 'Understanding adolescent female prostitution: A literature review', *British Journal of Social Work* 23 (5), 1993; J. Green, *It's No Game*; V. Groocock, 'Streets ahead', *Social Work Today* 23 (5), 1992; S. M. Edwards, 'Prostitutes: Victims of law, social policy and organised crime', in P.Carlen and A. Worrall (eds) *Gender, Crime and Justice* (Buckingham: Open University Press, 1992); G. Rees, *Hidden Truths: Young people's experience of running away* (London: Children's Society, 1993); M. Stein, N. Frost and G. Rees, *Running the Risk: Young People on the Streets of Britain Today* (London: Children's Society, 1994); D. Barrett, 'Social work on the Streets: Responding to juvenile prostitution in Amsterdam, London and Paris', *Social Work in Europe* 1 (2), 1994; D. Barrett, *Child Prostitution in Britain*; M. O'Neill, 'Prostitution and the State: Towards a feminist practice', in C. Lupon and T. Gillespie (eds) *Working with Violence* (Basingstoke: Macmillan, 1994); M. O'Neill, 'Prostitute women now', in G. Scrambler and A. Scrambler (eds) *Rethinking Prostitution: Purchasing Sex in the 1990s* (London: Routledge, 1997); M. O'Neill, N. Goode and K. Hopkins, 'Juvenile prostitution: the experience of young women in residential care', *Childright* 113, 1995; J. O'Connell-Davidson, 'The anatomy of "free choice" prostitution', *Gender, Work and Organization* 2 (1), 1995; J. Pitts, 'Causes of youth prostitution';

J. Green *et al*, 'Young people and prostitution'; S. Crosby and D. Barrett, 'Poverty, drugs and youth prostitution', A. Marlow and J. Pitts (eds) *Managing Drugs and Young People* (Lyme Regis: Russell House Publications, 1999); M. Melrose *et al*, *One Way Street?*'; M. Melrose and D. Barrett, 'Report on a study'; M. Melrose, 'Not much juvenile justice'.

24 M. Melrose *et al*, *One Way Street?*; M. Melrose and D. Barrett, 'Report on a study'; M. Melrose, 'Not much juvenile justice'.

25 T.N.C. Gibbens cited in M. Collison, 'In search of the high life', p. 432.

26 M. Collison, 'In search of the high life', p. 436.

27 Ibid, p. 429.

28 M. Melrose *et al, One Way Street?*

29 I. Shaw and I. Butler, 'Understanding young people and prostitution: A foundation for practice', *British Journal of Social Work* 28, 1998; D. McNeish, 'An overview of agency views and service provision for young people abused through prostitution', in *Whose Daughter Next?* (Essex: Barnardo's, 1998); D. Barrett, 'Young people and prostitution: perpetrators in our midst', *International Review of Law, Computers and Technology* 12 (3), 1998; P. Ayre and D. Barrett, 'Young people and prostitution: an end to the beginning?', *Children and Society* 14, 1999.

30 R. Lee, *Doing Research on Sensitive Topics* (London: Sage, 1993).

31 M. Melrose, 'Labour pains: Some consideration of the difficulties of researching juvenile prostitution', *International Journal of Social Research Methodology, Theory and Practice*, 2001 forthcoming.

32 R. Lee, *Doing Research on Sensitive Topics*, p. 49.

33 I. Shaw and I. Butler, 'Understanding Young People'.

34 G. Scambler and A. Scambler, *Rethinking Prostitution*.

35 P. Aitchison and R. O'Brien, 'Redressing the balance: the legal contact of child prostitution', in D. Barrett (ed.) *Child Prostitution in Britain*.

36 Ibid.

37 R. Lee, *Doing Research on Sensitive Topics*; P. Ayre and D. Barrett, 'Young people and prostitution'.

38 M. Melrose *et al, One Way Streets?*; M. Melrose and D. Barrett, 'Report on a study of child prostitution'.

39 R. Lee, *Doing Research on Sensitive Topics*.

40 I. Shaw and I. Butler, 'Understanding young people'.

41 D. Barrett, 'Young people and prostitution'.

42 A. Thompson, 'Abuse by another name', Community Care 19–25 October 1995; S. Crosby and D. Barrett, 'Poverty, drugs and youth prostitution'.

43 D. Barrett, 'Young people and prostitution'.

44 B. Williams, 'Sold Out', *Young People Now*, February 1999.

45 Ibid.

46 J. O'Connell-Davidson, 'Sex tourism in Cuba'; D. Barrett, 'Young people and prostitution'.

47 J. Green, *It's No Game*; J. O'Connell-Davidson, 'Sex tourism in Cuba'; O. Calcetos-Santos, *Report of the special rapporteur on the sale of children, child prostitution and child pornography*, European Commission of Human Rights

53rd session, Item 21 (b) 1997; S. Kershaw, 'Sex for Sale'.

48 M. Melrose *et al, One Way Street?*

49 M. Melrose *et al, One Way Street?*; M. Melrose and D. Barrett, 'Report on a study of juvenile crime'; M. Melrose, 'Not much juvenile justice'.

50 M. Melrose *et al, One Way Street?*

51 M. Melrose *et al, One Way Street?*; M. Melrose and D. Barrett, 'Report on a study of juvenile prostitution'; M. Melrose, 'Not much juvenile justice'.

52 See E. Armstrong, 'Pondering pandering', *Deviant Behaviour* 4 (2).

53 See for example, J. Faugier and M. Sergeant, 'Boyfriends, "pimps" and clients', G. Scrambler and A. Scrambler, *Rethinking Prostitution*; S. Swan, 'A model for understanding abuse through prostitution', in *Whose Daughter Next?'*

54 P. Ayre and D. Barrett, 'Young people and prostitution'.

55 D. Barrett, 'Young people and prostitution', p. 478.

56 S. Kirby and J. Corzine, 'The contagion of stigma', *Qualitative Sociology* 4.

57 P. Ayre and D. Barrett, 'Young people and prostitution'.

58 M. Melrose *et al, One Way Street?*; M. Melrose and D. Barrett, 'Report on a study of juveniles prostitution'; M. Melrose and I. Brodie, 'Developing multi-agency responses to young people involved in prostitution', paper presented at Fourth International Conference on the Rights of the Child, Laval, Quebec, Canada, 13–15 October 1999.

59 P. Ayre and D. Barrett, 'Young people and prostitution'.

60 Ibid.

61 S. Wellard, 'Exit Strategy', *Community Care* 11–17 February 1999.

62 J. Pitts, 'Causes of youth prostitution'; M. Melrose *et al, One Way Streets?*; M. Melrose and D. Barrett, 'Report on a study of juvenile prostitution'; M. Melrose, 'Not much juvenile justice'.

63 M. Melrose *et al, One Way Street?*; P. Ayre and D. Barrett, "Young people and prostitution'.

64 Department of Health, Home Office, Department for Education and Employment and National Assembly for Wales, *Safeguarding Children Involved in Prostitution: Supplementary Guidance to Working Together to Safeguard Children*, London.

65 M. Melrose and I. Brodie, 'Developing multi-agency responses'.

66 T. Brain, T. Duffin, S. Anderson and P. Parchment, *Child Prostitution: A report on the ACPO guidelines and the pilot studies in Nottinghamshire and Wolverhampton*, Gloucestershire Constabulary, 1998.

67 M. Melrose *et al, One Way Street?*; M. Melrose and D. Barrett, 'Report on a study of juvenile prostitution'; M. Melrose and I. Brodie, 'Developing multi-agency responses'.

68 Ibid.

69 M. Melrose and D. Barrett, 'Report on a study of juvenile prostitution'; M. Melrose and I. Brodie, 'Developing multi-agency responses'; M. Melrose, 'Not much juvenile justice'.

70 M. Melrose and I. Brodie, 'Developing multi-agency responses'.

71 Ibid.

Postscript

Any society that fails to learn from its past will repeat its mistakes. Many lessons have been learned the hard way as the preceding chapters demonstrate. Few of those involved survive with their integrity and dignity fully intact with the sole exception of the most powerless, the children. MPs, social reformers, welfare workers and many more could learn from this history which records an emerging contribution to the health and well being of many communities. By neglecting to record both successes and failures a society leaves itself vulnerable to those who would impose on it policies that have been tried and found wanting in the past.

We think this book contributes to identifying those successes and failures and thus simultaneously contributes to the process of learning from our mistakes which consequently influence social policy. Via considerable archive research, we also pay homage to the pioneers in this field, whether they contributed at the policy, practice or purely social commentator debate level. All have helped to create a better understanding of contemporary practice and provide the means to help improve services for our vulnerable children. We hope the book is devoid of nostalgia. And further that by exploring these histories from the vantage point of contemporary practice the latter can receive critical scrutiny informed by knowledge from the former.

As, we believe, the first book on the subject of child prostitution covering the whole of the twentieth century, we acknowledge that it is very much a first step. However, as such we hope it will highlight a much neglected area of historical research. Of course, one of the reasons why this subject has been neglected is the scarcity of historical sources and certainly the problems this poses can be seen in our own work. Nonetheless, small but vital pieces of evidence on child prostitution are likely to be held in archives on related issues, such as adult prostitution, social work, child welfare, education, children's charities and may often be overlooked by researchers investigating other areas. We hope that this publication will serve to encourage others to utilise and piece together this evidence constructively and build upon the beginnings made here.

Margaret Melrose and Patrick Ayre have contributed the final chapter to this publication. Their analysis and commentary brings the issue up to date, including the new guidelines from the government in May 2000. They also talk of micro/macro economics and globalisation, they could have also easily expanded their contribution into commodification and cybercrime too, a paucity of space limited this opportunity. However, it is apparent that some of the causal issues remain as important at the beginning of the twenty-first century as they were at the beginning of the twentieth century, for example poverty/economics and class, war, gender and sexually transmitted diseases. In this respect, the final chapter effectively brings together and clarifies many of the issues discussed in the preceding chapters. Other matters are remarkably different, like the language of cybercrime and commodification.

One of the most consistent contributors to this field of development has been the relevant charities, hence the preface by the Chief Executive of a leading children's charity. We suspect they will be present at the beginning of the twenty-second century, this can be seen as both a success and a failure but most importantly services to children will continue to strive for further improvement.

For young people who are sexually exploited through their involvement in prostitution, the situation is dynamic and changing as we write. We are learning more about the issue and developing our responses to it all the time. We have learned more, for example, about how to overcome the difficulties of modern research in this field and are continually learning about routes of entry, mechanisms of involvement and models of good practice in this field.[1]

Home Office funded research in which one of the authors is presently involved suggests that there may be subtle and not-so-subtle regional variations in the organisation and management of child prostitution markets. In some areas young women may be forced into prostitution by other people, while in other areas they may be largely self-managed. Practitioners in different areas need to be sensitive to these variations, as they may require distinct practical responses and policy solutions at the local level. It is also possible, of course, that there will be regional variations in the ways in which the new government guidelines are implemented and in the ways in which professionals respond to the issue of child prostitution. This is a situation that will require careful monitoring over time and from which much may be learned for the future.

References

1 M. Melrose and D. Barrett, *Doing the Business: Effective interactions with young people involved in prostitution* (Lyme Regis: Russell House Publishing, forthcoming 2003).

References

Acton, W. *Prostitution,* P. Fryer (ed.) (London: MacGibbon and Kee, 1968).

Aitchison, P. and O'Brien, R. 'Redressing the balance: the legal context of child Prostitution', in D. Barrett (ed.) *Child Prostitution in Britain: Dilemmas and practical responses* (London: The Children's Society, 1997).

Aitken, J.K. 'Modern mothers', *Medical World* June 1956: 522–3.

Alexander, R. M. *The 'Girl Problem': Female Sexual Delinquency in New York, 1900–1930* (New York: Cornel University Press, 1995).

Alexander, S. 'Men's fears and women's work: responses to unemployment in London between the Wars', *Gender and Society* 10 (3) 2000: 401–25.

Allbeson, J. 'Seen but not heard: young people', in Ward. S. (ed.) *DHSS in Crisis: Social Security Under Pressure and Under Review* (London: Child Poverty Action, 1985).

Andrews, C. *Social Work Today,* 4 (12) 1974: 637.

Andrews, K. and Jacobs, J. *Punishing the Poor: Poverty under Thatcher* (Basingstoke: Macmillan, 1990).

Andrieu-Sanz, R. and Vasquez-Anton, K. 'Young women prostitutes in Bilbao', in M. Cain (ed.) *Growing Up Good: Policing the Behaviour of Girls in Europe* (London: Sage, 1989).

Anon. 'The cry of the children', *Quarterly Review* 205, 1906.

Anon. *Streetwalker* (London: Bodley Head, 1959).

Armstrong, E. 'Pondering pandering', *Deviant Behaviour* Vol. 4 (2) 1983. pp 203–17.

Ayre, P. 'Child abuse on the front page: learning from the British experience', Paper presented at the *Fourth International Conference on the Rights of the Child,* Laval, Quebec, Canada, 13–15th October 1999.

Ayre, P. and Barrett, D. 'Young people and prostitution: an end to the beginning?', *Children and Society* 14, 2000: 48–59.

Bailey, V. *Delinquency and Citizenship: Reclaiming the Young Offender, 1914–1948* (Oxford: Clarendon Press, 1987).

Bailey, V. and Blackbourn, S. 'The punishment of Incest Act 1908: a case study of law creation', *Criminal Law Review*, 1979: 708–718.

Banks, O. *Faces of Feminism: a Study of Feminism as a Social Movement* (Oxford: Blackwell, 1986).

Barbaret, R., Barrett, D. and O'Neill, M. 'Young people and prostitution: no respecter of boundaries in North Western Europe', *Social Work in Europe* 2 (2) 1995: 44–5.

Barclay, Sir P. *Inquiry into Income and Wealth, Vol. 1.* (York: Joseph Rowntree Foundation, 1995).

Barrett, D. (ed.). *Child Prostitution: in Britain: Dilemmas and Practical Responses* (London: Children's Society, 1997).

'Social work on the streets: responding to juvenile prostitution in Amsterdam, London and Paris', *Social Work in Europe* 1 (2) 1994: 29–32.

'Young people and prostitution: perpetrators in our midst', *International Review of Law, Computers and Technology* 12 (3) 1998: 475–86.

'Hard cases, hard lives', *The Guardian* 24 May 2000.

Barry, K. *Female Sexual Slavery* (London: Prentice-Hall, 1979).

Bartley, P. *Prostitution: Prevention and Reform in England, 1860–1914*, Women's and Gender History Series, (London: Routledge, 2000).

Behlmer, G. *Child Abuse and Moral Reform in England 1870–1908* (California: Stanford University Press, 1982).

Friends of the Family: The English Home and its Guardians, 1850–1940 (Stanford, California: Stanford University Press, 1998).

Bland, L. 'Cleansing the portals of life: the venereal disease campaign in the early Twentieth Century', in M.Langan and B.Scwartz (eds) *Crisis in the British State, 1880–1930* (London: Routledge, 1985).

BMA. *Cruelty to and Neglect of Children: Report of a Joint Committee of the British Medical Association and the Magistrates Association* (London: BMA, 1956).

Booth, C. *The Life and Labour of the People in London, First Series* (London: Macmillan, 1969).

Booth, W. *In Darkest England and the Way Out* (London: Carlyle Press, 1890).

Bottomley, V. 'The government and family policy: background note', *Report of the All Parliamentary Group on Parenting and International Year of the Family UK* (London: Parliamentary Hearings, HMSO, 1994).

Bourgois, P. *In Search of Respect: Selling Crack in El Barrio* (Cambridge: Cambridge University Press, 1996).

Bowerman, E.E. *The Law of Child Protection* (London: Pitman, 1933).

Bowlby, J. *Maternal Care and Mental Health* (Geneva: W.H.O, 1951).

Child Care and the Growth of Love (Harmondsworth: Penguin, 1953).

Boyle, H.R. 'Sexual morality', *Westminster Review* 166, 1906: 334–340.

Bradshaw, J. *Child Poverty and Deprivation in the UK* (London: National Children's Bureau, 1990).

Brain,T., Duffin, T., Anderson, S. and Parchment, P. *Child Prostitution: A report on the ACPO guidelines and the pilot studies in Nottinghamshire and Wolverhampton*, Gloucestershire Constabulary, 1998.

Briggs, J., Harrisson, C., McInnes, A. and Vincent, D. *Crime and Punishment in England: An Introductory History* (London: UCL Press, 1996).

Bristow, E. *Vice and Vigilance: Purity Movements in Britain since 1700* (Dublin: Gill and Macmillan, 1977).

Brown, M. E. 'Teenage prostitution', *Adolescence* 14, 1979: 665–680.

Bruley, S. *Women in Britain since 1900* (Basingstoke: Macmillan, 1999).

Burlingham, D. and Freud, A. *Young Children in Wartime* (London: Allen and Unwin, 1942).

Burnett, J. (ed). *Destiny Obscured: Autobiographies of Childhood, Education and Family from 1820s to the 1920s* (London: Routledge, 1982).

Burt, C. *The Young Delinquent, Vol.1* (London: University of London Press, 1925).

Butts, W. M. 'Boy prostitutes of the Metropolis', *Journal of Clinical Psychology* 8, 1946/7: 673–681.

Calcetas-Santos, O. *Report of the special rapporteur on the sale of children, child prostitution and child pornography*, European Commission of Human Rights 53rd session, Item 21 (b), 1997.

Cale, M. 'Girls and the perception of danger in the Victorian reformatory system', *Historical Association* 78 (253) 1993: 203–217.

Campbell, F. 'Journalistic construction of news: information gathering', *New Library World* 98 (1133), 1997: 60–4.

Caplan, G. M. (1982) 'The politics of prostitution' *History Workshop Journal* 13, 1982: 77–78.
'Teenage prostitution', *Crime and Delinquency* 30 (1) 1984: 69–74.

Carlen, P., Hicks, J., Christina, D. and Tchaikovsky, C. *Criminal Women* (Cambridge: Polity Press, 1985).
Jigsaw: A Political Criminology of Youth Homelessness (Buckingham: Open University Press, 1996).

Chow, K. 'Popular sexual knowledges and women's agency in 1920s England: Marie Stopes' Married Love and E.M.Hull's The Sheik', *Feminist Review* 63, 1999: 64–87.

Clarke, J., Hall, S., Jefferson, T. and Roberts, B. 'Subcultures, cultures and class,' in *Resistance Through Rituals: Youth Subcultures in Post War Britain* (London: Hutchinson, 1976).

Cohen, S. *Folk Devils and Moral Panics: The Creation of Mods and Rockers* (London: MacGibbon and Kee, 1972).

Coles, B. *Youth and Social Policy: Youth Citizenship and Young Careers* (London: UCL Press, 1995).

Coles, B. and Craig, G. 'Excluded youth and the growth of begging', H. Dean (ed.) *Begging Questions: Street-Level Economic Activity and Social Policy Failure* (Bristol: Policy Press, 1999).

Collison, M., 'In search of the high life: drugs, crime, masculinities and consumption', *British Journal of Criminology* 36 (3) Special Issue 1996.

Corbain, A. 'Commercial sexuality in nineteenth-century France: a system of images and regulations', *Representations* 14, spring 1986: 209–219.

Costello, J. *Love, Sex and War: Changing Values 1939–45* (London: Collins, 1985).

Cousins, S. *To Beg I am Ashamed* (London: George Routledge and Sons Ltd, 1938).

Cowie, J., Cowie, V. and Slater, E. *Delinquency in Girls*, (London: Heinemann, 1968).

Cox, P. 'Rescue and reform: girls, delinquency and industrial schools, 1908–1933', Ph.D Cambridge University, 1996.

Craft, M. 'Boy prostitutes and their fate' *British Journal of Psychiatry* (112) 1966: 1111–4.

Cree, V. E. *From Public Streets to Private Lives: the Changing Task of Social Work* (Avebury: Aldershot, 1995).

Crosby, S. and Barrett, D. 'Poverty, drugs and youth prostitution', in A. Marlow and J. Pitts (eds) *Managing Drugs and Young People* (Lyme Regis: Russell House Publishing, 1999).

Cunningham, H. *The Children of the Poor: Representations of Childhood since the Seventeenth Century* (Oxford: Blackwell, 1991).

D'Cruze, S. *Crimes of Outrage: Sex, Violence and Victorian Working Women*, Women's History Series (London: UCL Press, 1998).

Davidoff, L. *et al, The Family Story: Blood, Contract and Intimacy, 1830–1960*, (London: Longman, 1999).

Davin, A. 'What is a child?' in A. Fletcher and S. Hussey (eds) *Childhood in Question: Children, Parents and the State* (Manchester: Manchester University Press, 1999).

DeMause, L. 'The history of child abuse', *Journal of Psychohistory* 25 (3), 1998: 1–15.

Dean, H. *Begging Questions: Street-Level Economic Activity and Social Policy Failure* (Bristol: Polity Press, 1999).
'Underclassed or undermined? Young people and social citizenship', R. MacDonald (ed.) *Youth, the Underclass and Social Exclusion* (London: Routledge, 1997).

Dean, H. and Melrose, M. 'Unraveling citizenship: the significance of social security benefit fraud', *Critical Social Policy*, Issue 48 Vol. 16 (3) 1996: 3–32.
'Manageable discord: fraud and resistance in the social security system', *Social Policy and Administration* 31 (2) 1997: 103–118.
Poverty, Riches and Social Citizenship (Basingstoke: Macmillan, 1998).

Department of Health, Home Office, *Guidance on Children Involved in Prostitution* (London: Home Office/Department of Health, 1998).

Department of Health, Home Office, Department for Education and Employment and National Assembly for Wales. *Safeguarding Children Involved in Prostitution: Supplementary Guidance to Working Together to Safeguard Children* (London: Department of Health, 2000).

Dingwall, R., Eekelaar, J.M. and Murray, T. 'Childhood as a social problem: a survey of the history of legal regulation', *Journal of Law and Society* 11(2) 1984: 207–232.

Doshay, L. J. *The Boy Sex Offender and His Later Criminal Career* (New York: Grune and Stratton, 1943).

Douglas, A. and Gilroy, R. 'Young women and homelessness', R. Gilroy and R.Woods (eds) *Housing Women* (London: Routledge, 1994).

Douglas, M. *Purity and Danger: An Analysis of the Concepts of Pollution and Taboo* (London: Routledge, 1966).

Edwards, S. M. 'Prostitutes: victims of law, social policy and organized crime', P. Carlen and A. Worrall (eds) *Gender, Crime and Justice* (Buckingham: Open University Press, 1992).

'Abused and exploited – young girls in prostitution', in *Whose Daughter Next? Children Abused Through Prostitution* (Essex: Barnardo's).

Edwards, Q. *What is Lawful? Does Innocence Begin Where Crime Ends? Afterthought on the Wolfenden Report* (Westminster: Church Information Office, 1959).

Ennew, J. *The Sexual Exploitation of Children* (Cambridge: Polity Press, 1986).

Epps, P. 'A preliminary study of 300 female delinquents in Borstal institutions, '*British Journal of Delinquency* 1, 1951: 187–197.

'A further survey of female delinquents undergoing Borstal training', *British Journal of Delinquency* 4, 1954: 265–271.

Evan, E.J. *Social Policy 1830–1914: Individualism, Collectivism and the Origins of the Welfare State* (London: Routledge and Kegan Paul, 1978).

Evans, D. 'Tackling the 'hideous scourge': the creation of the venereal disease treatment centres in early twentieth–century Britain', *Social History of Medicine* 5, 1992: 413–33.

Fairfield, L. 'Notes on prostitution', *British Journal of Criminology* 9, 1959: 164–73.

Faugier, J. and Sergeant, M. 'Boyfriends, "pimps" and clients', G. Scambler and A. Scambler (eds) *Rethinking Prostitution: Purchasing Sex in the 1990s* (London: Routledge, 1997).

Fergusson, H. 'Cleveland in history: the abused child and child protection, 1880–1914', in R.Cooter (ed.) *In the Name of the Child, Health and Welfare, 1880–1914* (London: Routledge, 1992).

Flexner, A. *Prostitution in Europe* (New York: The Century Co, 1917).

Foucault, M. *Discipline and Punish: The Birth of the Prison*, translated by R. Sheridan (Harmondsworth: Penguin, 1977).

History of Sexuality Vol.1, translated by R. Hurley (Harmonsworth: Penguin, 1990).

The Danger of Child Sexuality, broadcast on April 1978. This version on internet (http://www.mindsprin.com/~rainbowchild/foucault.html). Also published as 'Sexuality, morality and the law', in L. D. Kritzman (ed.) *Michel Foucault: Politics, Philosophy, Culture, Interviews and other Writings* (New York: Routledge, 1992).

France, A. 'Youth citizenship in the 1990s', *Youth and Policy* 53, 1996: 28–44.

Fraser, D. *The Evolution of the British Welfare State* (Basingstoke: Macmillan, 1986).

Garland, D. *Punishment and Welfare: A History of Penal Strategies* (Aldershot: Gower, 1985).

Garrett, P. 'Producing the moral citizen: the looking after children system' and the regulation of children and young people in public care', *Critical Social Policy* 19 (3) no.60, 1999: 291–311.

Gibbens, T.N.C. 'Juvenile prostitution,' *British Journal of Criminology* 8, 1957: 3–12.
'The Wolfenden Report, Prostitution,' *Howard Journal* X (1) 1958: 25–9.

Gibbs Van Brunschot, E., Sydie, R.A. and Krull, C. 'Images of prostitution: the prostitute and print media', *Women and Criminal Justice* 10 (4) 1999: 47–72.

Glover, E. *The Psychopathology of Prostitution* (London: Institute for the Study and Treatment of Delinquency, 1957 second edition).

Gordon, L. *Heroes of their Own Lives, the Politics and History of Family Violence: Boston 1880–1960* (New York: Viking, 1989).
'The politics of child sexual abuse, notes from American history', *Feminist Review* 28, 1998: 56–64.

Gorham, D. 'The "maiden tribute of modern Babylon" re-examined. Child prostitution and the idea of childhood in late-Victorian England', *Victorian Studies* 21, 1978: 353–79.

Gosling, J. and Warner, D. *The Shame of the City: An Inquiry into the Vice of London* (London: W.H.Allen, 1960).

Green, J. *It's No Game: Responding to the needs of young women at risk or involved in prostitution* (Leicester: National Youth Agency, 1992).

Green, J., Mulroy, S. and O'Neill, M. 'Young people and prostitution from a Youth Service perspective', in D. Barrett (ed.) *Child Prostitution in Britain: Dilemmas and Practical Responses* (London: Children's Society, 1997).

Groocock, V. 'Streets ahead', *Social Work Today*, Vol. 23 (5) 1992.

Hall, G. M. *Prostitution: a Survey and a Challenge* (London: Williams and Northgate, 1933).

Hall, J. G. 'The prostitute and the law', *British Journal of Delinquency* 9, 1959: 174–81.

Hall, L. A. *Hidden Anxieties: Male Sexuality 1900–1950* (Cambridge: Polity, 1991).
Sex, Gender and Social Change in Britain since 1880, European Culture and Society Series (Basingstoke: Macmilan, 2000).
Impotent ghosts from no man's land, flappers' boyfriends, or crypto-patriarchs? Men, sex and social change in 1920s Britain Social History 21(1), 1996: 54–70.
'80 Years of the Medical Women's Federation', *Medical Woman, Bulletin of the Medical Women's Federation* 16 (2) 1997: 6–9.

Hall-Williams, J. E. 'The Wolfenden Report – An appraisal', *Political Quarterly* 29, 1958: 132–143.

Haste, C. *Rules of Desire: Sex in Britain: World War 1 to the Present* (London: Chatto and Windus Ltd, 1992).

Hattersley, R. 'Skill for scandal', *The Guardian* 16 October 1999.

Hatton, T. 'Unemployment and the labour market in inter-war Britain', in R. Floud and D. McCloskey (eds) *The Economic History of Britain since 1700* (Cambridge: Cambridge University Press, 1994 second edition).

Hecht, T. 'In search of Brazil's street children', in C. Panther-Brick and M.T.Smith (eds) *Abandoned Children* (Cambridge: Cambridge University Press, 2000).

Hendrick, H. *Child Welfare, England 1872–1989* (London: Routledge, 1994).
Children, Childhood and English Society 1880–1990, New Studies in Economic and Social History (Cambridge: Cambridge University Press, 1997).

Heywood, J. S. *Children in Care: The Development of the Service for the Deprived Child* (London: Routledge and Kegan Paul, 1978 third edition).

Hills, A. 'How the press see you' *Social Work Today* 11 (36) 20 May 1980: 19–20.

Hills, J. *Inquiry into Income and Wealth* 2 (York: Joseph Rowntree Foundation, 1995).

Holman, B. 'Fifty years ago: the Curtis and Clyde Reports,' *Children and Society* 10, 1996: 197–209.

Hood, R. and Joyce, K. 'Three generations: oral testimonies on crime and social change in London's East End,' *British Journal of Criminology* 39 (1) 1999: 136–60.

Hooper, C. 'Child sexual abuse and the regulation of women, variations on a theme', in C.Smart (ed.) *Regulating Womanhood: Historical Essays on Marriage, Motherhood and Sexuality* (London: Routledge, 1992).

Humphries, S. *Hooligan or Rebel? An Oral History of Working Class Childhood and Youth 1880–1939* (Oxford: Open University Press, 1981).
A Secret World of Sex: Forbidden Fruit, the British Experience 1900–1950 (London: Sedgwick and Jackson, 1988).

Humphries, S. and Gordon, P. *Forbidden Britain: Our Secret Past 1900–1950* (London: BBC Books, 1994).

Jackson, L. A. Women's and Gender History Series, *Child Sexual Abuse in Victorian England* (London: Routledge, 2000).
''Singing birds as well as soap suds': The Salvation Army's work with sexually abused girls in Edwardian England', *Gender and History* 12 (1) 2000: 107–126.
'Children of the streets: rescue, reform and the family in Leeds, 1850–1914', *Family and Community History* 3 (2) 2000: 135–145.

James, A. and Jenks, C. 'Public perceptions of childhood criminality', *British Journal of Sociology* 47, 1996.

James, A. and Prout, A. (eds). *Constructing and Reconstructing Childhood: Contemporary Issues in the Sociological Study of Childhood* (London: Falmer Press, 1997 second edition).

Jeffreys, S. *The Spinster and her Enemies: Feminism and Sexuality 1880–1930* (London: Pandora, 1985).

Jesson, J. 'Understanding adolescent female prostitution: A literature review', *British Journal of Social Work* 23 (5) 1993: 517–30.

Jessop, B. 'The transition to post-Fordism and the Schumpetarian workfare state', R. Burrows and B. Loader (eds) *Towards a Post-Fordist Welfare State?* (London: Routledge, 1994).

Jones, A. E. 'The law versus prostitution', *Criminal Law Review* 1960: 704–9.

Jordan, B. *A Theory of Poverty and Social Exclusion* (Polity, Cambridge, 1996).

Jordan, T. *Growing up in the 50s* (London: Optima, 1990).

Joseph, C. 'Scarlet wounding: issues of child prostitution', *Journal of Psychohistory* 23 (1) 1995: 2–17.

Joseph Rowntree Foundation, *Findings – Monitoring Poverty and Social Exclusion* (York: Joseph Rowntree Foundation, 1998).

Kershaw, S. 'Sex for sale: a profile of young male sex workers' circumstances, choices and risks', *Youth and Policy* 63, spring 1999.

Kincaid, J. R. *Child-Loving: The Erotic Child and Victorian Culture* (London: Routledge, 1992).

Kingsley Kent, S. *Sex and Suffrage in Britain 1860–1914* (London: Routledge, 1987).

Kinnel, H. *Prostitutes' Experiences of Being in Care: Results of a Safe Project investigation* (Birmingham: Birmingham Community Health Trust, Safe Project, 1991).

Kirby, S. and Corzine, J. 'The contagion of stigma', *Qualitative Sociology* 4: 3–20.

Kumar, V. *Poverty and Inequality in the UK: The Effects on Children* (London: National Children's Bureau, 1993).

Kitzinger, J. 'Who are you kidding? Children, power, and the struggle against sexual abuse', in A. James and A. Prout (eds) *Constructing and Reconstructing Childhood* (London: Falmer Press, 1997 second edition).

League of Nations, Advisory Committee on Social Questions, *Prevention of Prostitution: A Study of Measures Adopted or Under Consideration Particularly with regard to Minors* IV.Social.1943.IV.2 (C.26.M.26.1943.IV).

Lee, R., *Doing Research on Sensitive Topics* (London: Sage, 1993).

Leeson, J. 'Understanding adolescent female prostitution: a literature review', *British Journal of Social Work* 23, 1993: 517–530.

Levine, P. 'Rough usage: prostitution, law and the social historian', in A.Wilson (ed.) *Rethinking Social History, English Society 1570–1920 and its Interpretation* (Manchester: Manchester University Press, 1993).

Lewis, J. 'Anxieties about the family and the relationships between parents, children and the state in twentieth century England,' in M. Richards and P. Light (eds), *Children of Social Worlds: Development in a Social Context* (Cambridge Mass: Harvard University Press, 1986).
Women in Britain since 1945 (Oxford: Blackwell, 1992).
'Gender, the family and women's agency in the building of 'welfare states': the British case', *Social History* 19 (1) 1994: 37–55.
'The boundaries between marriage, non-marriage and parenthood: changes in behaviour and policy in postwar Britain' *Journal of Family History* 21 (3) 1996: 372–87.

Lewis, J. and Welshman, J. 'The issue of the never-married mother in Britain, 1920–70', *Social History of Medicine* 10, 1997: 401–18.

Linehan, T. 'Pollution and purification: child prostitution and the age of consent in late Victorian England' MA Dissertation, London School of Economics, 2000.

Lloyd, R. *Playland: A Study of Boy Prostitution* (London: Blond and Briggs, 1977).

Loewe, L. L. *Basil Henriques: A portrait based on his diaries, letters and speeches as collated by his widow, Rose Henriques* (London: Routledge and Kegan Paul, 1976).

Macnicol, J. 'In pursuit of the underclass', *Journal of Social Policy* 16 (3) 1987: 293–318.
'Eugenics and the campaign for voluntary sterilization in Britain between the Wars', *Social History of Medicine* 2, 1989: 147–169.

Mahood, L. *The Magdalenes: Prostitution in the Nineteenth Century* (London: Routledge, 1990).
Policing Gender, Class and Family, England 1850–1940 (London: UCL Press, 1995).

Marks, L. 'The luckless waifs and strays of humanity': Irish and Jewish immigrant unwed mothers in London, 1870–1939', *Twentieth Century British History* 3 (2) 1992: 113–137.

Marwick, A. *The Deluge* (London: Macmillan, 1965).

Mason, M. H. 'Public morality: some constructive suggestions', *The Nineteenth Century* LXXXII (485) 1917: 185–94.

Matthews, R. 'Beyond Wolfenden? Prostitution, politics and the law', in R. Matthews and J. Young (eds), *Confronting Crime* (London: Sage, 1986).

Mauruce, F. 'Where to get men', *Contemporary Review* 1902.
'National health: a soldier's study', *Contemporary Review* 1903.

May, M., Dawkins, M. and Kratz, M. 'Comments on special problems of delinquent and maladjusted girls,' *British Journal of Criminology* 11 (3) 1964: 145–8.

McIntosh, A. *Asian Child Prostitution on the Rise Despite New Laws*, 29 October 1995, Reuters.

McLaren, A. *Twentieth-Century Sexuality: A History* (Oxford: Blackwell, 1999).

McLaughlin, E. and Glendenning, C. 'Paying for care in Europe: is there a feminist approach?' L. Hantrais and S. Mangen (eds) *Family Policy and the Welfare of Women* (Loughborough: Cross-National Research Papers, University of Loughborough, 1994).

McMullen, R. J. 'Youth prostitution: a balance of power', *Journal of Adolescence* 10 (1) 1997: 35–43.

McNeish, D. 'An overview of agency views and service provision for young people abused through prostitution', in *Whose Daughter Next?* (Essex: Barnardo's, 1998).

Mearns, A. *The Bitter Cry of Outcast London: An Enquiry into the Conditions of the Abject Poor* with an introduction by A. S. Wohl (Leicester: Leicester University Press, 1970).

Melrose, M. 'Not much juvenile justice in these neighbourhoods: report on a study of juvenile prostitution', Paper presented at *British Criminology Conference*, Liverpool, 13–15 July 1999.
'Labour pains: Some considerations of the difficulties of researching juvenile prostitution', *International Journal of Social Research Methodology, Theory and Practice*, 2001 forthcoming.

Melrose, M. and Barrett, D. 'Report on a study of juvenile prostitution', Paper presented at *National Vice Conference*, Portishead 29–30 June 1999. *Doing the Business: Effective interactions with young people involved in prostitution* (Lyme Regis: Russell House Publishing, 2003).

Melrose, M. and Brodie, I. 'Developing multi-agency responses to young people involved in prostitution', Paper presented at *Fourth International Conference on the Rights of the Child*, Laval, Quebec, Canada, 13–15 October 1999.

Melrose, M., Barrett, D. and Brodie, I. *One Way Street? Retrospectives on Childhood Prostitution* (London: Children's Society, 1999).

Merrick, G.P. *Work Among the Fallen: As Seen in the Prison Cell* (London: Ward, Lock and Co, 1890).

Midwinter, E. *Development of Social Welfare in Britain* (Buckingham: Open University Press, 1994).

Mitchell, M. 'The effects of unemployment on the social condition of women and children in the 1930s', *History Workshop Journal* 19, spring 1985: 105–127.

Montgomery, H. 'Abandonment and child prostitution in a Thai slum community', in C. Panther-Brick and M. T. Smith (eds) *Abandoned Children* (Cambridge: Cambridge University Press, 2000).

Mort, F. *Dangerous Sexualities: Medico-Moral Politics in England since 1830* (London: Routledge and Kegan Paul, 1987).

Neal, L. *Victorian Babylon: People Streets and Images in Nineteenth–Century* (New Haven: Yale University Press, 2000).

Nield, K. *Prostitution in the Victorian age: debates on the issues from 19th century critical journals* (Farnborough: Gregg, 1973).

Newburn, T. *Permission and Regulation: Law and Morals in Post-War Britain* (London: Routledge, 1992).

O'Connell-Davidson, J. 'The anatomy of "free choice" prostitution', *Gender, Work and Organization* 2 (1) 1995: 1–10. 'Sex tourism in Cuba', *Race and Class* 38 (1) 1996: 39– 48. *Prostitution, Power and Freedom* (Cambridge: Polity Press, 1998).

O'Neill, M. 'Prostitution and the state: towards a feminist practice', in C. Lupton and T. Gillespie (eds) *Working with Violence* (Basingstoke: Macmillan, 1994).

O'Neill, M. 'Prostitute women now', in G. Scambler and A. Scambler (eds.) *Rethinking Prostitution: Purchasing Sex in the* 1990s (London: Routledge, 1997).

O'Neill, M., Goode, N. and Hopkins, K. 'Juvenile prostitution: the experience of young women in residential care', *Childright* 113, 1995: 14–16.

Osgerby, B. *Youth in Britain since 1945* (Oxford: Oxford University Press, 1998)

Packman, J. *The Child's Generation: Child Care Policy from Curtis to Houghton* (London: Basil Blackwell, 1975).

Padel, U. and Stevenson, P. *Insiders: Women's Experience of Prison* (London: Virago, 1988).

Parker, R. A. 'The gestation of reform: the Children Act 1948', in P. Bean and S. MacPherson (eds) *Approaches to Welfare* (London: Routledge and Kegan Paul, 1983).

Parson, T. and Bales, R. F. *Family Socialization and Interaction Process* (Glencoe, III: Free Press, 1955).

Parton, N. *The Politics of Child Abuse* (London: Macmillan, 1985).

Pearsall, R. *The Worm in the Bud: The World of Victorian Sexuality* (London: Weidenfeld and Nicholson, 1969).

Pearson, M. *The Age of Consent* (London: David and Charles, 1972).

Petrow, S. *Policing Morals: The Metropolitan Police and the Home Office 1870–1914*, (Oxford: Clarendon Press, 1994).

Picton, W. 'Male prostitution in Berlin', *Howard Journal* 3 (2) 1931: 89–92.

Pinchbeck, I. and Hewitt, M. *Children in English Society*, Vol. II (London: Routledge and Kegan Paul, 1973).

Pitts, J. 'Causes of youth prostitution: new forms of practice and political responses', in D. Barrett (ed.) *Child Prostitution in Britain: Dilemmas and Practical* Responses (London: Children's Society, 1997).

Plowden, A. *The Case of Eliza Armstrong, 'A Child of 13 Bought for £5'* (London: BBC, 1974).

Porter, R. and Hall, L. *The Facts of Life: The Creation of Sexual Knowledge in Britain, 1650–1950* (New Haven: Yale University Press, 1995).

Power, M.J., Ash, P.M., Shoenberg, E. and Siney, E.C. 'Delinquency and the family', *British Journal of Social Work, 1974.*

Prout, A. and James, A. 'A new paradigm for the sociology of childhood? Provenance, promise and problems', in A. James and A. Prout (eds) *Constructing and Reconstructing Childhood* second edition, Contemporary Issues in the Sociological Study of Childhood (London: Falmer Press, 1997).

Railton, G. S. *The Truth about the Armstrong Case and the Salvation Army* (London: Salvation Army, 1885).

Raven, S. 'Boys will be boys: the male prostitute in London' in H.M. Ruitenbeek (ed.) *The Problem of Homosexuality in Modern Society* (New York: E.P. Dutton and Co, 1963).

Rees, G. *Hidden Truths: Young People's Experiences of Running Away* (London: Children's Society, 1993).

Reiss Jr, A. J. 'The social integration of queers and peers' in H.M. Ruitenbeek (ed.) *The Problem of Homosexuality in Modern Society* (New York: E.P. Dutton and Co, 1963).

Roberts, N. *Whores in History: Prostitution in Western Society* (London: Grafton, 1993).

Roberts, R. *The Classic Slum: Salford Life in the First Quarter of the Century* (Manchester: Manchester University Press, 1971).

Robinson, I. 'Globalization: Nine thesis on our epoch', *Race and Class* 38 (2) 1996: 13–32.

Roche, J. and Tucker, S. (eds). *Youth in Society: Contemporary Theory, Policy and Practice* (London: Sage, 1997).

Rolf, C. H. (ed.). *Women of the Streets: A Sociological Study of the Common Prostitute* (London: Secker and Warburg, 1955).

Ross, E. *Love and Toil: Motherhood in Outcast London, 1870–1918* (Oxford: Oxford University Press, 1993).

Rowntree, B. S. *Poverty: A Study of Town Life* (London: Macmillan, 1901).

Ruitenbeek, H. M (ed.). *The Problem of Homosexuality in Modern Society* (New York: E.P. Dutton and Co, 1963).

'Men alone: the male homosexual and the disintegrated family', in H. M. Ruitenbeek (ed.) *The Problem of Homosexuality in Modern Society* (New York: E.P. Dutton and Co, 1963).

Samuel, R. *East End Underworld: Chapters in the Life of Arthur Harding* (London: Routledge and Kegan Paul, 1981).

Saunders, G. M. 'Should mothers go out to work?' *Nursery World* 29 June 1957: 919.

Scambler, G. and Scambler, A (eds). 'Rethinking prostitution', in *Rethinking Prostitution: Purchasing Sex in the 1990s* (London: Routledge, 1997).

Scott, G. R. *A History of Prostitution from Antiquity to the Present Day* (London: Torchstream Books, 1954 revised from 1936).

Sempkins, F. *Unemployment and Prostitution of Young Girls* (London: BSHC, 1933).

Shaw, I. and Butler, I. 'Understanding young people and prostitution: a foundation for practice? *British Journal of Social Work* 28, 1998: 177–96.

Showalter, W. *The Female Malady: Women, Madness and English Culture, 1830–1980* (London: Virago, 1987).

Sidorenko-Stephenson, S. 'Moscow street children and emerging urban marginality', paper presented to panel on *Youth and Cultural Globalization in Post-Soviet Russia*, BASEES Conference, Fitzwilliam College, Cambridge, 27–29 March 1999.

Simmons, H. G. 'Explaining social policy: the English Mental Deficiency Act of 1913', *Journal of Social History* 3, 1978: 387–403.

Sivanandan, A. 'New circuits of imperialism', in A. Sivanandan (ed.) *Communities of Resistance* (London: Verso, 1990).

Skidmore, P. 'Telling tales: media power, ideology and the reporting of child sexual abuse in Britain', in D. Kidd–Hewitt and R. Osbourne (eds) *Crime and the Media: The Post-Modern Spectacle* (London: Pluto Press, 1995).

Smart, C. 'Disruptive bodies and unruly sex: The regulation of reproduction and sexuality in the nineteenth century' in C. Smart (ed.) *Regulating Womanhood: Historical Essays on Marriage, Motherhood and Sexuality* (London: Routledge, 1992).

(ed.) *Regulating Womanhood: Historical Essays on Marriage, Motherhood and Sexuality* (London: Routledge, 1992).

'Legal subjects and subject objects: ideology, law and female sexuality', in C. Smart, *Law, Crime and Sexuality: Essays in Feminism* (London: Sage, 1995).

'The historical struggle against child abuse', occasional paper the University of Leeds 1998.

'A history of ambivalence and conflict in the discursive construction of the "child victim" of sexual abuse', *Social and Legal Studies* 8 1999: 391–409.

'Reconsidering the recent history of child sexual abuse, 1910–1960', *Journal of Social Policy* 29 (1) 2000: 55–71.

Smith, F. B. 'Labouchere's amendment to the Criminal Law Amendment Bill', *Historical Studies* 67, 1976: 165–75.

Smith, J.D. 'The voluntary tradition: philanthropy and self-help in Britain 1500–1945', in Smith, J.D., Rochester, C. and Hedley, R. (eds) *An Introduction to the Voluntary Sector* (London: Routledge, 1995).

Snitow, A., Stansell, C. and Thompson, E. (eds). *Powers of Desire: The Politics of Sexuality* (New York: New Feminist Library, 1983).

Soothill, K. and Walby, S. *Sex Crimes in the News* (London: Routledge, 1991).

Sparks, I. 'Age of Innocence', *The Guardian* 24 May 2000.

Springhall, J. *Coming of Age: Adolescence in England 1860–1960* (Dublin: Gill and Macmillan, 1986).

Stanley, L. *Sex Surveyed 1949–1994: From Mass-Observation's 'Little Kinsey' to the National Survey and the Hite Reports* (London: Taylor and Francis, 1995).

Steedman, C. 'Bodies, figures and physiology: Margaret McMillan and the late nineteenth-century remaking of working-class childhood', in R. Cooter (ed.) *In the Name of the Child: Health and Welfare 1880–1940* (London: Routledge, 1992).

Stein, M., Frost, N. and Rees, G. *Running the Risk: Young People on the Streets of Britain Today* (London: Children's Society, 1994).

Stevenson, J. *British Society 1914–45* (Harmondsworth: Penguin, 1984).

Stevenson, O. 'It was more difficult than we thought: a reflection on 50 years of child welfare practice' *Child and Family Social Work* (3) 1998: 153–61.

Stewart, J. 'Children, parents and the state: the Children Act 1908' *Children and Society* 9 (1) 1995: 90–99.

Stroud, J. *Thirteen Penny Stamps: The Story of the Church of England Children's Society (Waifs and Strays) from 1881 to the 1970s* (London: Hodder and Stoughton, 1971).

Summers, A. 'The constitution violated: the female body and the female subject in the campaigns of Josephine Butler', *History Workshop Journal* 48, 1999: 1–15.

Swan, S. A model for understanding abuse through prostitution', in whose daughter next? Children abused through prostitution (Essex: Barnardo's).

Taylor, K. J. 'Venereal disease in nineteenth-century children', *Journal of Psychohistory* 12 (4) 1985: 431–63.

Terrot, C. *The Maiden Tribute: A Study of the White Slave Traffic of the Nineteenth-Century* (London: Frederick Muller, 1959).

Thane, P. 'Towards equal opportunities? Women in Britain since 1945', in T.R. Gourvish and A.O. 'Day (eds) *Britain since 1945* (Basingstoke: Macmillan, 1991).

Thomas, T. *Sex Crime: Sex Offending and Society* (Devon: Willan Publishing, 2000).

Thompson, A. 'Abuse by another name', *Community Care* 19–25 October 1995: 16–18.

Trudgill, E. (1973) 'Prostitution and Paterfamilias', in H. J. Dyos and M. Wolff (eds) *The Victorian City: Images and Realities Vol.2* (London: Routledge and Kegan Paul, 1973).

Van Meeuwen, A. 'Introduction: setting the scene', in *Whose Daughter Next? Children Abused Through Prostitution* (Essex: Barnardo's, 1998).

Vincent, A. W. 'The Poor Law reports of 1909 and the social theory of the Charity Organisation Society', in D. Gladstone (ed.) *Before Beveridge: Welfare Before the Welfare State* (London: IEA, 1999).

Walby, S., Hay, A. and Soothill, K. 'The social construction of rape', *Theory, Culture and Society* 2 (1) 1983: 86–98.

Walker, A. 'Special problems of delinquent and maladjusted girls', *British Journal of Criminology* 11 (2) 1963: 27–36.

Walker, D. 'Are social workers badly treated by the newspapers?' *Social Work Today* 7 (9) 5 August 1976: 292–3.

Walkowitz, J. R. *Prostitution and Victorian Society: Women, Class and the State* (Cambridge: Cambridge University Press, 1980).

'The politics of prostitution' in C.R. Stimpson and E.S. Person (eds) *Women, Sex and Sexuality* (Chicago: University of Chicago Press, 1980).

'Male vice and feminist virtue: feminism and the politics of prostitution in nineteenth-century England,' *History Workshop Journal* 13, 1982: 79–93.

City of Dreadful Delight. Narratives of Sexual Danger in Late-Victorian London (London: Virago Press, 1992).

Webster, C. 'Health, welfare and unemployment during the Depression', *Past and Present* 109, 1985: 204–30.

Weeks, J. *Sex, Politics and Society: The Regulation of Sexuality since 1800* (Harlow: Longman, 1989).

'Inverts, perverts and mary-annes: male prostitution and the regulation of homosexuality in England in the nineteenth and early twentieth centuries', in J. Weeks, *Against Nature: Essays on History, Sexuality and Identity* (London: Rivers Oram Press, 1991).

Wiener, M. 'New women vs old men?: sexual danger and "social narratives" in later Victorian England' Roundtable on Walkowitz, *City of Dreadful Delight, Journal of Victorian Culture* 2 (2), 1997: 302–310.

Wellard, S. 'Exit strategy', *Community Care* 11–17 February 1999: 22–23.

Welshman, J. 'In search of the "problem family": Public health and social work in England and Wales 1940–70', *Social History of Medicine* 9, 1996: 447–465.

Whitehouse, J. H. 'Street trading by children' in Whitehouse, J.H. (ed.) *Problems of Boy Life* (London: King, 1912).

Whose Daughter Next? Children Abused Through Prostitution (Essex: Barnardo's, 1998).

Wildeblood, P. *Against the Law: The Classic Account of a Homosexual in 1950s Britain* (London: Phoenix, 2000) first published 1955.

Williams, B. 'Sold out', *Young People Now* February 1999: 21–23.

Willmott, P. *Adolescent Boys in East London* (London: Routledge and Kegan Paul, 1966).

Winnicott, D. *The Child and the Family: First Relationships*, J. Hardenberg (ed.) (London: Tavistock Press, 1957).

Young, E. Rev. *et al*, Vice increase in Stepney, report in NVA Archives 1957.
Younghusband, E. *Social Work in Britain: 1950–1975, Vol.1* (London: George Allen and Unwin, 1978).

Zedner, L. *Women, Crime, and Custody in Victorian England* (Oxford: Oxford University Press, 1991).

Parliamentary papers

Hansards Parliamentary Debates.
Evidence of House of Lords Committee of Inquiry, PP 1881, IX, p. 355.
Final Report of the Royal Commissioners on Venereal Diseases, PP 1916 (Cd. 8189) XVI, p.1 and appendix p.215.
Committee on Sexual Offences Against Young Persons, PP 1924–5 [Cmd. 25611] XV, p.905.
Street Offences Committee Report, PP 1928–9 (Cmd. 3231) IX, p.735.
Report of the Departmental Committee on Adoption Societies and Agencies, PP 1936–7 (Cmd. 5499) IX, p.1.
Report of the Departmental Committee on Adoption Societies and Agencies, PP 1936–7 (Cmnd. 5499) IX, p.1.
Social Insurance and Allied Services, PP 1942 (Cmnd. 6404), p.53.
Report of the Departmental Committee on the Adoption of Children, PP 1953–4 (Cmd. 9248) VIII, p.1
Report of the Departmental Committee on Homosexual Offences and Prostitution PP, 1957 (Cmnd. 247) XIV.
Criminal Law Revision Committee Report, PP 1958–59 (Cmnd. 835) XVI, p.869.
The Child, the Family and the Young Offender 1964–65, PP August 1965 (Cmnd 2742) XXIX, p.193.
Report on the Work of the Children's Department 1964–66, PP July 1967 (Cmd. 603) XXIV, p.1.
Children in Trouble April 1968, PP, 1967–68 (Cmnd. 3601) XXXIX, p.149.

Newspapers and magazines

Holborn Guardian
Jewish Chronicle
Medical World
New Society
News Chronicle
Picture Post

Sunday Pictorial
The Birmingham Post
The Child's Guardian, the supporters magazine of the NSPCC, NSPCC Archive, Curtail Road, London.
The Contemporary Review
The Daily Express
The Daily Herald
The Daily Mail
The Daily Telegraph
The Guardian
The Nineteenth-Century
The Quarterly Review
The Shield, magazine of the Association for Moral and Social Hygiene (later the Josephine Butler Society), The Fawcett Library, University of London.
The Sunday Express
The Sunday People
The Sunday Times
The Times
Tit Bits
Waifs and Strays: The Monthly Paper of the Church of England Central Society for Providing Homes for Waifs and Strays
Women's Sunday Mirror

Archives

Association of Moral and Social Hygiene, Fawcett Library, The University of London.
Barnardo's, The University of Liverpool.
Mass Observation, The University of Sussex.
Medical Women's Federation, The Wellcome Institute, London.
National Vigilance Association, Fawcett Library, The University of London.
NSPCC, Curtain Road, London.
Public Record Office London, material from the Cabinet, the Central Criminal Court, the Home Office, the Cabinet, the Metropolitan Police and the Ministry of Health.
The Children's Society, Bermondsey, London.

Index

Incest, 7, 15, 17, 28, 53, 58
Industrial schools, 38, 48, 75, 77, 106, 109
Ingleby Report (1960), 165, 167
International Bureau, 76
Irish, 133

Jarrett, Rebecca, 21–2, 25, 26, 27
Jewish Association, 76
Joint Committee on Sexual Offences Against Children (1932), 100–1
Josephine Butler Society – see *Association for Moral and Social Hygiene*
Juvenile delinquency, 30, 75, 77, 93, 107–8, 109, 111, 114, 117, 121, 124–5, 151, 156, 157, 166, 183
Juvenile offenders – see *juvenile delinquency*

Ladies Association for the Care of Friendless Girls, 16
Ladies National Association, 16
League of Nations, 76, 77, 114, 115
Leeds, 164
Liberal welfare reforms, 42
Lincoln, 67
Liverpool, 18, 23
Local Authority Social Services Act (1970), 163, 167
London Committee for Suppressing the Traffic in British Girls, 20
London Society for the Prevention of Cruelty to Children, 15

Magdalenes, 7
Magistrates Association, 79, 124, 139
Maiden Tribute, 14, 15, 16, 18, 20–22, 25, 26, 27
Maisons Tolerees – see brothels
Manchester, 56–7, 137, 155, 164
Mass Observation, 118, 126–7
Massage parlour, 45, 147, 148
Maternal deprivation, 124, 125
Medical Women's Federation, 117, 137

Mental Deficiency Act (1913), 56, 57, 104, 135
Mentally defective – see *feebleminded*
Metropolitan Police Act (1839), 77
Middlesborough, 126

National Association of Probation Officers, 132
National Children's Home and Orphanage, 84
National Council for the Unmarried Mother and Her Child, 116
National Society for the Prevention of Cruelty to Children (NSPCC), 38, 40, 42, 43, 44, 50, 53, 54, 59, 68, 83, 116, 117, 119, 122
And the family, 29, 30, 40–1, 50
And police, 40, 54
Annual Reports, 45, 54, 74, 109
Campaigns, 29, 41, 42, 58, 60, 74, 80, 85
Inspectors, 67, 81, 82, 85–7
Prosecutions, 53, 54, 58, 75, 81, 110
National Union of Societies for Equal Citizenship (NUSEC), 93
National Union of Women's Suffrage Societies, 93
National Vigilance Association (NVA) (renamed British Vigilance Association 1953) 54, 58, 71, 76, 78, 94, 97, 98, 100, 102, 105, 106, 107, 120, 132, 133
New Labour, 182
New morality, 96
New Right, 161, 167, 171
New York, 54, 77, 157, 158, 171
Nottinghamshire, 54, 159, 182

Offences Against the Person Act (1861), 14
Orphans, 19, 31

Permissiveness, 147, 160, 161, 164
Pimps, 44–5, 114, 115, 130, 136, 153, 171, 180
Playland, 148, 152, 153, 156, 160, 161